THE VISION BOOK OF FOOTBALL RECORDS 2019

BY CLIVE BATTY

VSP

Published by Vision Sports Publishing in 2018

Vision Sports Publishing
19-23 High Street
Kingston upon Thames
Surrey
KT1 1LL

www.visionsp.co.uk

© Clive Batty

ISBN: 978-1909534-87-2

Editors: Ed Davis and Jim Drewett
Design: Neal Cobourne
Kit images: David Moor, www.historicalkits.co.uk
All pictures: Getty Images

Printed and bound in Slovakia by Neografia
A CIP catalogue record for this book is available from the British Library

MIX
Paper from
responsible sources
FSC® C020353
FSC
www.fsc.org

All statistics in the *Vision Book of Football Records 2019*
are correct up until the start of the 2018/19 season

Welcome to the 2019 edition of the *Vision Book of Football Records*. Since this book last appeared on the shelves 12 months ago billions of people around the globe have enjoyed one of the most thrilling World Cups ever. Highlights included Germany's unexpected (and, it has to be said, really rather amusing) elimination at the group stage, England's epic run to the semi-finals, and a thoroughly entertaining final between France and Croatia.

Along with the likes of Kylian Mbappe, Luka Modric and Harry Kane, referees were also in the spotlight, taking centre stage every so often to review their decisions by watching slow-motion replays on a handily placed television set by the side of the pitch. Depending on your view of the new, much-discussed 'VAR' system, the sight of a man in a light blue shirt staring intently at a TV screen was either nail-biting, not-to-be-missed edge-of-the-seat drama... or was an utterly tedious spectacle, about as exciting as watching the grass grow back in a patchy six-yard box!

Putting that debate to one side, in the domestic season that preceded the glorious Russian footy fest Manchester City rewrote the Premier League record books on their way to winning the Title, while Celtic's achievement in landing the 'Double-Treble' north of the border also deserves mention. There were equally predictable championship successes for European giants like Barcelona, Bayern Munich, Juventus and Paris Saint-Germain, creating a sense that the race for the title could do with becoming a bit more competitive in some countries.

Still, while the big guns were sweeping up yet more silverware they were also breaking records aplenty and these have all been included in this new edition, along with all the many records that were smashed at the World Cup. Perhaps the biggest change this year, though, is the inclusion for the first time of individual entries for some of the leading figures in the women's game, among them England captain Steph Houghton, Barcelona striker Toni Duggan and Brazilian superstar Marta. The women's game has grown hugely in recent years, decent crowds being attracted not just by the excellent standard of football but the sportsmanship of the players – you don't see many 'Neymar-style' dives when the girls are out on the pitch!

Along with the top women players, more Premier League stars than ever before make the cut this time round, including all of England's World Cup heroes, the most intriguing new signings and a smattering of cult figures at clubs outside the 'Top Six' like Marko Arnautovic, Troy Deeney and Jonjo Shelvey. To create space for these various newcomers, all the great players of yesteryear have had to make way, but you can still read about the achievements of the likes of Johan Cruyff, Diego Maradona and Pele in the mini-articles about their respective countries; the legends of the past are gone but by no means forgotten.

As in previous editions, you'll also find entries for the top managers, the best foreign-based stars, all 92 English league clubs, the top-flight Scottish sides and the most famous European club outfits. In addition, there are entries for the leading football nations, the most important domestic and international competitions, and individual aspects of the game such as hat-tricks, headers, free kicks and, of course, penalties.

There's much more too, including loads of 'wild card' entries on subjects as diverse as 'Animals' (remember those pesky midges that attacked Gareth Southgate's boys out in Volgograd?), 'Relegation' (any idea which Football League club has suffered the drop a record 16 times?) and 'Twitter' (one world-famous player has even more 'followers' than President Trump – you can probably guess who he is!).

All in all, then, you should find plenty here to keep you occupied during those increasingly rare moments when there is no actual live football on the box. You could even dip into the book during games as, sad to say, there are often tiresome breaks in play these days while players roll around feigning injury or trudge off to the touchline at a snail-like pace after being substituted. Not forgetting, of course, the long minutes that tick by while the referee watches his own personal TV set to determine whether a goal should stand or a penalty be awarded, leaving the two sets of players scratching their heads in the middle of the pitch!

CLIVE BATTY

ABANDONED MATCHES

Since the Premier League was formed in 1992, only six matches have had to be abandoned. The most recent was on 30th December 2006 when Watford's game with Wigan Athletic was called off after 56 minutes due to a waterlogged pitch. The score at the time was 1-1, as it was when the match was replayed later in the season.

• The shortest ever Football League game took place in 1894, when a raging blizzard caused the match between Stoke and Wolves at the Victoria Ground to be called off after just three minutes. Only 400 hardy fans had braved the elements, and even they must have been secretly relieved when the referee, Mr Helme, called the game off.

• The French league match between Bastia and Lyon on 16th April 2017 was abandoned at half-time after home fans twice invaded the pitch and attacked opposition players. Lyon were subsequently awarded a 3-0 win, contributing to Bastia's relegation at the end of the season.

• In a rare case of a football match being abandoned early in the season because of bad weather, Croatia's World Cup qualifier with Kosovo in

Aberdeen have never been relegated from the Scottish top flight

Zagreb on 2nd September 2017 was called off in the 21st minute due to torrential rain making the pitch unplayable. The match resumed the following day, Croatia winning 1-0.

• The Turkish Cup semi-final between Fenerbahce and Besiktas on 19th April 2018 was abandoned after 58 minutes when Besiktas coach Senol Gunes was hit on the head by an object thrown from the stands. The Turkish Football Federation ruled that the remaining 32 minutes should be played behind closed doors, but Besiktas decided to boycott the fixture giving Fenerbahce a bye to the final.

ABERDEEN

Year founded: 1903
Ground: Pittodrie Stadium (20,866)
Nickname: The Dons
Biggest win: 13-0 v Peterhead (1923)
Heaviest defeat: 0-9 v Celtic (2010)

Aberdeen were founded in 1903, following the amalgamation of three city clubs, Aberdeen, Orion and Victoria United. The following year the club joined the Scottish Second Division, and in 1905 the Dons were elected to an expanded First Division. Aberdeen have remained in the top flight ever since, a record shared with just Celtic, and were runners-up in the Scottish

Premiership behind Celtic in 2015, 2016, 2017 and 2018.

• The club was originally known as the Whites and later as the Wasps or the Black and Golds after their early strips, but in 1913 became known as the Dons. This nickname is sometimes said to derive from the involvement of professors at Aberdeen University in the foundation of the club, but is more likely to be a contraction of the word 'Aberdonians', the term used to describe people from Aberdeen.

• Aberdeen first won the Scottish title in 1955, and later enjoyed a trio of championship successes in the 1980s under manager Alex Ferguson. Before he moved on to even greater triumphs with Manchester United, Fergie also led the Dons to four victories in five years in the Scottish Cup, which included a record run of 20 cup games without defeat between 1982 and 1985.

• The club's finest hour, though, came in 1983 when the Dons became only the second Scottish club (after Rangers in 1972) to win the European Cup Winners' Cup, beating Real Madrid 2-1 in the final. Later that year Aberdeen defeated Hamburg over two legs to claim the European Super Cup and remain the only Scottish side to win two European trophies.

• In 1984 Aberdeen became the first club outside the 'Old Firm' to win the Double, after finishing seven points clear at the top of the league and beating Celtic 2-1 in the Scottish Cup final.

• Aberdeen's record of 16 appearances in the Scottish Cup final (including seven wins) is only bettered by Celtic and Rangers.

- Scottish international defender Willie Miller has made more appearances for the club than any other player, an impressive 560 games between 1973 and 1990. Hotshot striker Joe Harper is the Dons' record goalscorer, with 199 during two spells at Pittodrie (1969-72 and 1976-81).
- Aberdeen were the first team ever to be knocked out of a European competition in a penalty shoot-out, losing 5-4 to Hungarian outfit Honved in the first round of the European Cup Winners' Cup in 1970.
- Ginger-haired central defender Alex McLeish made a club record 77 appearances for Scotland between 1980 and 1993.

HONOURS
Premier Division champions 1980, 1984, 1985
Division 1 champions 1955
Scottish Cup 1947, 1970, 1982, 1983, 1984, 1986, 1990
League Cup 1956, 1977, 1986, 1990, 1996, 2014
European Cup Winners' Cup 1983
European Super Cup 1983

AC MILAN

Year founded: 1899
Ground: San Siro (80,018)
Nickname: Rossoneri
League titles: 18
Domestic cups: 5
European cups: 14
International cups: 4

One of the giants of European football, the club was founded by British expatriates as the Milan Cricket and Football Club in 1899. Apart from a period during the fascist dictatorship of Benito Mussolini, the club has always been known as 'Milan' rather than the Italian 'Milano'.
- Milan were the first Italian side to win the European Cup, beating Benfica in the final at Wembley in 1963, and have gone on to win the trophy seven times – a record surpassed only by Real Madrid, with 13 victories.
- In 1986 the club was acquired by the businessman

and future Italian President Silvio Berlusconi, who invested in star players like Marco van Basten, Ruud Gullit and Frank Rijkaard. Milan went on to enjoy a golden era under coaches Arrigo Sacchi and Fabio Capello, winning three European Cups and four Serie A titles between 1988 and 1994. Incredibly, the club were undefeated for 58 league games between 1991 and 1993, a record run in Italian football.
- Another star of that AC Milan team was legendary defender Paolo Maldini, who made a record 647 appearances in Serie A between 1985 and 2009.
- British players to wear AC Milan's famous red and black stripes include goal poacher supreme Jimmy Greaves, Scottish international striker Joe Jordan and England midfielder Ray Wilkins, who sadly died in April 2018.

Gonzalo Higuain on the ball for AC Milan

HONOURS
Italian champions 1901, 1906, 1907, 1951, 1955, 1957, 1959, 1962, 1968, 1979, 1988, 1992, 1993, 1994, 1996, 1999, 2004, 2011
Italian Cup 1967, 1972, 1973, 1977, 2003
European Cup/Champions League 1963, 1969, 1989, 1990, 1994, 2003, 2007
European Cup Winners' Cup 1968, 1973
European Super Cup 1989, 1990, 1994, 2003, 2007
Club World Cup/Intercontinental Cup 1969, 1989, 1990, 2007

ACCRINGTON STANLEY

Year founded: 1968
Ground: Crown Ground (5,057)
Nickname: The Stans
Biggest win: 10-1 v Lincoln United (1999)
Heaviest defeat: 2-8 v Peterborough (2008)

Accrington Stanley were founded at a meeting in a working men's club in Accrington in 1968, as a successor to the former Football League club of the same name which had folded two years earlier.
- Conference champions in 2006, Stanley were promoted to the Football League in place of relegated Oxford United. After more than a decade in League Two the club finally went up to the third tier as champions in 2018, thanks in part to 25 goals from striker Billy Kee, the division's top scorer.
- The original town club, Accrington, were one of the 12 founder members of the Football League in 1888, but resigned from the league after just five years.
- Midfielder Romuald Boco, the scorer of the Stans' first ever league goal, made a club record 17 international appearances for Benin between 2005 and 2008.

HONOURS
League Two champions 2018
Conference champions 2006

AFC WIMBLEDON

Year founded: 2002
Ground: Kingsmeadow (4,850)
Nickname: The Dons
Biggest win: 9-0 v Chessington United (2004) and v Slough Town (2007)
Heaviest defeat: 0-5 v York City (2010)

AFC Wimbledon were founded in 2002 by supporters of the former Premier League club Wimbledon, who opposed the decision of the FA to sanction the 'franchising' of their club when they allowed it to move 56 miles north from their south London base to Milton Keynes in Buckinghamshire (the club later becoming the MK Dons).

• **In October 2006 an agreement was reached with the MK Dons that the honours won by the old Wimbledon would return to the London Borough of Merton. This was an important victory for the AFC fans, who view their club as the true successors to Wimbledon FC.**

• In their former incarnation as Wimbledon the club won the FA Cup in 1988, beating hot favourites Liverpool 1-0 at Wembley. Incredibly, the Dons had only been elected to the Football League just 12 years earlier, but enjoyed a remarkable rise through the divisions, winning promotion to the top flight in 1986. Dubbed the 'Crazy Gang' for their physical approach on the pitch and madcap antics off it, Wimbledon remained in the Premier League until 2000.

• **In 2011 the Dons gained promotion to League Two after beating Luton Town on penalties in the Conference play-off final. Then, in 2016, AFC became the first club formed in the 21st century to play in the Football League play-offs and delighted their fans by beating Plymouth Argyle 2-0 in the League Two final at Wembley.**

• With a capacity of just 4,850, the club's tiny Kingsmeadow Stadium is the smallest in the Football League.

• **Defender Barry Fuller has made a club record 203 league appearances for the Dons since 2013. The club's record scorer is Montserrat international striker Lyle Taylor with 44 league goals.**

> HONOURS
> *Division 4 champions 1983 (as Wimbledon FC)*
> *FA Cup 1988 (as Wimbledon FC)*
> *FA Amateur Cup 1963 (as Wimbledon FC)*

AFRICA CUP OF NATIONS

The Africa Cup of Nations was founded in 1957. The first tournament was a decidedly small affair consisting of just three competing teams (Egypt, Ethiopia and hosts Sudan) after South Africa's invitation was withdrawn when they refused to send a multi-racial squad to the finals. Egypt were the first winners, comfortably beating Ethiopia 4-0 in the final in Khartoum.

• **With seven victories, Egypt are the most successful side in the history of the competition. In second place overall are Cameroon with five victories, the most recent of which came in 2017 when they beat Egypt 2-1 in the final in Libreville, Gabon, thanks to a late winner from striker Vincent Aboubakar.**

• Egypt's Hassan El-Shazly is the only player to score two hat-tricks at the finals, notching trebles against Nigeria in 1963 and Ivory Coast in 1970.

• **The top scorer in the history of the competition is Cameroon striker Samuel Eto'o, who hit a total of 18 goals in the tournament between 2000 and 2010. Pierre Ndaye Mulamba of Zaire holds the record for the most goals in a single tournament, with nine in 1974.**

• Holders Cameroon will host the next edition of the competition in June 2019.

Cameroon's 2017 Africa Cup of Nations victory party was a low-key affair...

AFRICAN FOOTBALLER OF THE YEAR

The African Footballer of the Year award was established by the Confederation of African Football in 1992. The 2017 winner was Liverpool and Egypt striker Mohamed Salah, who topped the poll ahead of his team-mate, Senegal forward Sadio Mane.

• Ivory Coast midfielder Yaya Toure enjoyed a record four wins on the trot between 2011 and 2014. Legendary Cameroon striker Samuel Eto'o has also won the award four times, including a hat-trick between 2003 and 2005.

• The first Premier League-based player to win the award was Arsenal's Nigerian striker Kanu in 1999. Altogether, players at English clubs have won the award a record 11 times.

• **Players from nine different African countries have won the award, with Ivory Coast (six wins in total) enjoying the most success.**

AGE

The oldest player in the history of English football is Neil McBain, the New Brighton manager, who had to go in goal for his side's Division Three (North) match against Hartlepool aged 51 and 120 days during an injury crisis in 1947.

• **Striker Jordan Allan became the youngest player ever in British football history when he came on as a sub for Airdrie United against Livingston in April 2014 aged 14 and 189 days. At the time he was still a pupil at the Calderside Academy in South Lanarkshire.**

• The oldest international in British football is Wales' Billy Meredith, who played against England in 1920 at the age of 45. Outside forward Meredith scored in his side's 2-1 win, and remains the oldest goalscorer ever in international football.

• **The youngest player to score in international football is Aung Kyaw Tun of Myanmar, who found the net in a 3-1 defeat against Thailand in November 2000 aged 14 and 93 days.**

• The youngest player to score in the Premier League is Everton's James Vaughan, who was aged 16 and 270 days when he hit the target against Crystal Palace on 10th April 2005. At the opposite end of the age scale, former England international Teddy Sheringham was 40 and 268 days when he scored his last Premier League goal for West Ham against his former club Portsmouth on Boxing Day 2006.

• **The oldest professional footballer to score a goal is former Japan international Kazuyoshi Miura, who slotted home from inside the six-yard box for Yokohama FC against Thespa Kusatsu in the J2 League (Japanese second division) on 12th March 2017, aged 50 and 14 days.**

• The youngest player to appear in international football is Lucas Knecht, who turned out for the Northern Mariana Islands against Guam two days after his 14th birthday in 2007. The 'oldie's' record is held by Barrie Dewsbury, who was 52 and 11 days when he played in Sark's 16-0 defeat by Greenland in 2003.

Super striker Sergio Aguero is flying high at Manchester City

SERGIO AGUERO

Born: Quilmes, Argentina, 2nd June 1988
Position: Striker
Club career:
2003-06 Independiente 54 (23)
2006-11 Atletico Madrid 175 (74)
2011- Manchester City 206 (143)
International record:
2006- Argentina 89 (39)

Manchester City's all-time top scorer with 201 goals in all competitions, Sergio Aguero is also the highest-scoring non-European in Premier League history with 143 goals, and one of just four players (along with Alan Shearer, Thierry Henry and Harry Kane) to hit 20 or more goals in four consecutive Premier League seasons, achieving this feat with 21 in 2017/18 to help City win a third title in his seven years at the Etihad.

• Known as 'El Kun' because of his resemblance to a Japanese cartoon character, Aguero became the youngest ever player to appear in Argentina's top flight when he made his debut for Independiente in 2003 aged just 15 years and 35 days. The previous record was set by the legendary Diego Maradona, Aguero's former father-in-law.

• Aguero moved on to Atletico Madrid in 2006 aged 17, helping the Spanish club win the inaugural Europa League in 2010. The following year he joined Manchester City for £38 million, becoming the second most expensive player in British football history at the time.

• The fee proved to be a bargain as Aguero banged in 23 Premier League goals – including a dramatic title-clinching winner against QPR on the last day of the season – as City topped the table for the first time since 1968. Two years later he contributed another 17 goals as City won the title again, and in 2015 he became the first Manchester City player to win the Premier League Golden Boot outright after topping the scoring charts with an impressive total of 26 goals. The following season he became only the fifth player in Premier League history to score five goals in a game, doing so in record time – just 23 minutes and 34 seconds – during a 6-1 hammering of Newcastle. When added to his four-goal tallies against Tottenham in 2014 and Leicester City in 2018, the Argentinian is the only player to have scored four goals or more in three Premier League matches.

• A quicksilver attacker who possesses excellent close control, Aguero made his international debut for Argentina in a 2006 friendly against Brazil at Arsenal's Emirates Stadium. In 2008 he was a key figure in the Argentina team that won gold at the Beijing Olympics, and he is now third on his country's list of all-time top scorers with 39 goals.

AIR CRASHES

On 28th November 2016 a plane carrying the Brazilian team Chapecoense on their way to play Colombian side Atletico Nacional in the first leg of the Copa Sudamericana finals crashed into a hillside near Medellin after running out of fuel. A total of 71 people were killed in the disaster, including 19 players and the team's coach, Luiz Carlos Saroli.

• On 6th February 1958 eight members of the Manchester United 'Busby Babes' team, including England internationals Roger Byrne, Duncan Edwards and Tommy Taylor, were killed in the Munich Air Crash. Their plane crashed while attempting to take off in a snowstorm at Munich Airport, where it had stopped to refuel after a European Cup tie in Belgrade. In total, 23 people died in the incident, although manager Matt Busby and Bobby Charlton were among the survivors. Amazingly, United still managed to reach the FA Cup final that year, but lost at Wembley to Bolton Wanderers.

• The entire first team of Torino, the strongest Italian club at the time, were wiped out in an air disaster on 4th May 1949. Returning from a testimonial match in Portugal, the team's plane crashed into the Basilica of Superga outside Turin. Among the 31 dead were 10 members of the Italian national side and the club's English manager, Leslie Lievesley. Torino fielded their youth team in their four remaining fixtures and, with their opponents each doing the same as a mark of respect, won a joint-record fifth consecutive league title at the end of the season.

AJAX

Year founded: 1900
Ground: Johan Cruyff Arena (54,033)
Nickname: De Godenzonen (the sons of the Gods)
League titles: 33
Domestic cups: 18
European cups: 8
International cups: 2

Founded in 1900 in Amsterdam, Ajax are named after the Greek mythological hero. The club is the most successful in Holland, having won the league a record 33 times and the Dutch Cup a record 18 times.

• The Dutch side's most glorious decade was in the 1970s when, with a team featuring legends like Johan Cruyff, Johan Neeskens and Johnny Rep, Ajax won the European Cup three times on the trot, playing a fluid system known as 'Total Football'. In 1995 a young Ajax team won the trophy for a fourth time, Patrick Kluivert scoring the winner in the final against AC Milan.

• When Ajax beat Torino in the final of the UEFA Cup in 1992 they became only the second team, after Juventus, to win all three major European trophies. In 2017 Ajax reached their first European final for two decades, but lost 2-0 in the Europa League final to Manchester United.

• Ajax's most successful manager was the Englishman Jack Reynolds, who won eight league titles during three spells with the club between 1915 and 1947. His haul might have been bigger, too, but for the German invasion of the Netherlands in 1940 which resulted in Reynolds being interned in a camp in Poland for the duration of the Second World War.

• In 2018 Ajax's home, the largest stadium in the Netherlands, was renamed the Johan Cruyff Arena in recognition of their greatest ever player, who died in March 2016.

HONOURS
Dutch champions 1918, 1919, 1931, 1932, 1934, 1937, 1939, 1947, 1957, 1960, 1966, 1967, 1968, 1970, 1972, 1973, 1977, 1979, 1980, 1982, 1983, 1985, 1990, 1994, 1995, 1996, 1998, 2002, 2004, 2011, 2012, 2013, 2014
Dutch Cup 1917, 1943, 1961, 1967, 1970, 1971, 1972, 1979, 1983, 1986, 1987, 1993, 1998, 1999, 2002, 2006, 2007, 2010
European Cup/Champions League 1971, 1972, 1973, 1995
UEFA Cup 1992
European Cup Winners' Cup 1987
European Super Cup 1973, 1995
Intercontinental Cup 1972, 1995

NATHAN AKE

Born: The Hague, Netherlands, 18th February 1995
Position: Defender
Club career:
2012-17 Chelsea 7 (0)
2015 Reading (loan) 5 (0)
2015-16 Watford (loan) 24 (1)
2016-17 Bournemouth (loan) 10 (3)
2017- Bournemouth 38 (2)
International record:
2017- Netherlands 7 (1)

Dreadlocked Bournemouth defender Nathan Ake became the Cherries' record signing at the time when he joined for the club from Chelsea in June 2017 for £20 million, having impressed at the Vitality Stadium during a loan spell on the south coast the previous season.

• A calm and composed player who has the knack of timing his tackles and interceptions to perfection, Ake started out as a defensive midfielder in the youth programmes at Den Haag and Feyenoord before signing for Chelsea as a 16-year-old in 2011.

• However, his opportunities at Stamford Bridge were limited, and he had to go out on loan to Reading and Watford to gain valuable first-team experience. In January 2017 then Chelsea boss Antonio Conte recalled Ake from another loan at Bournemouth and later that season he played in the Blues' 4-2 defeat of Tottenham in the FA Cup semi-final at Wembley.

For just a few weeks Alisson was the world's most expensive goalkeeper

Skilful defender Nathan Ake has established himself down on the south coast

• In 2012 Ake was part of the Dutch Under-17 team which won the European Championships, scoring in the shoot-out in the final against Germany. He made his senior debut in a 2-1 friendly win against Morocco in May 2017.

ALISSON

Born: Novo Hamburgo, Brazil, 2nd October 1992
Position: Goalkeeper
Club career:
2013-16 Internacional 44
2016-18 Roma 37
2018- Liverpool
International record:
2015- Brazil 31

Brazil international Alisson became the world's most expensive goalkeeper ever when he joined Liverpool from Roma for £66.8 million in July 2018. However, he only held top spot for a few weeks before Chelsea signed Kepa Arrizabalaga from Athletic Bilbao for £71.6 million.

• A tall and commanding goalkeeper who is adept with his feet, Alisson started out as back-up to his brother, Muriel, at Internacional, a club based in Porto Alegre in southern Brazil. After breaking into the first team he won four consecutive

regional titles before moving to Roma for around £6 million in 2016.

• Alisson spent his first season in the Italian capital as understudy to Wojciech Szczesny and had to wait until the Polish international joined Juventus before making his Serie A debut on the opening day of the 2017/18 campaign in a 1-0 win against Atalanta. However, he enjoyed a superb season with I Lupi, helping them reach the semi-finals of the Champions League where they lost 7-6 on aggregate to Liverpool.

• Alisson made his debut for Brazil in a 3-1 defeat of Venezuela in 2015 and was his country's No 1 at the 2018 World Cup in Russia.

DELE ALLI

Born: Milton Keynes, 11th April 1996
Position: Midfielder
Club career:
2011-15 Milton Keynes Dons 62 (18)
2015- Tottenham Hotspur 106 (37)
2015 Milton Keynes Dons (loan) 12 (4)
International record:
2015- England 30 (3)

An attacking midfielder who loves making runs into the opposition box, Dele Alli became only the fourth player to win the PFA Young Player of the Year award twice when he topped the poll in 2017, a year after his first success. The Tottenham star, who scored a

Dele Alli was signed for Tottenham for a bargain £5 million

career best 18 league goals in 2016/17, was also voted into the PFA Team of the Year for the second consecutive season. Alli failed to hit the same heights in 2017/18, but he did score two goals in a 3-1 defeat of London rivals Chelsea which gave Tottenham their first win at Stamford Bridge for 28 years.

• **Alli joined his local club MK Dons as an 11-year-old, making his first-team debut aged just 16 in November 2012 against Cambridge City in the FA Cup. After helping the Dons win promotion to the Championship in 2015 he was voted the Football League Young Player of the Year.**

• Alli moved to Tottenham for a bargain £5 million during the 2015 winter transfer window, but was loaned back to MK Dons for the rest of the season. He eventually made his Spurs debut in August 2015 and later that season scored with a brilliant effort against Crystal Palace at Selhurst Park that was voted the BBC's Goal of the Season.

• **First capped by England at Under-17 level, Alli's eye-catching displays for Tottenham soon earned him a call up to the senior squad and he marked his first start for England in fine style with a blistering long-range strike past Spurs team-mate Hugo Lloris in a 2-0 friendly victory over France at Wembley in November 2015. A**

niggling thigh injury prevented him from showing his best form at the 2018 World Cup in Russia, but he still managed to get on the scoresheet in the 2-0 quarter-final defeat of Sweden with a well-taken header.

ANIMALS

Turkish club Besiktas were fined £30,000 by UEFA after a ginger cat wandered onto the pitch during their last 16 Champions League home tie with Bayern Munich in March 2018. The Bavarian giants won 3-1, but their fans still voted the moggy as their 'Man of the Match' on Twitter.

• **The Bolivian Premier League match between Blooming and Nacional de Potosi in October 2017 was held up for a few minutes when a police dog ran onto the pitch and punctured the ball, much to the amusement of the spectators.**

• The most famous dog in football, Pickles, never appeared on the pitch but, to the relief of fans around the globe, discovered the World Cup trophy which was stolen while on display at an exhibition in Central Hall, Westminster, on 20th March 1966. A black and white mongrel, Pickles found the trophy under a bush while out for a walk on Beulah Hill in south London with his owner. He was hailed as a national hero but, sadly, later that same year he was strangled by his lead while chasing after a cat.

• **The Uruguayan first division match between Fenix and Racing in March 2018 was briefly halted when two chickens painted in the green and white colours of the visitors were let loose on the pitch by protesting fans. Fenix director Gaston Alegari reacted angrily, booting one of the chickens off the turf to land himself in hot water with animal rights groups.**

• In April 2018 Russian third-tier club Mashuk were also condemned by animal rights activists after using a circus-trained bear to hand the match ball to the referee before the start of their game against KMV and Angusht.

APPEARANCES

Goalkeeping legend Peter Shilton holds the record for the most Football League appearances, playing 1,005 games between 1966 and 1997. His total was made up as follows: Leicester City (286 games), Stoke City (110), Nottingham Forest (202), Southampton (188), Derby County (175), Plymouth (34), Bolton (1) and Leyton Orient (9). Shilton is followed in the all-time list by Tony Ford (931 appearances, 1975-2001), who holds the record for an outfield player.

• **Shilton also holds the world record for first-class appearances in all competitions for his various clubs and England, with an incredible total of 1,390.**

• Swindon Town stalwart John Trollope holds the record for the most league appearances for a single club, with 770

IS THAT A FACT?

Before England's match with Tunisia at the 2018 World Cup in Russia Gareth Southgate's men had to spray themselves with insect repellent after a swarm of aggressive midges descended on the stadium in Volgograd. However, the little blighters couldn't prevent the Three Lions from winning 2-1 thanks to skipper Harry Kane's last-gasp header.

between 1960 and 1980. Manchester United legend Ryan Giggs appeared in 672 league games for the Red Devils between 1991 and 2014, a record for the same club in the top flight.

• Former England midfielder Gareth Barry holds the Premier League appearance record, with a total of 653 appearances for Aston Villa, Manchester City, Everton and West Brom since 1998.

• Spain goalkeeper Iker Casillas holds the record for the most appearances in the Champions League with 167 for Real Madrid and Porto from 1999.

ARGENTINA

First international: Uruguay 2 Argentina 3, 1901
Most capped player: Javier Mascherano, 147 caps (2003-18)
Leading goalscorer: Lionel Messi, 65 goals (2005-)
First World Cup appearance: Argentina 1 France 0, 1930
Biggest win: Argentina 12 Ecuador 0, 1942
Heaviest defeat: Argentina 1 Czechoslovakia 6 (1958) and Argentina 1 Bolivia 6 (2009)

Outside Britain, Argentina is the oldest football nation on the planet. The roots of the game in this football-obsessed country go back to 1865, when the Buenos Aires Football Club was founded by British residents in the Argentine capital. Six clubs formed the first league in 1891, making it the oldest anywhere in the world outside Britain.

• Losing finalists in the first World Cup in 1930, Argentina had to wait until 1978 before winning the competition for the first time, defeating Holland 3-1 on home soil. Another success, inspired by brilliant captain Diego Maradona, followed in 1986 and Argentina came close to retaining their trophy four years later, losing 1-0 in the final to West Germany. After a 24-year wait they reached the final again in 2014, but narrowly lost to Germany.

• Argentina's oldest rivals are neighbours Uruguay. The two countries first met in 1901, in the first official international to

An Argentina fan who clearly believes two heads are better than one

be played outside Britain, with Argentina winning 3-2 in Montevideo. In the ensuing years the two sides have played each other 188 times, making the Argentina-Uruguay fixture the most played in the history of international football.

• With 14 victories to their name, Argentina have the second best record in the Copa America. In 2015 and 2016 Messi and co. had a great chance to equal Uruguay's record of 15 wins but frustratingly lost both finals to Chile on penalties.

HONOURS
World Cup winners *1978, 1986*
Copa America winners *1921, 1925, 1927, 1929, 1937, 1941, 1945, 1946, 1947, 1955, 1957, 1959, 1991, 1993*
World Cup Record
1930 Runners-up
1934 Round 1
1938 Did not enter
1950 Did not enter
1954 Did not enter
1958 Round 1
1962 Round 1
1966 Quarter-finals
1970 Did not qualify
1974 Round 2
1978 Winners
1982 Round 2
1986 Winners
1990 Runners-up
1994 Round 2
1998 Quarter-finals
2002 Round 1
2006 Quarter-finals
2010 Quarter-finals
2014 Runners-up
2018 Round 2

MARKO ARNAUTOVIC

Born: Vienna, Austria 19th April 1989
Position: Striker
Club career:
2006-10 Twente 44 (12)
2009-10 Inter Milan (loan) 3 (0)
2010-13 Werder Bremen 72 (14)
2013-17 Stoke City 125 (22)
2017- West Ham United 31 (11)
International record:
2008- Austria 72 (19)

A skilful, imaginative and unpredictable striker, Marko Arnautovic became West Ham's then record signing when he joined the east Londoners from Stoke City for £23 million in July 2017. The Austrian repaid some of the hefty fee by scoring 11 goals to help his new club pull clear of the relegation zone and at the end of the campaign he was voted 'Hammer of the Year'.

• Born in Vienna to an Austrian mother and Serbian father, Arnautovic started out with Twente in the Dutch league. His impressive performances caught the eye of Inter Milan, where he went on loan in 2009. However, his time in Italy was blighted by injury and sparked occasional frustrated outbursts which did not go down well with then Inter manager Jose Mourinho, who said: "Marko is a fantastic person but he has the attitude of a child."

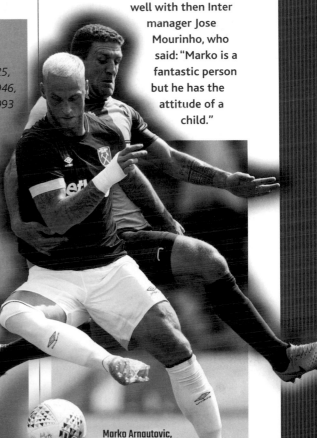

Marko Arnautovic, West Ham's Austrian 'bad boy'

• After a three-year spell in Germany with Werder Bremen, Arnautovic joined Stoke City for a bargain £2 million in September 2013. His technical ability and some stunning strikes made him a fans' favourite in the Potteries, while his total of 33 goals for Stoke and West Ham is a record for an Austrian player in the Premier League.

• Dubbed 'the bad boy of Austrian football' in his homeland, Arnautovic made his debut for his country against the Faroe Islands in October 2008 and has now won over 70 caps.

KEPA ARRIZABALAGA

Born: Ondarroa, Spain, 3rd October 1994
Position: Goalkeeper
Club career:
2012-13 Basconia 31
2013-16 Bilbao Athletic 50
2015 Ponferradina (loan) 20
2015-16 Valladolid (loan) 39
2016-18 Athletic Bilbao 53
2018- Chelsea
International record:
2017- Spain 1

Spain international Kepa Arrizabalaga became the most expensive goalkeeper in the world and Chelsea's record signing when he joined the Blues from Athletic Bilbao in August 2018 for £71.6 million – about £5 million more than the previous benchmark set by Brazilian shot-stopper Alisson's move from Roma to Liverpool just a few weeks earlier.

• A tall goalkeeper who commands his box with authority, Arrizabalaga

Kepa Arrizabalaga is the world's most expensive goalkeeper

joined the Athletic Bilbao youth set-up aged 10, progressing to make his debut for the Basque outfit's feeder club, Basconia, in January 2012 when still a teenager. The following year he moved up to the reserve side, Bilbao Athletic. After successful loan spells at two second-tier clubs, Ponferradina and Valladolid, the young goalie finally made his debut for Bilbao in a 1-0 away win at Deportivo la Coruna in September 2016.

• After playing for Spain at Under-18 level, Arrizabalaga was a key member of the Spanish team which won the Under-19 European Championships in Estonia in 2012. His stand-out performance came in the semi-final against France when he saved two penalties in a penalty shoot-out.

• Arrizabalaga made his senior debut for Spain in a 5-0 hammering of Costa Rica in Malaga in November 2017. He was picked for his country's World Cup squad the following year but spent the entire tournament in Russia on the bench as back-up to David de Gea.

ARSENAL

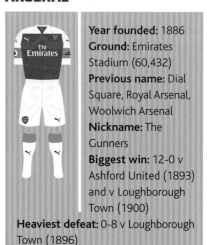

Year founded: 1886
Ground: Emirates Stadium (60,432)
Previous name: Dial Square, Royal Arsenal, Woolwich Arsenal
Nickname: The Gunners
Biggest win: 12-0 v Ashford United (1893) and v Loughborough Town (1900)
Heaviest defeat: 0-8 v Loughborough Town (1896)

Founded as Dial Square in 1886 by workers at the Royal Arsenal in Woolwich, the club was renamed Royal Arsenal soon afterwards. Another name change, to Woolwich Arsenal, followed in 1891 when the club turned professional. Then, a year after moving north of the river to the Arsenal Stadium in 1913, the club became simply 'Arsenal'.

• One of the most successful clubs in the history of English football, Arsenal enjoyed a first golden period in the 1930s under innovative manager Herbert Chapman. The Gunners won the FA Cup for the first time in 1930 and later in the decade became only

the second club to win three league titles on the trot. The first was the club Chapman managed in the 1920s, Huddersfield Town.

• Arsenal were the first club from London to win the league, topping the table in 1931 after scoring an incredible 60 goals in 21 away matches – an all-time record for the Football League.

• Arsenal are the most successful club in the history of the FA Cup with 13 victories to their name, the most recent coming in 2017 when the Gunners beat London rivals Chelsea 2-1 in the final at Wembley. Seven of those cup triumphs were achieved during the long reign of former boss Arsène Wenger, the best haul of any manager in FA Cup history. Wenger also led the Gunners to the Double in both 1998 and 2002, and their total of three Doubles (including an earlier triumph in 1971) is only matched by Manchester United.

• Wenger's greatest achievement, though, came in the 2003/04 season when his team were crowned Premier League champions after going through the entire campaign undefeated. Only Preston North End had previously matched this feat, way back in 1888/89, but they had only played 22 league games compared to the 38 of Wenger's 'Invincibles'.

• The following season Arsenal extended their unbeaten run to 49 matches – setting an English league record in the process – before crashing to a bad-tempered 2-0 defeat against Manchester United at Old Trafford on 24th October 2004.

• One of the stars of that great Arsenal side was striker Thierry Henry, who is the Gunners' all-time leading scorer with 228 goals in all competitions in two spells at the club between 1999 and 2012. His total includes 42 goals in European competition, another club record. The former fans' favourite is also the most capped Arsenal player, appearing 81 times for France during his time with the club.

• In 1989 Arsenal won the closest ever title race by beating Liverpool 2-0 at Anfield in the final match of the season to pip the Reds to the championship on goals scored (the two sides had the same goal difference). But for a last-minute goal by Gunners midfielder Michael Thomas, after Alan Smith had scored with a second-half header, the title would have stayed on Merseyside.

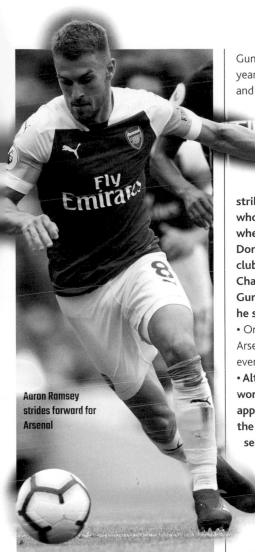

Aaron Ramsey strides forward for Arsenal

Gunners' hotseat for an incredible 21 years and 224 days between 1996 and 2018, a tenure only bettered by Manchester United's Alex Ferguson in the Premier League era.

• Arsenal's most expensive signing is Gabonese striker Pierre-Emerick Aubameyang, who cost the Gunners £55 million when he joined them from Borussia Dortmund in January 2018. The club's record sale is Alex Oxlade-Chamberlain, who boosted the Gunners' coffers by £35 million when he signed for Liverpool in 2017.

• On their way to the title in 2002 Arsenal became the first club to score in every Premier League fixture in a season.

• Although the Gunners have never won the Champions League they appeared in the group stages of the competition for 19 consecutive seasons from 1998/99 to 2016/17 – a record for an English club and one which is only bettered by Real Madrid. However, Arsenal also hold the record for the worst defeat suffered by an English side in the competition, 10-2 on aggregate in the last 16 against Bayern Munich in 2017.

• Irish international defender David O'Leary made a club record 722 first-team appearances for Arsenal between 1975 and 1993.

• **Arsenal endured a nightmare season in 1912/13, finishing bottom of Division One and winning just one home game during the campaign – an all-time record. However, the Gunners returned to the top flight in 1919 and have stayed there ever since – the longest unbroken run in the top tier.**

• Arsenal tube station on the Piccadilly Line is the only train station in Britain to be named after a football club. It used to be called Gillespie Road, until Herbert Chapman successfully lobbied for the name change in 1932.

• **Three years later, on 14th December 1935, Arsenal thrashed Aston Villa 7-1 at Villa Park. Incredibly, centre-forward Ted Drake grabbed all seven of the Gunners' goals to set a top-flight record that still stands to this day. The previous season Drake scored a club best 44 goals, including 42 in the league.**

• Arsene Wenger is easily Arsenal's longest serving manager, sitting in the

HONOURS
Premier League champions 1998, 2002, 2004
Division 1 champions 1931, 1933, 1934, 1935, 1948, 1953, 1971, 1989, 1991
FA Cup 1930, 1936, 1950, 1971, 1979, 1993, 1998, 2002, 2003, 2005, 2014, 2015, 2017
League Cup 1987, 1993
Double 1971, 1998, 2002
Fairs Cup 1970
European Cup Winners' Cup 1994

ASTON VILLA

32Red

Year founded: 1874
Ground: Villa Park (42,660)
Nickname: The Villans
Biggest win: 13-0 v Wednesbury Old Athletic (1886)
Heaviest defeat: 0-8 v Chelsea (2012)

One of England's most famous and distinguished clubs, Aston Villa were founded in 1874 by members of the Villa Cross Wesleyan Chapel in Aston, Birmingham. The club were founder members of the Football League in 1888, winning their first title six years later.

• **The most successful team of the Victorian era, Villa became only the second club to win the league and FA Cup Double in 1897 (Preston North End were the first in 1889). Villa's manager at the time was the legendary George Ramsay, who went on to guide the Villans to six league titles and six FA Cups – a trophy haul which has only been surpassed by Liverpool's Bob Paisley and former Manchester United boss Sir Alex Ferguson.**

• Ramsay is also the second longest serving manager in the history of English football, taking charge of the Villans for an incredible 42 years between 1884 and 1926. Only West Brom's Fred Everiss has managed a club for longer, racking up 46 years' service at the Hawthorns.

• **Although they slipped as low as the old Third Division in the early 1970s, Villa have spent more time in the top flight than any other club apart from Everton (105 seasons compared to the Toffees' 116). The two clubs have played each other 202 times to date, making Aston Villa v Everton the most played fixture in the entire history of league football.**

• Villa won the last of their seven league titles in 1980/81, when manager Ron Saunders used just 14 players throughout the whole campaign – equalling Liverpool's record set in 1965/66. The following season Villa became only the fourth English club to win the European Cup when they beat Bayern Munich 1-0 in the final in Rotterdam.

• **In 1961 Villa won the League Cup in the competition's inaugural season,** beating Rotherham 3-2 in a two-legged final. The Villans are the joint-second most successful side in the tournament behind Liverpool with five triumphs, their most recent success coming in 1996.

• Villa's most capped international is former Republic of Ireland defender Steve Staunton, who played 64 times for his country while at Villa Park between 1991 and 1998. His team-mate Gareth Southgate, now England manager, played a club record 42 times for the Three Lions between 1995 and 2001.

• **Stalwart defender Charlie Aitken made more appearances for the club than any other player, turning out in 657 games between 1959 and 1976. Villa's all-time top goalscorer is Billy Walker, who found the back of the net an incredible 244 times between 1919 and 1933.**

• Walker helped Villa bang in 128 league goals in the 1930/31 season, a record for the top flight which is unlikely ever to be broken. In the same campaign, Tom 'Pongo' Waring scored a club record 49 league goals.

> HONOURS
> **Division 1 champions** *1894, 1896, 1897, 1899, 1900, 1910, 1981*
> **Division 2 champions** *1938, 1960*
> **Division 3 champions** *1972*
> **FA Cup** *1887, 1895, 1897, 1905, 1913, 1920, 1957*
> **Double** *1897*
> **League Cup** *1961, 1975, 1977, 1994, 1996*
> **European Cup** *1982*
> **European Super Cup** *1982*

ATLETICO MADRID

Year founded: 1903
Ground: Wanda Metropolitana (67,703)
Previous names: Athletic Club de Madrid, Athletic Aviacion de Madrid
Nickname: El Atleti
League titles: 10
Domestic cups: 10
European cups: 7
International cups: 1

The club was founded in 1903 by breakaway members of Madrid FC (later Real Madrid). In 1939, following a merger with the Spanish air force team, the club

Pacy French midfielder Thomas Lemar joined Atletico from Monaco for the 2018/19 season

became known as Athletic Aviacion de Madrid before becoming plain Atletico Madrid eight years later.

• **Atletico are the third most successful club in Spanish football history with 10 La Liga triumphs under their belt. The most recent of these came in 2014 when Atleti drew 1-1 at runners-up Barcelona on the last day of the season to become the first side for a decade to break the usual Barca/Real Madrid duopoly.**

• Atletico have enjoyed great success in Europe recent years, winning the inaugural Europa League in 2010 after a 2-1 win against Fulham in the final in Hamburg. Another triumph followed in 2012 and in 2018 Atleti became only the second club to win the new competition three times following a 3-0 thrashing of Marseille in the final in Lyon. Less impressively, Atletico are the only club to reach three finals of the European Cup/Champions League and lose them all.

• **In September 2017 Atletico played their first match at their new near 68,000-capacity Wanda Metropolitana stadium, the venue for the 2019 Champions League final, beating Malaga 1-0 in front of King Felipe VI of Spain.**

> HONOURS
> **Spanish champions** *1940, 1941, 1950, 1951, 1966, 1970, 1973, 1977, 1996, 2014*
> **Spanish Cup** *1960, 1961, 1965, 1972, 1976, 1985, 1991, 1992, 1996, 2013*
> **Europa League** *2010, 2012, 2018*
> **European Cup Winners' Cup** *1962*
> **European Super Cup** *2010, 2012, 2018*
> **Intercontinental Cup** *1974*

ATTENDANCES

The Maracana Stadium in Rio de Janeiro holds the world record for a football match attendance, 199,854 spectators having watched the final match of the 1950 World Cup between Brazil and Uruguay. Most of the fans, though, went home in tears after Uruguay came from behind to win 2-1 and claim the trophy for a second time.

• **The biggest crowd at a match in Britain was probably for the first ever FA Cup final at Wembley in 1923. The official attendance for the match between Bolton and West Ham was 126,047, although, with thousands more fans gaining entry without paying, the actual crowd was estimated at 150,000-200,000. The record official attendance for a match in Britain is 149,547, set in 1937 for Scotland's 3-1 victory over England in the Home International Championship at Hampden Park.**

• In 1948 a crowd of 83,260 watched Manchester United entertain Arsenal at Maine Road (United's temporary home in the post-war years after Old Trafford suffered bomb damage), a record for the Football League. However, the biggest attendance ever for an English club's home fixture is 85,512, set on 2nd November 2016 for Tottenham's Champions League group game with Bayer Leverkusen at Wembley.

• **On 15th April 1970 the biggest crowd ever to watch a European Cup tie, 135,826, crammed into Hampden Park in Glasgow to see Celtic beat Leeds United 2-1 in the semi-final second leg.**

• A record Premier League crowd of 83,222 watched Tottenham beat Arsenal 1-0 in the north London derby

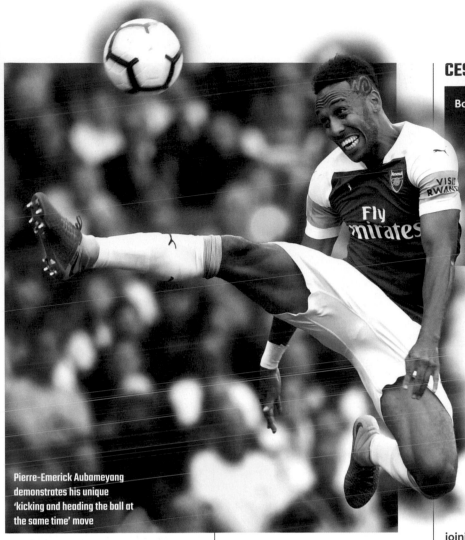

Pierre-Emerick Aubameyang demonstrates his unique 'kicking and heading the ball at the same time' move

CESAR AZPILICUETA

Born: Pamplona, Spain, 28th August 1989
Position: Defender
Club career:
2006-07 Osasuna B 27 (1)
2007-10 Osasuna 99 (0)
2010-12 Marseille 47 (1)
2012- Chelsea 197 (5)
International record:
2013- Spain 22 (0)

A defender who loves to get forward and float in dangerous crosses, Chelsea's Cesar Azpilicueta came up with an impressive six assists in the 2017/18 Premier League season. Remarkably, all half dozen goals were scored by Blues striker Alvaro Morata, making the Spanish pair one of the most productive partnerships in the league.

• **Equally at home at full-back or as part of a back three, Azpilicueta started out with Osasuna in northern Spain before joining Marseille for around £6 million in 2010. Two years later he signed for Chelsea for a bargain £7 million.**

• Dubbed 'Dave' by Chelsea fans as his surname is a bit of a mouthful, Azpilicueta has won a host of honours with the Blues, including two league titles, the Europa League (2013), the League Cup (2015) and the FA Cup (2018).

• **Azpilicueta was part of the Spanish Under-19 team that won the European Championship in 2007. He made his senior debut against Uruguay in 2013 and has since represented his country at the 2014 and 2018 World Cups.**

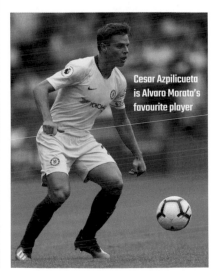

Cesar Azpilicueta is Alvaro Morata's favourite player

at Wembley on 10th February 2018. Less impressively, Wimbledon against Everton at Selhurst Park on 26th January 1993 drew the lowest Premier League attendance ever, just 3,039.
• **Manchester United attracted a record average home crowd of 75,821 in their impressive title-winning 2006/07 campaign.**

PIERRE-EMERICK AUBAMEYANG

Born: Laval, France 18th June 1989
Position: Striker
Club career:
2008-11 AC Milan 0 (0)
2008-09 Dijon (loan) 34 (8)
2009-10 Lille (loan) 14 (2)
2010-11 Monaco (loan) 19 (2)
2011 Saint-Etienne (loan) 33 (8)
2011-13 Saint-Etienne 54 (29)
2013-18 Borussia Dortmund 144 (98)
2018- Arsenal 13 (10)
International record:
2009- Gabon 56 (23)

African Player of the Year in 2015, Pierre-Emerick Aubameyang became Arsenal's record signing in January 2018 when he joined the Gunners from Borussia Dortmund in a £55 million deal. The Gabonese striker immediately repaid some of that fee by scoring five times in his first six league games, a record for an Arsenal player in the Premier League era.

• **Born in France, Aubameyang began his career with AC Milan but was subsequently loaned out to four French clubs before making a permanent move to Saint-Etienne with whom he won the French League Cup in 2013. In the same year he was voted into the Ligue 1 Team of the Season after coming second in the goalscoring charts.**

• He joined Borussia Dortmund in 2013, enjoying a golden season in 2016/17 when he was top scorer in the Bundesliga with 31 goals and scored the winning goal in the German Cup final from the penalty spot in Dortmund's 2-1 victory against Eintracht Frankfurt.

• **Aubameyang played for the French Under-21 side in a friendly against Tunisia in February 2009 but the following month committed his international future to Gabon, for whom his father, Pierre, had previously played. He is now his country's captain and all-time leading scorer with 23 goals.**

BADGES

Rye United of the Sussex County League claim to have the world's oldest club crest, dating back to the 13th century. Their badge features the three lions which appeared on the coat of arms of the Confederation of the Cinque Ports – which provided for the defence of the realm before the formation of a permanent navy – and was established by Royal Charter in 1155.

• Juventus were the first club to add a star to their badge, representing their achievement in winning a then record tenth Italian title in 1958. Other clubs and nations have followed suit, a famous example being the five stars above Brazil's badge to represent their five World Cup triumphs.

• In January 2018 Leeds United were forced to scrap plans for a new badge after 77,000 unhappy fans signed a petition condemning the unpopular design, which featured a nondescript figure giving the 'Leeds salute'.

• In May 2018 Real Sociedad replaced their usual badge with the face of long-serving midfielder Xabi Prieto to mark his final home game for the club, a 3-2 victory against Leganes.

GARETH BALE

Born: Cardiff, 16th July 1989
Position: Winger/striker
Club career:
2006-07 Southampton 40 (5)
2007-13 Tottenham Hotspur 146 (22)
2013- Real Madrid 126 (70)
International record:
2006- Wales 70 (29)

In 2018 Gareth Bale became only the second British player (after Liverpool defender Phil Neal) to win the European Cup/Champions League four times, when he scored twice in Real Madrid's 3-1 defeat of Liverpool in the final in Kiev.

Gareth Bale – the top scoring Brit in Spanish football history

He also equalled Neal's British record of scoring in two finals, having previously netted in Real's 4-1 defeat of Atletico Madrid in 2014. For good measure, Bale also scored in Real's shoot-out victory against their city rivals in the 2016 final.

• Bale began his career at Southampton, where he became the second youngest player to debut for the club (behind Theo Walcott) when he appeared in a 2-0 win against Millwall in the Championship in April 2006. The following season his superb displays for the Saints earned him the Football League Young Player of the Year award.

• In the summer of 2007 Bale joined Tottenham for an initial fee of £5 million and was soon being hailed as one of the most exciting talents in the game. He enjoyed an outstanding season with Spurs in 2010/11 and at the end of the campaign he was named PFA Player of the Year – only the fourth Welshman to receive this honour. He was also the only Premier League player to be voted into the UEFA Team of the Year for 2011. He had an even better season in 2012/13, picking up both Player of the Year gongs and the PFA Young Player of the Year award – only the second player, after Cristiano Ronaldo, to collect this individual treble.

• Bale joined Real for a then world record fee of £86 million in August 2013 and has scored more goals in La Liga, 70, than any other British player. The record was previously held by Gary Lineker, who notched 43 goals for Barcelona in the 1980s.

• When Bale scored his first international goal, in a 5-1 home defeat by Slovakia in 2006, he became his country's youngest ever scorer aged 17 and 35 days. He starred for Wales on their unlikely run to the semi-finals of Euro 2016 and in March 2018 became his country's all-time top scorer when he banged in a hat-trick in a 6-0 rout of China.

BALL BOYS

Ball boys developed from a gimmick employed by Chelsea in the 1905/06 season. To emphasise the extraordinary bulk of the team's 23-stone goalkeeper, William 'Fatty' Foulke, two young boys would stand behind his goal. They soon proved themselves useful in retrieving the ball when it went out of play, and so the concept of the ball boy was born.

• Amazingly, a ball boy scored a goal in a match between Santacruzense and Atletico Sorocaba in Brazil in 2006. Santacruzense were trailing 1-0 when one of their players fired wide in the last minute. Instead of handing the ball back to the Atletico goalkeeper, the ball boy kicked it into the net and the goal was awarded by the female referee despite the angry protests of the Atletico players.

• Seventeen-year-old Swansea ball boy Charlie Morgan helped his side reach the League Cup final in 2013 by falling on top of the ball when Chelsea's Eden

Hazard wanted to take a corner kick. Frustrated at the lad's refusal to return the ball quickly, Hazard kicked it out from under him and was promptly shown a red card that pretty much ended Chelsea's chances of overhauling a two-goal deficit from the first leg.

• Shakhtar Donetsk striker Fecundo Ferreyra sparked a mass brawl during his side's last 16 Champions League tie with Roma in March 2018 when he rushed to get the ball from a ball boy and angrily pushed the youngster over the advertising hoardings. He escaped with a yellow card and later apologised for his actions.

• A 16-year-old Bournemouth ball boy was ticked off by an assistant referee during the Cherries' home match with Tottenham in March 2018 when he initially refused to return the ball to Spurs defender Jan Vertonghen and then threw the ball hard at the Belgian international's knees.

BALLS

The laws of football specify that the ball must be an air-filled sphere with a circumference of 68-70cm and a weight before the start of the game of 410-450g. Before the first plastic footballs appeared in the 1950s, balls were made from leather and in wet conditions would become progressively heavier, sometimes actually doubling in weight.

• **Most modern footballs are made in Pakistan, especially in the city of Sialkot, and are usually stitched from 32 panels of waterproofed leather or plastic. In the past child labour was often used in the production of the balls but, following pressure from UNICEF and the International Labour Organisation, manufacturers agreed in 1997 not to employ underage workers.**

• Adidas have supplied the official ball for the World Cup since the iconic black-and-white Telstar in 1970. The ball for the 2018 tournament in Russia, the

Adidas Telstar 18, featured six textured panels seamlessly glued together and was produced by Forward Sports in Sialkot.

• **Nike are the official supplier of balls for the Premier League, taking over the role from Mitre in 2000. A winter 'Hi-Vis' yellow ball has been used in the league since the 2004/05 season.**

• Nike are the official suppliers of the ball for FA Cup matches. The ball for the 137th final in 2018 between Chelsea and Manchester United, the Nike Ordem V, featured the names of 137 different goalscorers from that season's competition from the extra preliminary round onwards.

• **A ball accidentally kicked off the pitch during a match at Scottish Under-19 side Banks O' Dee FC was discovered over 1,000 miles away on an island off Norway in April 2017. The club by the River Dee has lost** numerous balls in the water, but this was the first one to turn up in the Arctic Circle.

BARCELONA

	Year founded: 1899 **Ground:** Nou Camp (99,354) **Nickname:** Barça **League titles:** 25 **Domestic cups:** 30 **European cups:** 17 **International cups:** 3

One of the most famous and popular clubs in the world, Barcelona were founded in 1899 by bank worker Joan Gamper, a former captain of Swiss club Basel. The club were founder members and first winners of the Spanish championship, La Liga, in 1928 and have remained in the top flight of Spanish football ever since.

• **For the people of Catalonia, Barcelona is more like a national team than a mere club. As former manager Bobby Robson once succinctly**

Everyone wanted to get their hands on the official ball for the 2018 World Cup

put it, "Catalonia is a country and FC Barcelona is their army." The hierarchy of the club and many of its fans are strong supporters of Catalan independence, demonstrating their backing for the cause on the day of the 2017 referendum on the issue by playing their La Liga match against Las Palmas behind closed doors.

• With a capacity of 99,354 Barcelona's Nou Camp stadium is the largest in Europe. Among the stadium's many facilities are a museum which attracts over one million visitors a year, mini training pitches and even a chapel for the players.

• For many years Barcelona played second fiddle to bitter rivals Real Madrid. Finally, in the 1990s, under former player-turned-coach Johan Cruyff, Barça turned the tables on the team from the Spanish capital by winning four La Liga titles on the trot between 1991 and 1994. Cruyff also led the Catalans to a first taste of glory in the European Cup, Barcelona beating Sampdoria at Wembley in 1992. The club have since won the Champions League on four more occasions, most recently beating

Juventus 3-1 in the 2015 final to become the first European club to win the Treble twice (the first occasion was in 2009).

• Reigning Spanish champions, Barcelona were unbeaten for a La Liga record 43 consecutive league games between 15th April 2017 and 9th May 2018.

HONOURS
Spanish champions *1929, 1945, 1948, 1949, 1952, 1953, 1959, 1960, 1974, 1985, 1991, 1992, 1993, 1994, 1998, 1999, 2005, 2006, 2009, 2010, 2011, 2013, 2015, 2016, 2018*
Spanish Cup *1910, 1912, 1913, 1920, 1922, 1925, 1926, 1928, 1942, 1951,1952, 1953, 1957, 1959, 1963, 1968, 1971, 1978, 1981, 1983, 1988, 1990, 1997, 1998, 2009, 2012, 2015, 2016, 2017, 2018*
European Cup/Champions League *1992, 2006, 2009, 2011, 2015*
Fairs Cup *1958, 1960, 1961*
European Cup Winners' Cup *1979, 1982, 1989, 1997*
European Super Cup *1992, 1997, 2009, 2011, 2015*
Club World Cup *2009, 2011, 2015*

Lionesses goalkeeper Karen Bardsley

KAREN BARDSLEY

Born: Santa Monica, USA, 14th October 1984
Position: Goalkeeper
Club career:
2007 Ajax America Women
2008 Pali Blues 5
2009-11 Sky Blue FC 17
2011-12 Linkopings FC 3
2013 Lincoln Ladies 14
2014- Manchester City 47
International record:
2005- England 73

Born in California to parents from Greater Manchester, Karen Bardsley opted to play for England rather than the USA and she has been a fixture between the posts for the Lionesses for a number of years, representing her country at two World Cups.

• **The tall shot-stopper came through the college system in America to play for clubs on both the west and east coast before moving to Sweden and then on to England, signing first for Lincoln Ladies and then, in November 2013, for Manchester City.**

• Bardsley was part of the City side which won the Women's Super League in 2016 and the Women's FA Cup the following year, after a crushing 4-1 defeat of Birmingham City in the final at Wembley.

• **England's number one since the 2011 World Cup, Bardsley has had some bad luck playing for the Lionesses in recent years. At the 2015 World Cup she had to be subbed off in the quarter-final against hosts Canada after suffering a mysterious eye inflammation and two years later she broke her leg against France at the same stage of the European Championships in the Netherlands.**

Mohican? Check! Bushy beard? Check! Tattoo? Check! Barcelona's Arturo Vidal is all in when it comes to fashion

FC Bayern München... better known as German giants Bayern Munich

BARNSLEY

Year founded: 1887
Ground: Oakwell (23,009)
Previous name: Barnsley St Peter's
Nickname: The Tykes
Biggest win: 9-0 v Loughborough United (1899)
Heaviest defeat: 0-9 v Notts County (1927)

Founded as the church team Barnsley St Peter's in 1887 by the Rev. Tiverton Preedy, the club changed to their present name a year after joining the Football League in 1898.

• Although they were relegated from the Championship in 2018, the Tykes have spent more seasons (75) in the second tier of English football than any other club and had to wait until 1997 before they had their first taste of life in the top flight. Unfortunately for their fans, however, it lasted just one season.

• The Yorkshiremen's finest hour came in 1912 when they won the FA Cup, beating West Bromwich Albion 1-0 in a replay. The club were nicknamed 'Battling Barnsley' that season as they played a record 12 games during their cup run, including six 0-0 draws, before finally getting their hands on the trophy. Barnsley came close to repeating this feat in 2008, but were beaten in the semi-finals by fellow Championship side Cardiff City after they had sensationally knocked out Liverpool as well as cup holders Chelsea.

• The youngest player to appear in the Football League is Barnsley striker Reuben Noble-Lazarus, who was 15 years and 45 days old when he faced Ipswich Town in September 2008. Afterwards, Barnsley boss Simon Davey joked Noble-Lazarus would be rewarded with a pizza as he was too young to be paid!

• Stalwart defender Barry Murphy made a club record 569 league appearances for the Tykes between 1962 and 1978. Striker Ernie Hine scored a club record 131 goals in two spells with the Tykes between 1921 and 1938.

• The club's most decorated international is defender Gerry Taggart, who played 35 times for Northern Ireland between 1990 and 1995.

HONOURS
Division 3 (North) champions 1934, 1939, 1955
FA Cup 1912
Football League Trophy 2016

BAYERN MUNICH

Year founded: 1900
Ground: Allianz Arena (75,000)
Nickname: The Bavarians
League titles: 28
Domestic cups: 18
European cups: 7

The biggest and most successful club in Germany, Bayern Munich were founded in 1900 by members of a Munich gymnastics club. Incredibly, when the Bundesliga was formed in 1963, Bayern's form was so poor that they were not invited to become founder members of the league. But, thanks to the emergence in the mid-1960s of legendary players like goalkeeper Sepp Maier, sweeper Franz Beckenbauer and prolific goalscorer Gerd Muller, Bayern rapidly became the dominant force in German football. The club won the Bundesliga for the first time in 1969 and now have a record 28 German championships to their name, including a record six on the trot between 2013 and 2018.

• In 1974 Bayern became the first German club to win the European Cup, defeating Atletico Madrid 4-0 in the

TOP 10

TOTAL BUNDESLIGA MATCHES WON

1.	Bayern Munich	1,070
2.	Werder Bremen	771
3.	Borussia Dortmund	761
4.	Hamburg	746
5.	Stuttgart	733
6.	Borussia Monchengladbach	685
7.	Schalke	673
8.	FC Cologne	629
9.	Eintracht Frankfurt	606
10.	FC Kaiserslautern	575

only final to go to a replay. **Skippered by the imperious Beckenbauer, the club went on to complete a hat-trick of victories in the competition.**

• In winning the Bundesliga title in 2012/13, Bayern set numerous records, including highest points total (91), most wins (29) and best goal difference (+80). They then beat Borussia Dortmund 2-1 at Wembley in the first all-German Champions League final, before becoming the first ever German team to win the Treble when they beat Stuttgart 3-2 in the final of the German Cup.

• **Former French international Franck Ribery is the only foreign player to win eight Bundesliga titles, achieving this feat with Bayern between 2008 and 2018.**

• Gerd Muller scored a German record 365 league goals for Bayern between 1965 and 1979, finding the net in a record 16 consecutive matches in the 1969/70 season.

HONOURS

German champions 1932, 1969, 1972, 1973, 1974, 1980, 1981, 1985, 1986, 1987, 1989, 1990, 1994, 1997, 1999, 2000, 2001, 2003, 2005, 2006, 2008, 2010, 2013, 2014, 2015, 2016, 2017, 2018
German Cup 1957, 1966, 1967, 1969, 1971, 1982, 1984, 1986, 1998, 2000, 2003, 2005, 2006, 2008, 2010, 2013, 2014, 2016
European Cup/
Champions League
1974, 1975, 1976, 2001, 2013
UEFA Cup 1996
European Cup Winners' Cup 1967
European Super Cup 2013
Club World Cup 2013

BELGIUM

First international: Belgium 3 France 3, 1904
Most capped player: Jan Vertonghen, 108 caps (2007-)
Leading goalscorer: Romelu Lukaku, 40 goals (2010-)
First World Cup appearance: Belgium 2 Germany 5, 1934
Biggest win: Belgium 10 San Marino 1, 2001
Heaviest defeat: England amateurs 11 Belgium 2, 1909

A rising force in the world game, Belgium are yet to win a major trophy but they came mighty close in the 1980 European Championships in Italy. After topping their group ahead of Italy, England and Spain, Belgium went straight through to the final against West Germany where they were unfortunate to go down 2-1 in a close encounter.

• Belgium's best performance at the World Cup came in 2018 when, after beating Japan and Brazil in the earlier knock-out rounds, they lost 1-0 to eventual winners France in the semi-final in St Petersburg. The defeat ended the country's best ever run of 24 games without defeat, but the Belgians were soon back to winning ways, beating England 2-0 in the third place play-off match thanks to well-worked goals by wing-back Thomas Meunier, who became his team's record 11th scorer at the 2018 finals, and skipper Eden Hazard.

• Belgium also reached the semi-finals in 1986 but came up against a Diego Maradona-inspired Argentina and went down 2-0 in Mexico City. After losing 4-2 in the third place match to France, Belgium had to be content with fourth place at the tournament.

• **On 10th October 2016 Belgium scored the fastest ever goal in the World Cup, when Christian Benteke netted after just 8.1 seconds in a qualifier against Gibraltar.**

Belgium enjoyed their best ever World Cup in 2018

World Cup Record
1930 Round 1
1934 Round 1
1938 Round 1
1950 Withdrew
1954 Round 1
1958 Did not qualify
1962 Did not qualify
1966 Did not qualify
1970 Round 1
1974 Did not qualify
1978 Did not qualify
1982 Round 2
1986 Fourth place
1990 Round 2
1994 Round 2
1998 Round 1
2002 Round 2
2006 Did not qualify
2010 Did not qualify
2014 Quarter-finals
2018 Third place

BENFICA

Year founded: 1904
Ground: Estadio Da Luz, Lisbon (64,642)
Nickname: The Eagles
League titles: 36
Domestic cups: 29
European cups: 2

Portugal's most successful club, Benfica were founded in 1904 at a meeting of 24 football enthusiasts in south Lisbon. The club were founder members of the Portuguese league in 1933 and have since won the title a record 36 times.

• Inspired by legendary striker Eusebio, Benfica enjoyed a golden era in the 1960s when the club won eight domestic championships. In 1961 Benfica became the first team to break Real Madrid's dominance in the European Cup when they beat Barcelona 3-2 in the final. The following year, the trophy stayed in Lisbon after the Eagles sensationally beat star-studded Real 5-3 in the final in Amsterdam.

• In 1972/73 Benfica went the whole season undefeated – the first Portuguese team to achieve this feat – winning a staggering 28 and drawing just two of their 30 league matches. Along the way, Benfica set a still unbroken European

record by winning 29 consecutive domestic league matches.

• **In 2015/16 Benfica won the Portuguese league with a record 88 points. The club also hold records for the most wins in the league overall (1,613) and the most goals scored in total (5,709).**

• Benfica hold the record for the biggest ever aggregate win in the European Cup/Champions League with an astonishing 18-0 thrashing of Luxembourg minnows Stade Dudelange in 1965.

HONOURS
Portuguese champions 1936, 1937, 1938, 1942, 1943, 1945, 1950, 1955, 1957,1960, 1961, 1963, 1964, 1965, 1967, 1968, 1969,1971, 1972, 1973, 1975,1976, 1977, 1981, 1983, 1984, 1987, 1989, 1991, 1994, 2005, 2010, 2014, 2015, 2016, 2017
Portuguese Cup 1930, 1931, 1935, 1940, 1943, 1944, 1949, 1951, 1952, 1953, 1955, 1957,1959, 1962, 1964, 1969, 1970, 1972, 1980,1981,1983, 1985, 1986, 1987, 1993, 1996, 2004, 2014, 2017
European Cup 1961, 1962

RAFA BENITEZ

Born: Madrid, Spain 16th April 1960
Managerial career:
1993-95 Real Madrid B
1995-96 Real Valladolid
1996 Osasuna
1997-99 Extremadura
2000-01 Tenerife
2001-04 Valencia
2004-10 Liverpool
2010 Inter Milan
2012-13 Chelsea (interim)
2013-15 Napoli
2015-16 Real Madrid
2016- Newcastle United

Rafael Benitez's total of 302 Premier League games in charge of Liverpool, Chelsea and Newcastle, his current club, is only bettered by Arsene Wenger (828) among managers from outside the British Isles.

• **In a long and varied career in management, Benitez has won a host of top honours, including two Spanish league titles with Valencia, the Champions League with Liverpool in 2005, the FIFA Club World Cup with Inter Milan in 2010 and the Coppa Italia with Napoli in 2014.**

You'd never guess it, but Rafa Benitez is really quite popular on Tyneside!

• Despite being an unpopular choice as Chelsea interim manager thanks to his Liverpool connections, Benitez won the Europa League with the Blues in 2013 after a 2-1 victory against Benfica in the final in Amsterdam. That triumph meant that the Spaniard became only the second manager (after Giovanni Trapattoni) to win the competition with two different clubs, having previously won the UEFA Cup (as it was known then) with Valencia in 2004.

• After a disappointing six-month spell with Real Madrid, Benitez returned to England to take charge of Newcastle in March 2016. He couldn't prevent the Magpies being relegated at the end of the campaign, but then became a cult hero on Tyneside when he led the Geordies to the Championship title in 2017 and an impressive tenth-place finish in the Premier League the following year.

BIRMINGHAM CITY

Year founded: 1875
Ground: St Andrew's (29,409)
Previous name: Small Heath Alliance, Small Heath, Birmingham
Nickname: The Blues
Biggest win: 12-0 v Nottingham Forest (1899), Walsall Town Swifts (1892) and Doncaster Rovers (1903)
Heaviest defeat: 1-9 v Blackburn Rovers (1895) and Sheffield Wednesday (1930)

IS THAT A FACT?
In February 1979 Birmingham became the first British club to sell a player for £1 million, when striker Trevor Francis left St Andrew's for Nottingham Forest. The move worked well for Francis, who scored the winner in that year's European Cup final, but less well for the Blues, who were relegated to the old Second Division at the end of the campaign.

Founded in 1875 as Small Heath Alliance, the club were founder members and the first champions of the Second Division in 1892. Unfortunately, Small Heath were undone at the 'test match' stage (a 19th-century version of the play-offs) and failed to gain promotion to the top flight.

• **The club had to wait until 2011 for the greatest day in their history, when the Blues beat hot favourites Arsenal 2-1 in the League Cup final at Wembley,** on-loan striker Obafemi Martins grabbing the winner in the final minutes to spark ecstatic celebrations among Birmingham's long-suffering fans. City had previously won the competition back in 1963 after getting the better of arch rivals Aston Villa over a two-legged final, although that achievement was hardly comparable as half the top-flight clubs hadn't even bothered to enter.

• However, on the final day of the 2010/11 season Birmingham were relegated from the Premier League. It was the 12th time in their history that the Blues had fallen through the top-flight trapdoor, a record of misery unmatched by any other club. More positively, Birmingham share the distinction with near-neighbours Leicester of being promoted to the top tier a record 12 times.

• **Stalwart defender Frank Womack made a club record 491 league appearances for the Blues between 1908 and 1928. Incredibly, Womack played a total of 510 league games without once getting on the scoresheet – a Football League record for an outfield player.**

• On 15th May 1955 Birmingham became the first English club to compete in Europe when they drew 0-0 away to Inter Milan in the inaugural competition of the Fairs Cup. Five years later in the same tournament, Brum became the first British club to reach a European final but were beaten 4-1 on aggregate by Barcelona.

• **England international Joe Bradford scored a club record 249 league goals for the Blues between 1920 and 1935.**

• The Blues splashed out a club record fee in excess of £6 million in August 2017 to sign Brentford midfielder Jota. In July 2006 the club received a record £6.7 million when

English winger Jermaine Pennant moved to Liverpool.

BLACKBURN ROVERS

Year founded: 1875
Ground: Ewood Park (31,367)
Nickname: Rovers
Biggest win: 11-0 v Rossendale United (1884)
Heaviest defeat: 0-8 v Arsenal (1933)

Founded in 1875 by a group of wealthy local residents and ex-public school boys, Blackburn Rovers joined the Football League as founder members in 1888. Two years later the club moved to a permanent home at Ewood Park, where they have remained ever since.

• **Blackburn were a force to be reckoned with from the start, winning the FA Cup five times in the 1880s and 1890s. Of all league clubs Rovers were the first to win the trophy, beating Scottish side Queen's Park 2-1 in the final at Kennington Oval in 1884. The Lancashire side went on to win the cup in the two following years as well, remaining undefeated in a record 23 consecutive games in the competition between 1884 and 1886.**

• Rovers won the cup again in 1890, 1891 and 1928 to make a total of six triumphs in the competition. In the first of these victories they thrashed Sheffield Wednesday 6-1 in the final, with left winger William Townley scoring three times to become the first player to hit a hat-trick in the final.

• **Promoted back to the Championship in 2018, the club have won the league title three times: in 1912, 1914 and, most memorably, in 1995 when, funded by the millions of popular local steel magnate Jack Walker and powered by the deadly 'SAS' strikeforce of Alan Shearer and Chris Sutton, Rovers pipped reigning champions Manchester United to the Premiership title.**

Scottish international Charlie Mulgrew's eye for a goal has Rovers' fans dreaming of a return to the Premiership

• Derek Fazackerley made the most appearances for Blackburn, turning out in 596 games between 1970 and 1986. The club's all-time leading scorer is Simon Garner, with 168 league goals between 1978 and 1992, although England striker Alan Shearer's incredible record of 122 goals in just 138 games for the club is arguably more impressive.

• **Nineteenth-century striker Jack Southworth scored a record 13 hat-tricks for Rovers, including a seasonal best of five in 1890/91.**

• Defender Walter Crook played in a club record 208 consecutive league games between 1934 and 1936.

HONOURS
Premier League champions 1995
Division 1 champions 1912, 1914
Division 2 champions 1975
FA Cup 1884, 1885, 1886, 1890, 1891, 1928
League Cup 2002

BLACKPOOL

Year founded: 1887
Ground: Bloomfield Road (17,338)
Nickname: The Seasiders
Biggest win: 10-0 v Lanerossi Vicenza (1972)
Heaviest defeat: 1-10 v Small Heath (1901)

Founded in 1887 by old boys of St John's School, Blackpool joined the Second Division of the Football League in 1896. The club merged with South Shore in 1899, the same year in which Blackpool narrowly lost their league status for a single season.

• **Blackpool's heyday was in the late 1940s and early 1950s when the club reached three FA Cup finals in five years. The Seasiders lost in the finals of 1948 and 1951 but lifted the cup in 1953 after defeating Lancashire rivals Bolton 4-3 in one of the most exciting Wembley matches ever. Although centre-forward Stan Mortensen scored a hat-trick, the match was dubbed the 'Matthews Final' after veteran winger Stanley Matthews, who finally won a winner's medal at the grand old age of 38.**

• An apprentice at the time of the 'Matthews Final', long-serving right-back Jimmy Armfield holds the record for league appearances for Blackpool, with 569 between 1952 and 1971. Armfield, who died in January 2018, is also Blackpool's most capped player, having played for England 43 times. In 2011 a 9ft-high statue of the Seasiders legend was unveiled outside Bloomfield Road.

• **The club's record scorer is Jimmy Hampson, who hit 248 league goals between 1927 and 1938, including a season best 45 in the much-celebrated 1929/30 Second Division championship-winning campaign.**

• Blackpool were the first club to gain promotion from three different divisions via the play-offs. In total the Seasiders have played in a record seven play-off finals, most recently beating Exeter City 2-1 in the 2017 League Two decider at

Wembley, and with five wins they have the best record of any club in the finals.

• Blackpool used a club record 50 players in the 2014/15 season – just four short of the all-time Football League high set by Darlington in 2009/10.

HONOURS
Division 2 champions 1930
FA Cup 1953
Football League Trophy 2002, 2004

BOLTON WANDERERS

Year founded: 1874
Ground: University of Bolton Stadium (28,723)
Previous name: Christ Church
Nickname: The Trotters
Biggest win: 13-0 v Sheffield United (1890)
Heaviest defeat: 1-9 v Preston North End (1887)

The club was founded in 1874 as Christ Church, but three years later broke away from the church after a disagreement with the vicar and adopted their present name (the 'Wanderers' part stemmed from the fact that the club had no permanent home until moving to their former stadium, Burnden Park, in 1895).

• Bolton were founder members of the Football League in 1888, finishing fifth at the end of the campaign. The Trotters have since gone on to play more seasons in the top flight without ever winning the title, 73, than any other club.

• The club, though, have had better luck in the FA Cup. After defeats in the final in 1894 and 1904, Bolton won the cup for the first time in 1923 after beating West Ham 2-0 in the first Wembley final. In the same match, Bolton centre-forward David Jack enjoyed the distinction of becoming the first player to score a goal at the new stadium. The Trotters went on to win the competition again in 1926 and 1929.

• **In 1953 Bolton became the first team to score three goals in the FA Cup final yet finish as losers, going down 4-3 to a Stanley Matthews-inspired Blackpool. In 1958 Bolton won the cup for a fourth time, beating Manchester United 2-0 in the final at Wembley.**

- Bolton have twice reached the League Cup final but lost on both occasions, beaten 2-1 by Liverpool in 1995 and Middlesbrough in 2004.
- **Bolton's top scorer is legendary centre-forward Nat Lofthouse, who notched 285 goals in all competitions between 1946 and 1960. The Trotters' appearance record is held by another England international of the same era, goalkeeper Eddie Hopkinson, who turned out 578 times for the club between 1952 and 1970.**
- Ray Parry was the youngest Football League player ever at the time when he made his Bolton debut against Wolves in 1951 aged 15 and 267 days.

HONOURS
First Division champions 1997
Division 2 champions 1909, 1978
Division 3 champions 1973
FA Cup 1923, 1926, 1929, 1958
Football League Trophy 1989

BOOTS

The first record of a pair of football boots goes back to 1526 when Henry VIII, then aged 35, ordered "45 velvet pairs and one leather pair for football" from the Great Wardrobe. Whether he actually donned the boots for a royal kick-around in Hampton Court or Windsor Castle is not known.

IS THAT A FACT?
Around 60% of players at the 2018 World Cup in Russia wore Nike boots, including brand posterboys Cristiano Ronaldo, Neymar and Harry Kane.

- **Early leather boots were very different to the synthetic ones worn by modern players, having hard toe-caps and protection around the ankles. Studs were originally prohibited, but were sanctioned after a change in the rules in 1891. Lighter boots without ankle protection were first worn in South America, but did not become the norm in Britain until the 1950s, following the example of England international Stanley Matthews who had a lightweight pair of boots made for him by a Yorkshire company.**
- Herbert Chapman, later Arsenal's manager, is believed to be the first player to wear coloured boots, sporting a yellow pair in the 1900s. White boots first became fashionable in the 1970s when they were worn by the likes of Alan Ball (Everton), Terry Cooper (Leeds) and Alan Hinton (Derby County). In 1996,

Liverpool's John Barnes was the first player to wear white boots in an FA Cup final, but failed to dazzle in his side's 1-0 defeat to Manchester United.
- **In January 2016 Arsenal midfielder Mesut Ozil became the first player in Premier League history to wear laceless boots, the Adidas ACE16+PureControl.**
- Cristiano Ronaldo's incredible £1 billion lifetime sponsorship deal with boot manufacturers Nike is easily the biggest in the history of the game.

BOURNEMOUTH

Year founded: 1899
Ground: Dean Court (11,360)
Previous name: Boscombe, Bournemouth and Boscombe Athletic
Nickname: The Cherries
Biggest win: 11-0 v Margate (1970)
Heaviest defeat: 0-9 v Lincoln City (1982)

The Cherries were founded as Boscombe FC in 1899, having their origins in the Boscombe St John's club, which was formed in 1890. The club's

No prizes for guessing which Portuguese superstar has the most expensive boot deal in history

name changed to Bournemouth and Boscombe FC in 1923 and then to AFC Bournemouth in 1971, when the team's colours were altered to red-and-black stripes in imitation of AC Milan.

• Any similarity to the Italian giants was not obvious, though, until the 2014/15 season when the Cherries won promotion to the top flight for the first time in their history, clinching the Championship title in some style with a 3-0 victory at Charlton on the final day of the campaign.

• The Cherries' attack-minded team set a new record for the second tier by scoring 50 goals on their travels. They also set a new club record for goals scored in a season, with 115 in total in all competitions.

• The club recorded their biggest ever win in the FA Cup, smashing fellow seasiders Margate 11-0 at Dean Court in 1970. Cherries striker Ted MacDougall

Life's a bowl of cherries for Bournemouth these days

scored nine of the goals, an all-time record for an individual player in the competition. In the same season the prolific Scot scored a club record 42 league goals.

• Bournemouth enjoyed their best ever FA Cup run as a third-tier side in 1957, knocking out Tottenham in the fifth round before losing 2-1 at home to mighty Manchester United in the quarter-finals in front of a club record attendance of 28,799.

• The club's record scorer is Ron Eyre (202 goals between 1924 and 1933), while striker Steve Fletcher pulled on the Cherries' jersey an amazing 628 times in two spells at Dean Court between 1992 and 2013.

• In August 2018 Bournemouth splashed out a club record £25 million on Levante's Colombian international midfielder Jefferson Lerma, while two years earlier the Cherries received a record £12 million when winger Matt Ritchie joined Newcastle.

• Striker Joshua King is Bournemouth's most-capped player, having turned out 17 times for Norway since signing from Blackburn in 2015.

• Appointed Bournemouth manager for a second time in October 2012, Cherries boss Eddie Howe is now the longest-serving in the Premier League.

• In March 2018 midfielder Lewis Cook became the first current Bournemouth player to play for England, when he came on as a sub in a 1-1 draw against Italy at Wembley. His cameo appearance was especially good news for his grandfather who won £17,000 after betting £500 that Cook would represent the Three Lions while he was starting out in the Leeds reserve team.

HONOURS
Championship champions 2015
Division 3 champions 1987
Football League Trophy 1984

BRADFORD CITY

Year founded: 1903
Ground: Valley Parade (25,136)
Nickname: The Bantams
Biggest win: 11-1 v Rotherham United (1928)
Heaviest defeat: 1-9 v Colchester United (1961)

Bradford City were founded in 1903 when a local rugby league side, Manningham FC, decided to switch codes. The club was elected to Division Two in the same year before they had played a single match – a swift ascent into the Football League which is only matched by Chelsea.

• City's finest hour was in 1911 when they won the FA Cup for the only time in the club's history, beating Newcastle 1-0 in a replayed final at Old Trafford. There were more celebrations in Bradford in 1929 when City won the Third Division (North), scoring 128 goals in the process – a record for the third tier.

• In 2013 Bradford City became the first club from the fourth tier of English football to reach a major final at Wembley, losing 5-0 to Swansea City in the League Cup. Two years later the Bantams pulled off possibly the biggest FA Cup shock ever, coming back from 2-0 down to beat Chelsea 4-2 in the fourth round at Stamford Bridge.

• Sadly, City will forever be associated with the fire that broke out in the club's main stand on 11th May 1985 and killed 56 supporters. The official inquiry into the tragedy found that the inferno had probably been caused by a discarded cigarette butt which set fire to litter under the stand. As a permanent memorial to those who died, Bradford added black trimming to their shirt collars and sleeves.

• During a two-year spell in the Premier League, the Bantams made their record signing, splashing out £2.5 million on Leeds winger David Hopkin in 2000.

HONOURS
Division 2 champions 1908
Division 3 champions 1985
Division 3 (North) champions 1929
FA Cup 1911

BRAZIL

First international: Argentina 3 Brazil 0, 1914

Most capped player: Cafu, 142 caps (1990-2006)

Leading goalscorer: Pelé, 77 goals (1957-71)

First World Cup appearance: Brazil 1 Yugoslavia 2, 1930

Biggest win: Brazil 14 Nicaragua 0, 1975

Heaviest defeat: Brazil 1 Germany 7, 2014

The most successful country in the history of international football, Brazil are renowned for an exciting, flamboyant style of play which delights both their legions of drum-beating fans and neutrals alike.

• Brazil are the only country to have won the World Cup five times. The South Americans first lifted the trophy in 1958 (beating hosts Sweden 5-2 in the final) and retained the prize four years later in Chile. In 1970, a great Brazilian side featuring legends such as Pelé, Jairzinho, Gerson and Rivelino thrashed Italy 4-1 to win the Jules Rimet trophy for a third time. Further triumphs followed in 1994 (3-2 on penalties against Italy after a dour 0-0 draw) and in 2002 (after beating Germany 2-0 in the final).

• Brazil are the only country to have appeared at every World Cup (a total of 21) since the tournament began in 1930. The South Americans have also recorded the most wins (73) at the finals and scored the most goals (229). Less impressively, Brazil suffered the heaviest ever defeat by a host nation when they were trounced 7-1 by Germany in the semi-finals of the 2014 tournament.

• **Between February 1993 and January 1996 Brazil set a new world record when they were undefeated for 35 consecutive internationals.**

• With eight wins to their name, Brazil are the third most successful side in the history of the Copa America (behind Uruguay and Argentina, who have won the trophy 15 and 14 times respectively). However, the South Americans flopped at the most recent tournament in 2016, failing to reach the knock-out stages after a shock 1-0 defeat to Peru.

• **Brazil have the best record of any nation in the Confederations Cup, winning the trophy four times – most recently in 2013, when they beat Spain 3-0 in the final in Rio de Janeiro.**

TOP 10

BRAZIL GOALSCORERS

1. Pele (1957-71)	77
2. Ronaldo (1994-2011)	62
3. Neymar (2010-)	57
4. Romario (1987-2005)	55
5. Zico (1976-86)	48
6. Bebeto (1985-98)	39
7. Rivaldo (1993-2003)	35
8. Jairzinho (1964-82)	33
Ronaldinho (1999-2013)	33
9. Ademir (1945-53)	32
Tostao (1966-72)	32

HONOURS

World Cup winners 1958, 1962, 1970, 1994, 2002
Copa America winners 1919, 1922, 1949, 1989, 1997, 1999, 2004, 2007
Confederations Cup winners 1997, 2005, 2009, 2013

World Cup Record
1930 Round 1
1934 Round 1
1938 Semi-finals
1950 Runners-up
1954 Quarter-finals
1958 Winners
1962 Winners
1966 Round 1
1970 Winners
1974 Fourth place
1978 Third place
1982 Round 2
1986 Quarter-finals
1990 Round 2
1994 Winners
1998 Runners-up
2002 Winners
2006 Quarter-finals
2010 Quarter-finals
2014 Fourth place
2018 Quarter-finals

Brazil's exit from the 2018 World Cup was agony for their fans – and Neymar didn't enjoy it much, either!

BRENTFORD

Year founded: 1889
Ground: Griffin Park (12,763)
Nickname: The Bees
Biggest win: 9-0 v Wrexham (1963)
Heaviest defeat: 0-7 v Swansea Town (1926), v Walsall (1957) and v Peterborough (2007)

Brentford were founded in 1889 by members of a local rowing club and, after playing at a number of different venues, the club settled at Griffin Park in 1904.

• The club enjoyed its heyday in the decade before the Second World War. In 1929/30 Brentford won all 21 of their home games in the Third Division (South) to set a record which remains to this day. Promoted to the First Division in 1935, the Bees finished in the top six in the next three seasons before being relegated in the first post-war campaign. After plunging into the Fourth Division in 1962, Brentford became the first team to have played all the other 91 clubs in the Football League.

• Defender Ken Coote played in a club record 514 league games for the Bees between 1949 and 1964, while his team-mate Jim Towers scored a record 153 league goals.

• The Bees paid out a club record £2.5 million when they signed Norwich midfielder Sergi Canos in January 2017. In the same month the west Londoners received a record £9 million when striker Scott Hogan joined Aston Villa.

• In the 1974/75 season goalkeeper Steve Sherwood became the first ever on-loan player to be ever-present in a league campaign when he spent a year away from his parent club Chelsea at Griffin Park.

• Striker Jack Holliday scored a record nine hat-tricks for the Bees, including a club best five in 1932/33.

• In a League Cup first round tie against AFC Wimbledon in August 2017 Brentford's Justin Shaibu became the first ever fourth substitute to score a competitive goal.

HONOURS
Division 2 champions 1935
Division 3 (South) champions 1933
League Two champions 2009
Third Division champions 1999
Division 4 champions 1963

BRIGHTON AND HOVE ALBION

Year founded: 1900
Ground: AMEX Stadium (30,750)
Previous name: Brighton and Hove Rangers
Nickname: The Seagulls
Biggest win: 14-2 v Brighton Amateurs (1902)
Heaviest defeat: 0-9 v Middlesbrough (1958)

Yves Bissouma has become a key part of Albion's midfield since joining from Lille

Founded originally as Brighton and Hove Rangers in 1900, the club changed to its present name the following year. In 1920 Brighton joined Division Three as founder members, but had to wait another 38 years before gaining promotion to a higher level.

• Brighton enjoyed the greatest achievement in their history in 2017 when, under manager Chris Hughton, they were promoted to the Premier League for the first time, finishing just one point behind Championship title winners Newcastle. The following season the Seagulls confounded the doom mongers by staying up, securing their top-flight status with a 1-0 home win against Manchester United.

• The club reached the final of the FA Cup for the only time in their history in 1983, holding favourites Manchester United to a 2-2 draw at Wembley. The Seagulls were unable to repeat their heroics in the replay, however, and crashed to a 4-0 defeat. In the same year Brighton were relegated from the old First Division, ending a four-season stint in the top flight.

• A decade earlier, the Seagulls were briefly managed by the legendary Brian Clough. His time in charge of the club, though, was not a successful one and included an 8-2 thrashing by Bristol Rovers – the worst home defeat in Brighton's history.

• Brighton's record scorer is 1920s striker Tommy Cook, with 114 league goals. Cult hero Peter Ward, though, enjoyed the most prolific season in front of goal for the club, notching 32 times as the Seagulls gained promotion from the old Third Division in 1976/77. Ernie 'Tug' Wilson made the most appearances for the south coast outfit, with 509 between 1922 and 1936.

• The Seagulls' most expensive signing is Iran winger Alireza Jahanbakhsh, who cost £17 million from Dutch outfit AZ Alkmaar in July 2018. Argentinian striker Leonardo Ulloa boosted Brighton's coffers by a club record £8 million when he joined Leicester City in 2014.

• Brighton are the only club to have won the Charity Shield without ever winning the league title or FA Cup. In 1910 the Seagulls, then reigning Southern League champions, lifted the shield after beating title winners Aston Villa 1-0 at Stamford Bridge.

• Brighton defender Shane Duffy made more clearances, a mere 327, than any other Premier League player in the 2017/18 season.

> **HONOURS**
> *League One champions* 2011
> *Second Division champions* 2002
> *Division 3 (South) champions* 1958
> *Third Division champions* 2001
> *Division 4 champions* 1965

BRISTOL CITY

Year founded: 1894
Ground: Ashton Gate (27,000)
Previous name: Bristol South End
Nickname: The Robins
Biggest win: 11-0 v Chichester City (1960)
Heaviest defeat: 0-9 v Coventry City (1934)

Founded as Bristol South End in 1894, the club took its present name when it turned professional three years later. In 1900 City merged with Bedminster, whose ground at Ashton Gate became the club's permanent home in 1904.

• **The Robins enjoyed a golden decade in the 1900s, winning promotion to the top flight for the first time in 1906 after a campaign in which they won a club record 14 consecutive games. The following season City finished second, and in 1909 they reached the FA Cup final for the first and only time in their history, losing 1-0 to Manchester United at Crystal Palace.**

• Since then the followers of Bristol's biggest club have had to endure more downs than ups. The Robins returned to

IS THAT A FACT?
Between 1908 and 1996 Bristol City and Bristol Rovers met every year in the Gloucestershire Cup, the Robins winning 53 of these clashes while Rovers came out on top 27 times.

the top flight after a 65-year absence in 1976, but financial difficulties led to three consecutive relegations in the early 1980s (City being the first club ever to suffer this awful fate).

• **City's strikers were on fire in 1962/63 as the Robins scored 100 goals in Division Three. Sadly for their fans, however, City could only finish 14th in the league – the lowest place ever by a club hitting three figures.**

• England international striker John Atyeo is the Robins' top scorer with 315 goals between 1951 and 1966. In the history of league football only Dixie Dean (Everton) and George Camsell (Middlesbrough) scored more goals for the same club. Defender Louis Carey made a record 646 appearances for the club in two spells at Ashton Gate between 1995 and 2014.

• **Defender Billy 'Fatty' Wedlock won a club record 26 caps for England while with Bristol City between 1907 and 1914.**

• In the 2017/18 season the Robins beat Premier League clubs Watford, Stoke, Crystal Palace and Manchester United to reach the semi-finals of the League Cup for just the third time in their history. However, their dreams of reaching a first final were dashed by eventual winners Manchester City who won 5-3 on aggregate over the two legs.

> **HONOURS**
> *Division 2 champions* 1906
> *League One champions* 2015
> *Division 3 (South) champions* 1923, 1927, 1955
> *Football League Trophy* 1986, 2003, 2015
> *Welsh Cup* 1934

BRISTOL ROVERS

Year founded: 1893
Ground: Memorial Stadium (12,296)
Previous name: Black Arabs, Eastville Rovers, Bristol Eastville Rovers
Nickname: The Pirates
Biggest win: 15-1 v Weymouth (1900)
Heaviest defeat: 0-12 v Luton Town (1936)

Bristol Rovers can trace their history back to 1883 when the Black Arabs club was founded at the Eastville Restaurant in

Bristol. The club was renamed Eastville Rovers the following year in an attempt to attract more support from the local area, later adding 'Bristol' to their name before finally settling on plain old 'Bristol Rovers' in 1898.

• **Rovers have lived up to their name by playing at no fewer than nine different grounds. Having spent much of their history at Eastville Stadium, they have been based at the Memorial Stadium since 1996.**

• The only Rovers player to have appeared for England while with the Pirates, Geoff Bradford, is the club's record scorer, netting 242 times in the league between 1949 and 1964. The club's record appearance maker is central defender Stuart Taylor, who turned out in 546 league games between 1966 and 1980.

• **Rovers' Ronnie Dix is the youngest player ever to score in the Football League, notching against Norwich in 1928 when he was aged just 15 years and 180 days.**

• In 1989 Bristol Rovers' hero Nigel Martyn became the first British goalkeeper to command a seven-figure transfer fee when he joined Crystal Palace for £1 million.

> **HONOURS**
> *Division 3 champions* 1990
> *Division 3 (South) champions* 1953

LUCY BRONZE

> **Born:** Berwick-upon-Tweed, 28th October 1991
> **Position:** Defender
> **Club career:**
> 2007-10 Sunderland Ladies 23 (5)
> 2009 North Carolina Tar Heels 24 (3)
> 2010-12 Everton Ladies 24 (3)
> 2012-14 Liverpool Ladies 28 (3)
> 2014-17 Manchester City Women 34 (5)
> 2017- Lyon 17 (2)
> **International record:**
> 2013- England 57 (6)

An attacking right-back who often chips in with important goals, Lucy Bronze is the only player to win the PFA Women's Player of the Year award twice, topping the poll in both 2014 and 2017.

• **In 2018 Bronze became the first British player to win the Women's Champion League with a foreign club, when she played for Lyon in their 4-1 defeat of Wolfsburg in the final in Kiev.**

Lucy Bronze, the only two-time winner of the PFA Women's Player of the Year award

• After starting out with Sunderland, Bronze spent a year in the USA at the University of Carolina. She returned to England to play for Everton Ladies, before joining local rivals Liverpool in 2012. She won the Women's Super League title with the Reds in both 2013 and 2014, before moving on to Manchester City with whom she won the league in 2016 and the FA Women's Cup in 2017.

• **Bronze was part of the England Under-19 side that won the European championship in 2009. She made her full England debut in 2013 and two years later starred at the 2015 World Cup, scoring vital goals in the last 16 against Norway and in the quarter-final against hosts Canada.**

KEVIN DE BRUYNE

Born: Drongen, Belgium, 28th June 1991
Position: Midfielder
Club career:
2008-12 Genk 84 (14)
2012-14 Chelsea 3 (0)
2012 Genk (loan) 13 (2)
2012-13 Werder Bremen (loan) 33 (10)
2014-15 Wolfsburg 51 (13)
2015- Manchester City 98 (21)
International record:
2010- Belgium 68 (15)

For the second season running, Manchester City midfielder Kevin De Bruyne topped the Premier League assists chart in 2017/18 with 16 to help his club win the title. He also picked up a League Cup winners' medal after City crushed Arsenal 3-0 in the final at Wembley and was voted into the PFA Team of the Year.

• **An attacking midfielder who passes the ball well and loves to strike from distance, De Bruyne moved from Wolfsburg to Manchester City in August 2015 for a then club record £55 million, making him the second most expensive player in British football history at the time.**

• Before his move to Manchester, De Bruyne contributed a Bundesliga record 21 assists as Wolfsburg finished second in the league in 2014/15, and scored in his side's 3-1 German Cup final victory over Borussia Dortmund. After an outstanding campaign, De Bruyne was named German Footballer of the Year in 2015, the first Belgian to win this award.

• First capped in a friendly against Finland in 2010, De Bruyne was part of the Belgian team that came a best ever third at the 2018 World Cup in Russia, scoring a screamer in his country's 2-1 defeat of Brazil in the quarter-final and earning a place in the FIFA World Cup Dream Team.

BURNLEY

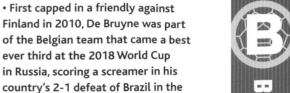

Year founded: 1882
Ground: Turf Moor (21,944)
Nickname: The Clarets
Biggest win: 9-0 v Darwen (1892), v New Brighton (1957) and v Penrith (1984)
Heaviest defeat: 0-11 v Darwen (1885)

One of England's most famous old clubs, Burnley were founded in 1882 when the Burnley Rovers rugby team decided to switch to the round ball game. The club was a founder member of the Football League in 1888 and has since won all

Kevin De Bruyne's 'teapot' impression is spot on!

four divisions of the league – a feat matched only by four other clubs.

• Burnley have twice won the league championship, in 1921 and 1960. The first of these triumphs saw the Clarets go on a 30-match unbeaten run, the longest in a single season until Arsenal went through the whole of 2003/04 undefeated. In its own way, Burnley's 1960 title win was just as remarkable, as the Clarets only ever topped the league on the last day of the season after a 2-1 win at Manchester City.

• The club's only FA Cup triumph came in 1914 when they defeated Liverpool 1-0. After the final whistle Burnley's captain Tommy Boyle became the first man to receive the cup from a reigning monarch, King George V.

• On 16th April 2011 Burnley defender Graham Alexander became only the second outfield player in the history of English football to make 1,000 professional appearances when he came on as a sub in the Clarets' 2-1 win over Swansea City. Alexander is also the most successful penalty taker ever in the domestic game, with a clinical 78 goals in 86 attempts from the spot.

• Burnley broke their transfer record in August 2017, signing New Zealand international striker Chris Wood from Leeds for £15 million. The Clarets made their record sale in July 2017 when England international defender Michael Keane moved to Everton for £25 million.

• **Club legend Jimmy McIlroy made a record 51 appearances for Northern Ireland between 1951 and 1962.**

• Burnley are the last club to score a century of goals in consecutive top-flight seasons, hitting the back of the net 102 times in 1960/61 and 101 in 1961/62.

• **England international goalkeeper Jerry Dawson made a club record 552 appearances for Burnley between 1907 and 1928. The club's record scorer is George Beel with 178 goals between 1923 and 1932.**

• Led superbly by their gravel-voiced manager Sean Dyche, Burnley achieved their best-ever Premier League finish, seventh, in the 2017/18 campaign. As a result, the Clarets qualified for Europe for the first time since 1966, when they went on to reach the quarter-finals of the Fairs Cup.

Burnley's players are a very close-knit bunch

HONOURS
Division 1 champions 1921, 1960
Championship champions 2016
Division 2 champions 1898, 1973
Division 3 champions 1982
Division 4 champions 1992
FA Cup 1914

Burton full-back Damien McCrory is always keen to lend his centre-back a hand

BURTON ALBION

Year founded: 1950
Ground: Pirelli Stadium (6,912)
Nickname: The Brewers
Biggest win: 12-1 v Coalville Town (1954)
Heaviest defeat: 0-10 v Barnet (1970)

Burton Albion were founded at a public meeting at the Town Hall in 1950. The town had previously supported two Football League clubs, Burton Swifts and Burton Wanderers, who merged to form Burton United in 1901 before folding nine years later.

• **The Brewers gained promotion to the Football League for the first time in 2009, going up as Conference champions. In 2015, managed by former Chelsea striker Jimmy Floyd Hasselbaink, Burton gained promotion to the third tier for the first time after winning the League Two title with a club record 94 points.**

• The following season, Burton earned another promotion as Nigel Clough, returning for a second spell at the Pirelli Stadium, took the Brewers into the Championship but their two-year sojourn in the second-tier ended in 2018.

• **In 2006 Burton achieved the greatest result in their history when they held mighty Manchester United to a 0-0 draw at home in the third round of the FA Cup. A record visiting contingent at**

Old Trafford of 11,000 Brewers fans attended the replay, but they had little to cheer about as United strolled to an emphatic 5-0 victory.

• Brewers defender Damien McCrory has played in a record 169 league games for Burton since 2012. The club's leading scorer is striker Billy Kee, with 39 league goals between 2011 and 2014.

• In June 2017 the Brewers splashed out a club record £500,000 on Ross County's Northern Ireland international striker Liam Boyce. Two months later Burton cashed a record cheque for £2 million when Australian midfielder Jackson Irvine joined Hull City.

BURY

Year founded: 1885
Ground: Gigg Lane (12,500)
Nickname: The Shakers
Biggest win: 12-1 v Stockton (1897)
Heaviest defeat: 0-10 v Blackburn Rovers (1887) and West Ham (1982)

The club with the shortest name in the Football League, Bury were founded in 1885 at a meeting at the Old White Horse Hotel in Bury, as successors to two other teams in the town, the Bury Unitarians and the Bury Wesleyans. Bury were founder members of the Lancashire League in 1889, joining the Football League five years later.

• Bury have won the FA Cup on two occasions. In 1900 the Shakers beat Southern League outfit Southampton 4-0 at Crystal Palace, and then three years later they thrashed Derby County 6-0 at the same venue to record the biggest ever victory in an FA Cup final.

• England international striker Norman Bullock made a record 539 appearances for Bury between 1920 and 1935. The club's all-time top scorer is Craig Madden, with 129 goals between 1977 and 1986.

• Relegated from League One in 2018, Bury became the first club to

Veteran Irish keeper Joe Murphy will be hoping to deliver plenty of clean sheets for Bury in League Two

be thrown out of the FA Cup in 2006 for fielding an ineligible player – Stephen Turnbull, a loan signing from Hartlepool United.

IS THAT A FACT?

On 27th August 2005 Bury became the first club to score 1,000 goals in all four tiers of the Football League when Brian Barry-Murphy netted in a 2-2 draw with Wrexham in a League Two fixture.

• Dual international defender Bill Gorman made a club record 11 appearances for Northern Ireland and the Republic of Ireland. Rather bizarrely, in September 1946 he represented both countries against England within just three days.

• In September 1999 Bury became the first European club to sign an Indian player when they bought Bhaichung Bhutia from East Bengal. He stayed five years at Gigg Lane before returning to India in 2004.

CAMBRIDGE UNITED

Year founded: 1912
Ground: Abbey Stadium (8,127)
Previous name: Abbey United
Nickname: The U's
Biggest win: 7-0 v Morecambe (2016)
Heaviest defeat: 0-7 v Sunderland (2002) and v Luton Town (2017)

Cambridge United were founded as Abbey United in 1912 before taking their current name two years after turning professional in 1949.

• **The club was elected to the Football League in 1970 and rose to the second tier a decade later. However, the U's soon returned to the basement division after being relegated in 1984 (setting a then league record of 31 consecutive games without a win) and in 1985 (losing 33 matches to equal the then league record).**

• Midfielder Steve Spriggs played in a record 416 league games for Cambridge between 1975 and 1987. The club's all-time top scorer is John Taylor with 86 goals in two spells at the Abbey Stadium between 1988 and 2004.

• **The U's reached the sixth round of the FA Cup in consecutive seasons in 1990 and 1991, frustratingly losing by a single goal to Crystal Palace and Arsenal respectively.**

HONOURS
Division 3 champions 1991
Division 4 champions 1977

CAPS

Legendary goalkeeper Peter Shilton has won more international caps than any other British player. 'Shilts' played for England 125 times between 1970 and 1990 and would have won many more caps if he had not faced stiff competition for the No. 1 shirt from his great rival Ray Clemence, who won 61 caps during the same period. In women's football, midfielder Fara Williams has won a record 168 caps for England since making her debut in 2001.

• **The first international caps were awarded by England in 1886, following a proposal put forward by the founder of the Corinthians, N.L. Jackson. To this day players actually receive a handmade 'cap' to mark**

Croatian caps are guaranteed to put a smile on the face of the wearer

the achievement of playing for their country. England caps are made by a Bedworth-based company called Toye, Kenning & Spencer, who also provide regalia for the Freemasons.

• The most capped player in the history of the game is Egypt midfielder Ahmed Hassan, who played an astonishing 184 times for his country between 1995 and 2012. The women's record is held by Kristine Lilly, who made 354 appearances for the USA between 1987 and 2010.

• **A record 17 players have won a century of caps for both the USA and Saudi Arabia. In the women's game, the USA lead the way with an incredible 36 female centurions.**

TOP 10

HIGHEST CAPPED BRITISH PLAYERS

1. Peter Shilton (England, 1970-90)	125
2. Pat Jennings (Northern Ireland, 1964-86)	119
Wayne Rooney (England, 2003-16)	119
4. David Beckham (England, 1996-2009)	115
5. Steven Gerrard (England, 2000-14)	114
6. Aaron Hughes (Northern Ireland, 1998-)	112
7. Bobby Moore (England, 1962-73)	108
8. Ashley Cole (England, 2001-14)	107
9. Bobby Charlton (England, 1958-70)	106
Frank Lampard (England, 1999-2014)	106

CARDIFF CITY

Year founded: 1899
Ground: Cardiff City Stadium (33,280)
Previous name: Riverside
Nickname: The Bluebirds
Biggest win: 16-0 v Knighton Town (1961)
Heaviest defeat: 2-11 v Sheffield United (1926)

Founded as the football branch of the Riverside Cricket Club, the club changed to its present name in 1908, three years after Cardiff was awarded city status.

• **Cardiff are the only non-English club to have won the FA Cup, lifting the trophy in 1927 after a 1-0 victory** over Arsenal at Wembley. Three years earlier the Bluebirds were pipped to the league title by Huddersfield on goal average, but if all-time leading scorer Len Davies had successfully converted a penalty in a 0-0 draw at Birmingham on the final day of the season the trophy would have gone to Wales.

• On 7th April 1947 a crowd of 51,621 squeezed into Cardiff's old Ninian Park Stadium for the club's match against Bristol City – an all-time record attendance for the third tier of English football.

• Cardiff have won the Welsh Cup 22 times, just one short of Wrexham's record. The Bluebirds' domination of the tournament in the 1960s and 1970s earned them regular qualification for the European Cup Winners' Cup and in 1968 they reached the semi-finals of the competition before losing 4-3 on aggregate to Hamburg.

• Cardiff's record appearance maker is midfielder Billy Hardy, who turned out 497 times for the club between 1911 and 1931.

• In the 2002/03 season Bluebirds striker Robert Earnshaw scored a club record 31 league goals. Earnshaw is the only player ever to have scored a hat-trick in the Premier League, all three divisions of the Football League, the FA Cup, the League Cup and an international match, achieving the bulk of these feats while with Cardiff between 1998 and 2004.

• Defender Alf Sherwood won a club record 39 caps for Wales while with Cardiff between 1946 and 1956.

• Promoted to the Premier League for a second time in 2018, Cardiff made their record signing in August 2013 when Gary Medel signed from Sevilla for £11 million. A year later the Chilean midfielder joined Inter Milan for £10 million to become Cardiff's record sale.

HONOURS
Championship champions 2013
Division 3 (South) champions 1947
Third Division champions 1993
FA Cup 1927
Welsh Cup 1912, 1920, 1922, 1923, 1927, 1928, 1930, 1956, 1959, 1964, 1965, 1967, 1968, 1969, 1970, 1971, 1973, 1974, 1976, 1988, 1992, 1993

Will life back in the Premier League be a hair-raising experience for Cardiff?

CARLISLE UNITED

Year founded: 1903
Ground: Brunton Park (18,202)
Nickname: The Blues
Biggest win: 8-0 v Hartlepool (1928) and v Scunthorpe (1952)
Heaviest defeat: 1-11 v Hull City (1939)

Carlisle United were formed in 1903 following the merger of two local clubs, Shaddongate United and Carlisle Red Rose. The Blues joined the Third Division (North) in 1928 and were long-term residents of the bottom two divisions until 1965, when they won promotion to the second tier for the first time.

• The club's greatest moment came in 1974 when, in their one season in the top flight, they sat on top of the old First Division after the opening three games. The Cumbrians, though, were quickly knocked off their lofty perch and ended the campaign rock bottom.

• In the same season the Blues enjoyed their best ever run in the FA Cup, reaching the quarter-finals before losing 1-0 at home to eventual competition runners-up Fulham.

• Carlisle have appeared in the Football League Trophy final on a record six occasions, and in 1995 became the first and only team to lose an English trophy on the 'golden goal' rule when they conceded in extra-time in the final against Birmingham City.

• Scottish goalkeeper Allan Ross made a club record 466 appearances for the Blues between 1963 and 1979.

• Following a long period of decline Carlisle were relegated from the Football League in 2004 to become the first club ever to play in all the top five divisions of English football.

• In the 2015/16 season Carlisle travelled a record total of 15,748 miles to away matches in all domestic competitions, including three 'home' games they had to play at other grounds after Brunton Park was flooded.

HONOURS
Division 3 champions 1965
League Two champions 2006
Third Division champions 1995
Football League Trophy 1997, 2011

EDINSON CAVANI

Born: Salto, Uruguay, 14th February 1987
Position: Striker
Club career:
2005-07 Danubio 25 (9)
2007-10 Palermo 109 (34)
2010-13 Napoli 104 (78)
2013- Paris St-Germain 165 (116)
International record:
2008- Uruguay 105 (45)

Long-haired Uruguayan striker Edinson Cavani is the all-time top scorer for Paris Saint-Germain with 167 goals in all competitions and only the second player – after his former PSG team-mate Zlatan Ibrahimovic – to notch 100 goals in both the Italian and French leagues.

• **In five seasons with PSG Cavani has helped the club from the French capital win four Ligue 1 titles and four French Cups, his most prolific season coming in 2016/17 when he topped the scoring charts with 35 goals and was named Ligue 1 Player of the Year.**

• Now a 31-year-old veteran, Cavani had to wait until 2012 before winning his first silverware, the Coppa Italia with Napoli. The following season he was top scorer in Serie A with 29 goals before joining PSG for a then French record £55 million.

• **Cavani scored against Colombia on his international debut in 2008 and three years later was a key figure in the Uruguay team which won the Copa America. He is now his country's second highest scorer of all time – behind Luis Suarez – with 45 goals.**

PETR CECH

Born: Pilzen, Czech Republic, 20th May 1982
Position: Goalkeeper
Club career:
1999-2001 Chmel Blsany 27
2001-02 Sparta Prague 27
2002-04 Rennes 70
2004-15 Chelsea 333
2015- Arsenal 103
International record:
2002-16 Czech Republic 124

A brilliant shot-stopper who dominates his penalty area with his imposing physique, Petr Cech is the only goalkeeper and the only non-British player to have won the FA Cup five times, although he was an unused substitute for the last of these triumphs with Arsenal in 2017. He has also won the Premier League four times with Chelsea and in the first of these triumphs, in 2004/05, set a record by keeping 24 clean sheets.

• **The giant goalkeeper also has the most clean sheets, 201, in the Premier League era, with 162 of those earned with Chelsea – a record for a single club. He reached his double century in a 3-0 home win against Watford in March 2018, preserving his clean sheet on the day with a penalty save from Troy Deeney. In 2015/16 Cech's 16 clean sheets with Arsenal**

Petr Cech holds the Premier League clean sheets record

earned him the Golden Glove award for a fourth time, equalling Joe Hart's record and making him the first player to win the award with two clubs.

• Cech was a member of the Czech Republic side which reached the semi-finals of Euro 2004 before losing to eventual winners Greece. By the time he announced his retirement from international football after Euro 2016 he had taken his caps tally to a Czech record 124.

• **In October 2006 Cech suffered a depressed fracture of the skull following a challenge by Reading's Stephen Hunt. He returned to action after three months out of the game wearing a rugby-style headguard for protection, and went on to make 494 appearances in all competitions for Chelsea – a club record for an overseas player – until he joined local rivals Arsenal for around £10 million in July 2015.**

• In 2012 Cech starred in the Blues' Champions League final victory over Bayern Munich, blocking a penalty from

Edinson Cavani celebrates a goal for Uruguay at the 2018 World Cup

former team-mate Arjen Robben in extra-time and then saving two more in the shoot-out. The following year he added more silverware to his collection when he helped Chelsea win the Europa League after the Blues beat Benfica in the final in Amsterdam.

CELTIC

Year founded: 1888
Ground: Celtic Park (60,411)
Nickname: The Bhoys
Biggest win: 11-0 v Dundee (1895)
Heaviest defeat: 0-8 v Motherwell (1937)

The first British team to win the European Cup, Celtic were founded by an Irish priest in 1887 with the aim of raising funds for poor children in Glasgow's East End slums. The club were founder members of the Scottish League in 1890, and have gone on to spend a record 123 seasons in the top flight.

• Celtic have won the Scottish Cup more times than any other club, with 38 victories. The Bhoys most recently won the cup in 2018, defeating Motherwell 2-0 in the final at Hampden Park.

• Under legendary manager Jock Stein Celtic won the Scottish league for nine consecutive seasons in the 1960s and 1970s, with a side featuring great names like Billy McNeill, Jimmy Johnstone, Bobby Lennox and Tommy Gemmell. This extraordinary run of success equalled a world record established by MTK Budapest of Hungary in the 1920s but, painfully for Celtic fans, was later matched by bitter rivals Rangers in the 1990s.

• The greatest ever Celtic side, managed by Stein and dubbed the 'Lisbon Lions', became the first British club to win the European Cup when they beat Inter Milan 2-1 in the Portuguese capital in 1967. Stein was central to the team's triumph, scoring an early point by sitting in

Celtic's Kieran Tierney is a master at dribbling without the ball!

Inter manager Helenio Herrera's seat and refusing to budge, and then urging his players forward after they went a goal down to the defensive-minded Italians. Sticking to their attacking game plan, Celtic fought back with goals by Gemmell and Steve Chalmers to spark jubilant celebrations at the end among the travelling fans. Remarkably, all the 'Lisbon Lions' were born and bred within a 30-mile radius of Celtic Park.

• That 1966/67 season was the most successful in the club's history as they won every competition they entered: the Scottish league, Scottish Cup and Scottish League Cup, as well as the European Cup. To this day, no other British side has won a similar 'Quadruple'.

• The skipper of the 'Lisbon Lions' was Billy McNeill, who went on to play in a record 790 games for Celtic in all competitions between 1957 and 1975. He later managed the club, leading Celtic to the Double in their centenary season in 1987/88. The club's most capped player is goalkeeper Pat Bonner, who made 80 appearances for the Republic of Ireland between 1981 and 1996.

• Jimmy McGrory, who played for the club between 1922 and 1938, scored a staggering 396 league goals for Celtic – a British record by a player for a single club. In 1932 he hit eight goals in a 9-0 thrashing of

Dunfermline, the biggest haul ever by a player in the top flight in Britain.

• In 1957 Celtic won the Scottish League Cup for the first time, demolishing Rangers 7-1 in the final at Hampden Park. The victory stands as the biggest by either side in an Old Firm match and is also a record for a major Scottish cup final. Celtic went on to enjoy more success in the League Cup, appearing in a world record 14 consecutive finals (winning six) between 1964 and 1978.

• In 2016/17 Celtic went through the entire league campaign unbeaten, only the third time this had happened in the Scottish top flight and the first time in a 38-game season. The Bhoys won the title with a record 106 points and finished an incredible 30 points clear of second-placed Aberdeen – just one point less than PSG's European record margin set a year earlier. In addition, Brendan Rodgers' 'Invincibles' were unbeaten in nine Scottish domestic cup matches as they clinched their third ever Treble.

• The following season Celtic extended their unbeaten run to a British record 69 matches before they lost 4-0 at Hearts in December 2017. Nevertheless, the Bhoys went on to win the Treble for a second consecutive campaign, to become the first British club ever to land the 'Double-Treble'.

• Celtic manager Willie Maley was in charge of the club for an incredible 43 years between 1897 and 1940 – a record of longevity only surpassed in European football by Guy Roux's 44-year tenure at Auxerre between 1961 and 2005 and Fred Everiss' 46-year reign at West Brom between 1902 and 1948.

IS THAT A FACT?
When Celtic beat Rangers 5-0 to clinch their seventh consecutive Scottish league title in April 2018 it was their biggest victory against their Old Firm rivals for 61 years.

- French striker Odsonne Edouard is Celtic's record signing, joining the club from Paris Saint-Germain for £9 million in June 2018. In July 2013 midfielder Victor Wanyama left Celtic Park for Southampton for a club record £12.5 million.

HONOURS
Premiership champions 2014, 2015, 2016, 2017, 2018
SPL champions 2001, 2002, 2004, 2006, 2007, 2008, 2012, 2013
Premier Division champions 1977, 1979, 1981, 1982, 1986, 1988, 1998
Division 1 champions 1893, 1884, 1896, 1898, 1905, 1906, 1907,1908, 1909, 1910, 1914, 1915,1916, 1917, 1919, 1922, 1926,1936, 1938, 1954, 1966, 1967,1968, 1969, 1970, 1971, 1972, 1973, 1974
Scottish Cup 1892,1899,1900, 1904,1907,1908, 1911, 1912,1914, 1923, 1925, 1927, 1931,1933,1937, 1951, 1954, 1965,1967, 1969,1971, 1972, 1974,1975, 1977, 1980, 1985, 1988,1989, 1995, 2001, 2004, 2005, 2007, 2011, 2013, 2017, 2018
League Cup 1957, 1958, 1966, 1967, 1968, 1969, 1970, 1975,1983, 1998, 2000, 2001, 2006, 2015, 2017, 2018
European Cup 1967

CHAMPIONS LEAGUE

The most prestigious competition in club football, the Champions League replaced the old European Cup in 1992. Previously a competition for domestic league champions only, runners-up from the main European nations were first admitted in 1997 and the tournament has subsequently expanded to include up to four entrants per country. In 2015 a new rule saw the Europa League winners qualify for the Champions League, with Manchester United becoming the first English club to take this route into the competition two years later.

- **Spanish giants Real Madrid won the first European Cup in 1956, defeating French side Reims 4-3 in the final in Paris. Real went on to win the competition the next four years as well, thanks largely to the brilliance of their star players Alfredo Di Stefano and Ferenc Puskas. With six wins in the European Cup and another seven in the Champions League, Real have won the competition a record 13 times.**
- The first British club to win the European Cup was Celtic, who famously beat Inter Milan in the final in Lisbon in 1967. The following year Manchester United became the first English club to triumph, beating Benfica 4-1 at Wembley. The most successful British club in the tournament, though, are Liverpool, with

five wins in 1977, 1978, 1981, 1984 and 2005, followed by Manchester United with three (1968, 1999 and 2008). Three other English clubs, Nottingham Forest (in 1979 and 1980), Aston Villa (in 1982) and Chelsea (in 2012) have also won the tournament, making England the only country to boast five different winners.

- **Portuguese superstar Cristiano Ronaldo is the leading scorer in the history of the competition with 120 goals (including a record 17 in the 2013/14 season for Real Madrid), and has been the tournament's leading scorer in a record seven seasons. Meanwhile, Real Madrid and Porto goalkeeper Iker Casillas has appeared in a record 167 games in the tournament, keeping a record 56 clean sheets.**
- Real Madrid winger Francisco Gento is the most successful player in the history of the competition with six winner's medals (1956-60 and 1966) while Cristiano Ronaldo is the only player to win the Champions League five times.
- **In 2017 Real Madrid became the first club to win the trophy three times on the trot in the Champions League era, after defeating Liverpool 3-1 in the final in Kiev.**
- Real were also involved in the highest-scoring final, when they thrashed Eintracht Frankfurt 7-3 at Hampden Park in 1960.
- **Feyenoord recorded the biggest win in the competition in 1969 when they thrashed KR Reykjavik 12-2 in the first round. In the Champions League era Liverpool and Real Madrid jointly hold the record with 8-0 tonkings of Besiktas (2007) and Malmo (2015) respectively.**
- Real legend Alfredo Di Stefano scored in a record five finals between 1956 and

Sergio Ramos posing with the Champions League trophy has become an annual event!

1960, while Cristiano Ronaldo is the only player to have scored in three Champions League finals (2008, 2014 and 2017).

• In the 2017/18 season Paris Saint-Germain scored a record 25 goals in the group stage of the Champions League. Less impressively, Deportivo la Coruna (2004), Maccabi Haifa (2009) and Dinamo Zagreb (2016) didn't manage a single goal in their six group matches.

• In 2005 Villarreal topped their group despite scoring just three goals in their six matches.

Champions League finals

1993 Marseille 1 AC Milan 0
1994 AC Milan 4 Barcelona 0
1995 Ajax 1 AC Milan 0
1996 Juventus 1* Ajax 1
1997 Borussia Dortmund 3 Juventus 1
1998 Real Madrid 1 Juventus 0
1999 Man United 2 Bayern Munich 1
2000 Real Madrid 3 Valencia 0
2001 Bayern Munich 1* Valencia 1
2002 Real Madrid 2 Bayer Leverkusen 1
2003 AC Milan 0* Juventus 0
2004 Porto 3 Monaco 0
2005 Liverpool 3* AC Milan 3
2006 Barcelona 2 Arsenal 1
2007 AC Milan 2 Liverpool 1
2008 Man United 1* Chelsea 1
2009 Barcelona 2 Man United 0
2010 Inter Milan 2 Bayern Munich 0
2011 Barcelona 3 Man United 1
2012 Bayern Munich 1 Chelsea 1*
2013 Bayern Munich 2 Borussia Dortmund 1
2014 Real Madrid 4 Atletico Madrid 1
2015 Barcelona 3 Juventus 1
2016 Real Madrid 1* Atletico Madrid 1
2017 Real Madrid 4 Juventus 1
2018 Real Madrid 3 Liverpool 1
* Won on penalties

CHANTS

The loudest recorded noise created by a football crowd is 131.76 decibels by Galatasaray fans during their home derby against Istanbul rivals Fenerbahce on 18th March 2011. Despite the raucous atmosphere created by the home fans, visitors Fenerbahce won the match 2-1.

• Fans back home in Mexico City chanting 'Mex-ico! Mex-ico! Mex-ico!' and jumping up-and-down in excitement set off sensitive earthquake sensors during the central Americans' shock 1-0 win over reigning champions Germany at the 2018 World Cup in Russia. In the same

Iceland fans' spine-chilling 'Viking' chant puts their rivals' efforts in the shade

match, however, 'homophobic chants' by fans in the stadium in Moscow led to the Mexican Football Federation being fined £7,615 by FIFA.

• Possibly the oldest football chant is 'Who ate all the pies?', which researchers at Oxford University have discovered dates back to 1894 when it was playfully directed by Sheffield United fans at their 22-stone goalkeeper William 'Fatty' Foulke. The chant stemmed from an incident when the tubby custodian got up early at the team hotel, sneaked down into the dining room and somehow munched his way through all the players' breakfast pies.

• In an unprecedented incident, Leipzig striker Timo Werner asked to be substituted after 32 minutes of his side's 2-0 defeat away to Besiktas in the Champions League in September 2017 because the chants and shrill whistles of the Turkish fans were making him feel dizzy.

CHARLTON ATHLETIC

Year founded: 1905
Ground: The Valley (27,111)
Nickname: The Addicks
Biggest win: 8-1 v Middlesbrough (1953)
Heaviest defeat: 1-11 v Aston Villa (1959)

Charlton Athletic were founded in 1905 when a number of youth clubs in the south-east London area, including East Street Mission and Blundell Mission, decided to merge. The club, whose nickname 'the Addicks' stemmed from the haddock served by a local chippy, graduated from minor leagues to join the Third Division (South) in 1921.

• Charlton's heyday was shortly before and just after the Second World War.

After becoming the first club to win successive promotions from the Third to First Division in 1935/36, the Addicks finished runners-up, just three points behind league champions Manchester City, in 1937. After losing in the 1946 FA Cup final to Derby County, Charlton returned to Wembley the following year and this time lifted the cup thanks to a 1-0 victory over Burnley in the final.

• Charlton's home ground, The Valley, used to be one of the biggest in English football with a capacity of around 75,000. In 1985, though, financial problems forced Charlton to leave The Valley and the Addicks spent seven years as tenants of West Ham and Crystal Palace before making an emotional return to their ancestral home in 1992.

• **Sam Bartram, who was known as 'the finest keeper England never had', played a record 623 games for the club between 1934 and 1956. Striker Derek Hales is Charlton's record goalscorer, notching 168 in two spells at the club in the 1970s and 1980s.**

• Midfielder Mark Kinsella won a club record 33 caps for the Republic of Ireland between 1998 and 2002.

• **On their way to the First Division title in 2000 Charlton won a club record 12 consecutive league games.**

HONOURS
First Division champions 2000
League One champions 2012
Division 3 (South) champions 1929, 1935
FA Cup 1947

CHEATING

The most notorious instance of on-pitch cheating occurred at the 1986 World Cup in Mexico when Argentina's Diego Maradona punched the ball into the net to open the scoring in his side's quarter-final victory over England. Maradona was unrepentant afterwards, claiming the goal was scored by "the hand of God, and the head of Diego".

• **In a similar incident in 2009 France captain Thierry Henry clearly handled the ball before crossing for William Gallas to score the decisive goal in a World Cup play-off against Ireland. "I will be honest, it was a handball – but I'm not the ref," a sheepish Henry admitted after the match.**

• In December 2015 Augsburg goalkeeper Marwin Hitz sneakily raked up the

penalty spot with his studs after home side Cologne were awarded a spot-kick. The ruse worked as Hitz saved the penalty, but he was later sent a bill by Cologne for 122 euros to repair damage to their pitch.

• **During the 2012/13 season Tottenham's Gareth Bale was booked a record seven times in all competitions for 'simulation' – more commonly known simply as 'diving'.**

• In 2017 Victor Moses became the first player to be sent off in the FA Cup final for diving, when he picked up a second yellow card for falling theatrically in the Arsenal penalty area during Chelsea's 2-1 defeat.

• **In 2010 Peruvian Second Division side Sport Ancash were accused of spiking the half-time drinks of opponents Hijos de Acosvinchos with sleeping pills when four of their players passed out in the second half of Ancash's 3-0 win.**

• The Brazilian Serie D play-off between Tupi and Aparecidense in 2013 ended in bizarre fashion when a Tupi striker rounded the goalkeeper and looked certain to score... until Aparecidense masseur Romildo da Silva ran onto the pitch and hoofed the ball clear. He

may have saved a goal, but his club were thrown out of the league as a punishment.

CHELSEA

Year founded: 1905
Ground: Stamford Bridge (41,631)
Nickname: The Blues
Biggest win: 13-0 v Jeunesse Hautcharage (1971)
Heaviest defeat: 1-8 v Wolves (1953)

Founded in 1905 by local businessmen Gus and Joseph Mears, Chelsea were elected to the Football League in that very same year. At the time of their election, the club had not played a single match – only Bradford City can claim a similarly swift ascent into league football.

• **Thanks to the staggering wealth of their Russian owner, Roman Abramovich, Chelsea are now one of the richest clubs in the world. Since taking over the Londoners in 2003,**

With the likes of Hazard, Pedro and Fabregas in their ranks, Chelsea certainly do not lack for attacking talent

Abramovich has pumped hundreds of millions into the club and has been rewarded with five Premier League titles, five FA Cups, three League Cups and the Double in 2010. After watching his team come agonisingly close on numerous occasions, Abramovich finally saw Chelsea win the Champions League in 2012 when, led by caretaker manager Roberto di Matteo, the Blues beat Bayern Munich on penalties in the final.

• The following year Chelsea won the Europa League after defeating Benfica 2-1 in the final in Amsterdam. That victory meant the Blues became the first British club to win all three historic UEFA trophies, as they had previously won the European Cup Winners' Cup in both 1971 and 1998. It was in the Cup Winners' Cup that Chelsea thrashed Luxembourg minnows Jeunesse Hautcharage 21-0 in 1971 to set a European record aggregate score.

• The Blues' recent success is in marked contrast to their early history. For the first 50 years of their existence Chelsea won precisely nothing, finally breaking their duck by winning the league championship in 1955. After a succession of near misses, the club won the FA Cup for the first time in 1970, beating Leeds 2-1 at Old Trafford in the first post-war final to go to a replay. Flamboyant striker Peter Osgood scored in every round of the cup run and remains the last player to achieve this feat.

• The club's fortunes declined sharply in the late 1970s and 1980s, the Blues spending much of the period in the Second Division while saddled with large debts. However, an influx of veteran foreign stars in the mid-1990s, including Gianfranco Zola, Ruud Gullit and Gianluca Vialli, sparked an exciting revival capped when the Blues won the FA Cup in 1997, their first major trophy for 26 years.

• On 26th December 1999 Chelsea became the first English club to field an entirely foreign line-up for their Premier League fixture at Southampton.

• Chelsea's arrival as one of England's top clubs was finally confirmed when charismatic manager Jose Mourinho led the Blues to the Premier League title in 2005. A second title followed in 2006, and Mourinho claimed another in 2015 in his second spell at the Bridge. When the club first won the championship way back in 1955, they did so with a record low of just 52 points.

• In 2007 Chelsea won the first ever FA Cup final at the new Wembley, Ivorian striker Didier Drogba scoring the only goal against Manchester United. In the same year the Blues won the League Cup, making them just the third English team after Arsenal (1993) and Liverpool (2001) to claim a domestic cup double. The Blues also won the FA Cup in 2009, 2010, 2012 and 2018, to give them the best record of any club in the competition at the new stadium.

• Hardman defender Ron 'Chopper' Harris is Chelsea's record appearance maker, turning out an incredible 795 times for the club between 1962 and 1980. Midfielder Frank Lampard, a key figure in the club's recent successes, scored a record 211 goals in all competitions between 2001 and 2014. Legendary striker Jimmy Greaves scored the most goals in a single season, with 41 in 1960/61.

• Between 2004 and 2008 the Blues were unbeaten in 86 consecutive home league matches, a record for both the Premier League and the Football League. The impressive run was eventually ended by Liverpool, who won 1-0 at Stamford Bridge on 26th October 2008.

• Club legend Frank Lampard is Chelsea's most-capped international, making 103 appearances for England while at Stamford Bridge between 2001 and 2014.

• The club's most expensive signing is Kepa Arrizabalaga, who moved to west London from Athletic Bilbao in August 2018 for £71.6 million – a world record fee for a goalkeeper. Chelsea sold Brazilian midfielder Oscar to Shanghai SIPG for a club record £60 million in January 2017.

HONOURS
Premier League champions 2005, 2006, 2010, 2015, 2017
Division 1 champions 1955
Division 2 champions 1984, 1989
FA Cup 1970, 1997, 2000, 2007, 2009, 2010, 2012, 2018
Double 2010
League Cup 1965, 1998, 2005, 2007, 2015
Champions League 2012
Europa League 2013
European Cup Winners' Cup 1971, 1998
European Super Cup 1998

CHELTENHAM TOWN

Year founded: 1892
Ground: Whaddon Road (7,266)
Nickname: The Robins
Biggest win: 12-0 v Chippenham Rovers (1935)
Heaviest defeat: 1-10 v Merthyr Tydfil (1952)

Cheltenham Town were founded in 1892 but had to wait over a century to join the Football League, eventually making their bow in 1999 after winning the Conference title. The Robins dropped out of the league in 2015, but bounced back the following year as the first winners of the National League.

• The Robins have twice gained promotion to the third tier via the play-offs, defeating Rushden 3-1 in the final at the Millennium Stadium in 2002 and Grimsby 1-0 four years later at the same venue, but they missed out on a hat-trick when they lost 2-0 to Crewe in the 2012 final at Wembley.

• Midfielder Dave Bird made a record 289 league appearances for the Robins between 2002 and 2012.

• When Kyle Haynes came on as a sub in a 1-1 draw with Oldham in March 2009 he became Cheltenham's youngest ever player, aged 17 and 85 days.

HONOURS
National League champions 2016
Conference champions 1999

IS THAT A FACT?
A record eight different Chelsea managers have won the FA Cup while with the club: Dave Sexton (1970), Ruud Gullit (1997), Gianluca Vialli (2000), Jose Mourinho (2007), Guus Hiddink (2009), Carlo Ancelotti (2010), Roberto di Matteo (2012) and Antonio Conte (2018).

CLEAN SHEETS

Arsenal's Petr Cech holds the Premier League clean sheet record with 201. Of these, 162 came with his former employers Chelsea – a record by a goalkeeper with a single club. Cech also kept a Premier League record 24 clean sheets in the 2004/05 season.

• The world record for consecutive clean sheets is held by Brazilian goalkeeper Mazaropi of Vasco de Gama, who went 1,816 minutes without conceding in 1977/78.

• Italy's long-serving goalkeeper Dino Zoff holds the international record, going 1,142 minutes without having to pick the ball out of his net between September 1972 and June 1974. Another Italian goalkeeper, Walter Zenga, holds the record for clean sheets at the World Cup, with a run of 518 minutes at the 1990 tournament. However, New Zealand's Richard Wilson did even better during the qualifying rounds for the 1982 tournament, going 921 minutes without conceding.

• The only goalkeeper to keep clean sheets in all four matches he played at the World Cup is Switzerland's Pascal Zuberbuhler at the 2006 finals in Germany.

• Former Manchester United goalkeeper Edwin van der Sar holds the British record for consecutive league clean sheets, keeping the ball out of his net for 14 Premier League games and a total of 1,311 minutes in the 2008/09 season. He was finally beaten on 4th March 2009 by Newcastle's Peter Lovenkrands in United's 2-1 victory at St James' Park.

TOP 10

PREMIER LEAGUE CLEAN SHEETS

1.	Petr Cech (2004-)	201
2.	David James (1992-2010)	169
3.	Mark Schwarzer (1997-2016)	151
4.	David Seaman (1992-2004)	140
5.	Nigel Martyn (1992-2006)	137
6.	Pepe Reina (2005-14)	134
7.	Edwin van der Sar (2001-11)	132
	Tim Howard (2003-16)	132
	Brad Friedel (1997-2015)	132
10.	Peter Schmeichel (1992-2008)	131

CLUB WORLD CUP

A competition contested between the champion clubs of all six continental confederations of FIFA, the Club World Cup was first played in Brazil in 2000 but has only been an annual tournament since 2005 when it replaced the old Intercontinental Cup.

• Manchester United's participation in the first Club World Cup led to the Red Devils pulling out of the FA Cup in 2000, a tournament they had won the previous season. United's decision attracted a lot of criticism at the time, not least from many of their own fans.

• Barcelona and Real Madrid have the best record in the competition with three triumphs each, Real most recently beating Gremio 1-0 in the 2017 final in Abu Dhabi.

• Manchester United became the first British winners of the tournament when a goal by Wayne Rooney saw off Ecuadorian side Quito in the 2008 final in Yokohama.

• Cristiano Ronaldo is the competition's top scorer with seven goals, including a hat-trick for Real Madrid in the 2016 final against Kashima Antlers. Ronaldo and his former Real team-mate Toni Kroos are the only two players to lift the trophy four times.

COLCHESTER UNITED

Year founded: 1937
Ground: The Colchester Community Stadium (10,105)
Nickname: The U's
Biggest win: 9-1 v Bradford City (1961) and v Leamington (2005)
Heaviest defeat: 0-8 v Leyton Orient (1989)

Founded as the successors to amateur club Colchester Town in 1937, Colchester United joined the Football League in 1950. The club lost its league status in 1990, but regained it just two years later after topping the Conference.

• The U's enjoyed their greatest day in 1971 when they beat then-mighty Leeds United 3-2 in the fifth round of the FA Cup at their old Layer Road ground. However, a 5-0 thrashing at Everton in the quarter-finals ended their hopes of an unlikely cup triumph.

• The first brothers to be sent off in the same match while playing for the same team were Colchester's Tom and Tony English against Crewe in 1986.

• In 1971, the U's became the first English club to win a tournament in a penalty shoot-out after defeating West Brom 4-3 on penalties in the final of the Watney Cup at the Hawthorns.

• Defender Micky Cook made a record 614 appearances for the U's between 1969 and 1984. Martyn King is the club's all-time top scorer with 130 league goals, including a joint-record five hat-tricks, between 1959 and 1965.

> HONOURS
> *Conference champions 1992*

COLOURS

In the 19th century, players originally wore different coloured caps, socks and armbands – but not shirts – to distinguish between the two sides. The first standardised kits were introduced in the 1870s, with many clubs opting for the colours of the schools or other sporting organisations from which they had emerged.

• Thanks largely to the longstanding success of Arsenal, Liverpool and Manchester United, teams wearing red have won more trophies in England than those sporting any other colour. Teams wearing stripes have fared less well, their last FA Cup success coming in 1987 (Coventry City) and their last league triumph way back in 1936 (Sunderland).

• In January 2018 Reading started their FA Cup third round replay against Stevenage in their normal blue-and-white hoops, only for the referee to rule that their kit clashed with the visitors' red-and-white outfit. At half-time Reading changed into orange shirts, and despite the kit confusion went on to win 3-0 thanks to a Jon Dadi Bodvarsson hat-trick.

• Miami-based River Plate fan Dan Goldfarb has an incredible 402 different shirts belonging to the Argentinian giants – the biggest single club collection of jerseys in the world.

IS THAT A FACT?

In a poll conducted by the EFL at the start of the 2017/18 season, Bristol City's purple and lime away kit was voted the best in the Football League.

"402 River Plate shirts, but I still want more!"

• In the summer of 2017 Wycombe Wanderers unveiled an eye-catching multi-coloured 'kaleidoscope-style' goalkeeper's kit with the aim of distracting opposition strikers' attention. The plan worked a treat as the Chairboys were promoted from League Two at the end of the season.

COMMUNITY SHIELD

Won by Manchester City in 2018, the Community Shield was originally known as the Charity Shield and since 1928 has been an annual fixture usually played at the start of the season between the reigning league champions and the FA Cup winners. Founded in 1908 to provide funds for various charities, the Charity Shield was initially played between the Football League First Division champions and the Southern League champions, developing into a game between select teams of amateurs and professionals in the early 1920s.

• **Manchester United were the first club to win the Charity Shield, defeating QPR 4-0 in a replay at Stamford Bridge. With 17 outright wins and four shared, United are also the most successful side in the history of the competition.**

• Manchester United's Ryan Giggs is the most successful player in the history of the Shield, with nine wins in 15 appearances (another record).

• **The 1974 Charity Shield between Leeds and Liverpool was the first to be held at Wembley and the first to be decided by penalties, the Reds winning 6-5. However, the game is best remembered for the dismissals of Liverpool's Kevin Keegan and Leeds'**

Winning the Community Shield is always a good excuse for cracking open the champagne!

Billy Bremner for fighting, the pair becoming the first British players to be sent off at the national stadium.

• Ipswich and QPR are the only clubs to appear in two Shield matches and lose them both. However, Newcastle have an even worse record, with just one win in six appearances.

COMPUTER GAMES

FIFA 13 sold more than 4.5 million copies worldwide in the first five days after its launch in 2012, leading publishers EA to claim it was the biggest-selling sports video launch of all time. The FIFA series as a whole has sold well over 100 million copies since it launched in 1993, making it the best selling football video game of all time.

• **The first football video game was created in 1973 by Tomohiro Nishikado, who later designed Space Invaders. Called simply Soccer, the**

ball-and-paddle game allowed two players to each control a goalkeeper and a striker.

• Wayne Rooney has appeared on the cover of FIFA the most times, seven in total. The cover star of FIFA 18 is Juventus and Portugal striker Cristiano Ronaldo.

IS THAT A FACT?
The longest ever game of Football Manager saw Lech Poznan fan Michal Leniec take charge of his club for 221 seasons over two actual years of playing time. During his mind-bogglingly long reign he boosted a win rate of 76% and led Poznan to an incredible 45 Champions League triumphs.

• Patrick Hadler, a 19-year-old from Hannover, holds the record for the biggest win in a computer football game. Playing as Germany on FIFA 14 he crushed the Cook Islands 321-0 in 2014, earning himself a place in *The Guinness Book of Records*.
• In August 2018 18-year-old Mosaad 'Msdossary' Aldossary from Saudi Arabia collected a cool $250,000 after being crowned the first winner of the FIFA eWorld Cup in a three-day tournament featuring 32 players at the O2 in London.

Chile may still be celebrating their 2016 Copa America triumph given how excited they were...

CONFEDERATIONS CUP

The Confederations Cup is a competition held every four years contested by the holders of each of the six FIFA confederation championships – such as the European Championships and the Copa America – plus the World Cup holders and host nation.
• **Since 2005 the Confederations Cup has been held in the country that will host the following year's World Cup, acting as a dress rehearsal for** the larger and more prestigious tournament.
• Brazil have the best record in the tournament with four victories to their name: in 1997 (after a 6-0 win over Australia in the final), in 2005 (4-1 against Argentina), 2009 (3-2 against the USA) and 2013 (3-0 against Spain). The only other country to win the Confederations Cup more than once are France (in 2001 and 2003). The holders are Germany, who beat Chile 1-0 in the 2017 final in St Petersburg.
• **Ronaldo (Brazil) and Cuauhtemoc Blanco (Mexico) are the leading scorers in the competition, with nine goals each. Brazilian striker Romario scored a record seven goals at the 1997 tournament in Saudi Arabia.**

Sorry, Germany fans, that's just the Confederations Cup – not the World Cup!

COPA AMERICA

The oldest surviving international football tournament in the world, the Copa America was founded in 1916. The first championships were held in Argentina as part of the country's independence centenary commemorations, with Uruguay emerging as the winners from a four-team field. Originally known as the South American Championship, the tournament was renamed in 1975. Previously, the Copa America was held every two years, but in 2007 it was decided to stage future tournaments at four-year intervals.
• **Uruguay have won the tournament a record 15 times, while Argentina are second in the winners' list, lifting the trophy on 14 occasions. The holders are Chile, who won the Centenary edition of the competition in 2016 after beating Argentina on penalties in the final.**
• Argentina hold the record for the biggest win at the finals, crushing Ecuador 12-0 in 1942.
• **The next finals, in 2019, will be held in Brazil and will be the last to be held in an odd-numbered year.**

COPA LIBERTADORES

The Copa Libertadores is the South American equivalent of the Champions League, played annually between top clubs from all the countries in the continent (in recent years, leading clubs from Mexico have also participated). Argentine club Independiente have the best record in the competition, winning the trophy seven times, including four in a row between 1972 and 1975.
• **Ecuadorian striker Albert Spencer is the leading scorer in the history of**

the competition with 54 goals (48 for Uruguayan club Penarol, helping them to win the first two tournaments in 1960 and 1961, and six for Ecuadorian outfit Barcelona de Guayaquil).

• Defender Francisco Sa won the competition a record six times in the 1970s – four times with Independiente and twice with Boca Juniors.

• **In 1970 Uruguayan giants Penarol recorded the biggest victory in the history of the competition, thrashing Venezuela's Valencia 11-2. Penarol also hold the record for the most emphatic aggregate win, destroying Ecuadorian minnows Everest 14-1 in 1963.**

• Argentinian clubs have won the trophy a record 24 times, while a record 10 different clubs from Brazil have raised the cup including 2017 winners Gremio.

CORNERS

Corner kicks were first introduced in 1872, but goals direct from a corner were not allowed until 1924. The first player to score from a corner in league football was Billy Smith of Huddersfield in the 1924/25 season. On 2nd October 1924 Argentina's Cesareo Onzari scored direct from a corner against reigning Olympic champions Uruguay in Buenos Aires, the first goal of this sort to occur in an international fixture.

• **Turkish striker Sukru Gulesin holds the record for the most goals scored direct from corners with an incredible 32 between 1940 and 1954 for a variety of clubs, including Besiktas, Lazio, Palermo and Galatasaray.**

• On 21st January 2012 Coleraine's Paul Owens became the first player ever to score two goals direct from a corner in the same match when his wind-assisted efforts sailed over the Glenavon

Nigeria's 2018 World Cup shirt might have been spectacular, but their corner routines definitely weren't

goalkeeper in his team's 3-1 Irish Premiership win.

• **Liverpool won a Premier League record 309 corners in the 2011/12 season.**

• Tottenham midfielder Christian Eriksen took a Premier League record 195 corners in the 2016/17 season.

DIEGO COSTA

Born: Lagarto, Brazil, 7th October 1988
Position: Striker
Club career:
2006 Braga 0 (0)
2006 Penafiel (loan) 13 (5)
2007-09 Atletico Madrid 0 (0)
2007 Braga (loan) 7 (0)
2007-08 Celta (loan) 30 (5)
2008-09 Albacete (loan) 34 (9)
2009-10 Valladolid 34 (8)
2010-14 Atletico Madrid 94 (43)
2012 Rayo Vallecano (loan) 16 (10)
2014-18 Chelsea 89 (52)
2018- Atletico Madrid 15 (3)
International record:
2013 Brazil 2 (0)
2014- Spain 24 (10)

After falling out with Chelsea boss Antonio Conte, fiery striker Diego Costa returned to Atletico Madrid for a club record £57 million in January 2018. He soon paid back some of that hefty fee by scoring the winner against Arsenal in the Europa League semi-final, and then helping Atleti lift the trophy after a 3-0 defeat of Marseille in the final in Lyon.

Premier League defenders aren't exactly unhappy that Diego Costa now plays in Spain

TOP 10

PREMIER LEAGUE CORNERS WON (SINCE 2006/07 SEASON)	
1. Liverpool	3,027
2. Arsenal	2,953
3. Manchester City	2,942
4. Chelsea	2,919
5. Manchester United	2,908
6. Tottenham Hotspur	2,905
7. Everton	2,518
8. West Ham United	2,148
9. Aston Villa	2,061
10. Newcastle United	1,885

• After a fairly undistinguished start to his career, Costa gradually developed into one of Europe's deadliest forwards after rejoining Atletico Madrid from Valladolid in 2010. Three years later he scored a vital goal in the Copa del Rey final as Atleti beat Real Madrid 2-1 to record their first victory over their glitzy city rivals since 1999.

• The following season Costa was third-top scorer in La Liga with 27 goals – only Cristiano Ronaldo and Lionel Messi were more prolific – as Atletico surprised everyone by lifting the title. Costa also helped Atleti reach the final of the Champions League for the first time, but had to limp out of the showpiece event against Real with a hamstring injury after just eight minutes. Later that summer he moved to Chelsea for £32 million and his goals powered the Blues to the Premier League title in both 2015 and 2017.

• Renowned for his aggressive approach on the pitch, Costa won the first of two caps for Brazil in 2013, but later that year gained Spanish citizenship and declared his intention to play for his adopted nation, much to the disgust of Brazilian fans. He made his debut for Spain in a 1-0 friendly win over Italy in March 2014 and was his country's top scorer at the 2018 World Cup with three goals.

THIBAUT COURTOIS

Born: Bree, Belgium, 11th May 1992
Position: Goalkeeper
Club career:
2009-11 Genk 41
2011-18 Chelsea 126
2011-14 Atletico Madrid (loan) 111
2018- Real Madrid
International record:
2011- Belgium 65

Rated by many as one of the best in his position in world football, Thibaut Courtois became the first Belgian goalkeeper ever to win the FA Cup when Chelsea beat Manchester United 1-0 in the 2018 final at Wembley. Previously, he was a key member of the Blues team which won the Premier League title in both 2015 and 2017, in the second of these campaigns winning the Golden Glove award for the first time. In August 2018 he joined Spanish giants Real Madrid for £35 million.

• A tall and well-built stopper who is especially adept at plucking crosses from the sky, Courtois came through the youth ranks at Genk to help the Belgian outfit win the league title in 2011, a season in which he was voted Goalkeeper of the Year.

• Courtois joined Chelsea for around £5 million in July 2011, but was immediately moved out on loan to Atletico Madrid. He enjoyed three great seasons with the Spanish outfit, helping Atletico win the Europa League in 2012, the Copa del Rey in 2013 and the league title in 2014. In addition, he became the first Atletico goalkeeper ever to retain the Ricardo Zamora trophy – awarded to the goalkeeper with the best goals-to-games ratio – when he topped the poll in both 2013 and 2014.

• **Courtois is the youngest ever goalkeeper to have played for Belgium, making his debut as a 19-year-old in a 0-0 friendly draw with France in 2011.**

At the 2018 World Cup he helped his country finish third and was awarded the Golden Glove as the tournament's top goalkeeper after making more saves, 25, than any of his rivals.

PHILIPPE COUTINHO

Quicksilver midfielder Philippe Coutinho became the third most expensive footballer in the history of the game

Philippe Coutinho is Barcelona's record signing

when he joined Barcelona from Liverpool for £142 million in January 2018. He didn't take long to settle in Catalonia, either, contributing eight league goals to help Barca win La Liga and scoring in his new side's 5-0 drubbing of Sevilla in the Spanish Cup final.

• Coutinho was less fortunate with Liverpool, collecting runners-up medals in the 2016 League Cup final, despite scoring against Manchester City at Wembley, and in that year's Europa League final, which the Reds lost to Sevilla. However, his 41 league goals for the Anfield outfit mean that he is the highest-scoring Brazilian ever in the Premier League.

• Coutinho moved to Italian giants Inter Milan from Vasco da Gama when he was just 18, but struggled to adapt to Serie A. A loan spell at Spanish outfit Espanyol in 2012 proved a turning point in his career and the following January he joined Liverpool in a £8.5 million deal.

• A typical Brazilian number 10 who combines vision, flair and creativity in equal measure, Coutinho made his debut for his country in a 3-0 friendly win against Iran in 2010 when he was aged just 18. At Russia 2018 he scored in group games against Switzerland and Costa Rica and was voted into the FIFA World Cup Dream Team.

Coventry bounced back into League One via the play-offs in 2017/18

COVENTRY CITY

Year founded: 1883
Ground: Ricoh Arena (32,609)
Previous name: Singers FC
Nickname: The Sky Blues
Biggest win: 9-0 v Bristol City (1934)
Heaviest defeat: 2-11 v Berwick Rangers (1901)

Coventry were founded in 1883 by workers from the local Singer's bicycle factory and were named after the company until 1898. The club was elected to the Second Division in 1919, but their league career started unpromisingly with a 5-0 home defeat to Tottenham Hotspur.

• A club with a history of ups and downs, Coventry were the first team to play in seven different divisions: Premier, Division One, Two, Three, Four, Three (North) and Three (South). They have also played in the Championship, League One and League Two, which they escaped from via the play-offs at the end of the 2017/18 season.

• Coventry's greatest moment came in 1987 when the club won the FA Cup for the only time, beating Tottenham 3-2 in an exciting Wembley final. Two years later, though, the Sky Blues were dumped out of the cup by non-league Sutton United in one of the competition's biggest ever upsets.

• In July 2000 the Sky Blues made their record sale when striker Robbie Keane joined Inter Milan for £13 million. The following month Coventry forked out a club record fee of £6.5 million for Norwich striker Craig Bellamy.

• Long-serving goalkeeper Steve Ogrizovic played in a club record 504 league games between 1984 and 2000. Sky Blues legend Clarrie Bourton scored a club record 173 league goals between 1931 and 1937, including a season's best 49 goals in 1931/32.

• Former England striker Cyrille Regis, who sadly died in January 2018, is one of just three City players to score five goals in a match, starring in a 7-2 demolition of Chester City in October 1985.

HONOURS
Division 2 champions 1967
Division 3 champions 1964
Division 3 (South) champions 1936
FA Cup 1987
Football League Trophy 2017

CRAWLEY TOWN

Year founded: 1896
Ground: Broadfield Stadium (6,134)
Nickname: The Red Devils
Biggest win: 8-0 v Droylsden (2008)
Heaviest defeat: 0-7 v Bath City (2000)

Founded in 1896, Crawley Town started out in the West Sussex League, eventually rising to the Conference in 2004. Dubbed the 'Manchester City of non-league', Crawley splashed out more than £500,000 on new players at the start of the 2010/11 season, an investment which paid off when the club won promotion to the Football League at the end of the campaign.

• **Runaway Conference champions, Crawley's haul of 105 points set a new record for the division, while they also equalled the records for fewest defeats (3) and most wins (31). The following season Crawley enjoyed a second successive promotion, after finishing third in League Two behind Swindon and Shrewsbury.**

• Crawley reached the fifth round of the FA Cup for the first time in their history in 2011 after knocking out Swindon, Derby and Torquay. To their fans' delight they were then paired with Manchester United, and their team did them proud, only losing 1-0 at Old Trafford.

• **Along with Accrington Stanley, Crawley are one of just two current Football League clubs never to have played at Wembley.**

• Crawley boss for a year until he joined Notts County in August 2018, Harry Kewell is the only Australian to have managed a Football League club.

> HONOURS
> *Conference champions 2011*

CREWE ALEXANDRA

Year founded: 1877
Ground: Gresty Road (10,153)
Nickname: The Railwaymen
Biggest win: 8-0 v Rotherham (1932)
Heaviest defeat: 2-13 v Tottenham Hotspur (1960)

Founded by railway workers in 1877, the Crewe Football Club added 'Alexandra' to their name in honour of Princess Alexandra, wife of the future king, Edward VII. The club were founder members of the Second Division in 1892, although they lost their league status four years later before rejoining the newly formed Third Division (North) in 1921.

• **Club legend Herbert Swindells scored a record 126 goals for Crewe between 1927 and 1937. Crewe's appearance record is held by Tommy** Lowry, who turned out in 437 league games between 1966 and 1977.

• Alex fans endured a miserable spell in the mid-1950s when their club failed to win away from home for a record 56 consecutive matches. The depressing run finally ended with a 1-0 win at Southport in April 1957.

• **Striker Tony Naylor is the only Crewe player to score five goals in a game, going nap in a 7-1 mauling of Colchester United in April 1993.**

• The Railwaymen made their record signing in July 1998, forking out £650,000 for Torquay United striker Rodney Jack. The club's coffers were boasted by a record £6 million when striker Nick Powell joined Manchester United in July 2012.

> HONOURS
> *Football League Trophy 2013*
> *Welsh Cup 1936, 1937*

CROATIA

First international: Croatia 2 USA 1, 1990
Most capped player: Darijo Srna, 134 caps (2002-16)
Leading goalscorer: Davor Suker, 45 goals (1992-2002)
First World Cup appearance: Croatia 3 Jamaica 1, 1998
Biggest win: Croatia 10 San Marino 0, 2016
Heaviest defeat: England 5 Croatia 1, 2009

With a population of just over four million, Croatia is the second smallest country (after Uruguay) to reach the World Cup final. However, luck was against them in Moscow in 2018 and they eventually went down 4-2 to France despite dominating the first half.

• **On their way to the final, the Crvena i bijela ('Red and white') showed great battling qualities, coming from behind against both Denmark and Russia to win on penalties, before beating England 2-1 in the semi-final despite going behind early on to a brilliant Kieran Trippier free kick. Croatia's superb campaign was masterminded by diminutive skipper Luka Modric, whose excellent midfield displays saw him rewarded with the Golden Ball.**

• Formerly part of Yugoslavia, Croatia gained independence in 1991. The new nation first competed at the World Cup in 1998 and performed extremely well, beating Germany 3-0 in the quarter-finals before losing 2-1 to hosts and eventual winners France in the semi-finals. However, the Croats overcame their disappointment to claim third place with a 2-1 win against the Netherlands. Striker Davor Suker, Croatia's most prolific player ever, was top scorer at the tournament with six goals.

• **Two years earlier, Croatia made their first international appearance at Euro 96 in England. A 3-0 defeat of reigning champions Denmark helped them get through the group stage, but they lost 2-1 to eventual winners Germany in the quarter-finals at Old Trafford. The Croats also reached the last eight of the European championships in 2008, losing on penalties to Turkey after a 1-1 draw in Vienna.**

Despite losing in the final, Croatia were pretty pleased to finish runners up at the 2018 World Cup

World Cup Record
1930-90 Competed as part of
Yugoslavia
1994 Did not qualify
1998 Third place
2002 Round 1
2006 Round 1
2010 Did not qualify
2014 Round 1
2018 Runners-up

CRYSTAL PALACE

Year founded: 1905
Ground: Selhurst Park
(26,255)
Nickname: The Eagles
Biggest win: 9-0 v
Barrow (1959)
Heaviest defeat: 0-9
v Burnley (1909) and v
Liverpool (1989)

The club was founded in 1905 by workers at the then cup final venue at Crystal Palace, and was an entirely separate entity to the amateur club of the same name which was made up of groundkeepers at the Great Exhibition and reached the first ever semi-finals of the FA Cup in 1872.

• **After spending their early years in the Southern League, Palace were founder members of the Third Division (South) in 1920. The club had a great start to their league career, going up to the Second Division as champions in their first season.**

• Crystal Palace are only the second club (after Scottish outfit Queen's Park in 1885) to reach two FA Cup finals and lose on both occasions to the same club. In 1990 the Eagles held Manchester

The Eagles of Crystal Palace love to fly high

United to a thrilling 3-3 draw at Wembley before losing 1-0 in the replay. Then, in 2016, the south London club endured more agony at the hands of United when they went down to a 2-1 defeat in extra-time despite taking the lead through substitute Jason Puncheon.

• **Pre-war striker Peter Simpson is the club's all-time leading scorer with 153 league goals between 1930 and 1936, including a club record six goals in a match against Exeter City in October 1930. Rugged defender Jim Cannon holds the club appearance record, turning out 660 times between 1973 and 1988.**

• Palace are the only club to have been promoted to the top flight four times via the play-offs, most recently in 2013. The Eagles are also the only club to have won play-off finals at four different venues: Selhurst Park (1989), old Wembley (1997), Millennium Stadium (2004) and new Wembley (2013).

• **Less happily for their fans, Palace have been relegated a joint-record four times from the Premier League, including a particularly unfortunate occasion in 1993 when they went**

down with a record 49 points (from 42 games).

• The club made their record signing in August 2016, when Belgium striker Christian Benteke signed from Liverpool for £27 million. In the same month the Eagles sold DR Congo winger Yannick Bolasie to Everton for a club record £25 million.

• **A record fourth-tier crowd of 37,774 watched Palace's home match with Millwall on 31st March 1961, but it proved to be a disappointing afternoon for the Selhurst faithful as the Eagles slumped to a 2-0 defeat.**

• Striker Andy Johnson scored a Premier League record 11 penalties for the Eagles in 2004/05, but his goals unfortunately could not prevent the south Londoners from being relegated.

• **Tough-tackling midfielder Mile Jedinak won a club record 37 caps for Australia while at Selhurst Park between 2011 and 2016.**

IS THAT A FACT?
Crystal Palace stayed up in 2017/18 despite enduring the worst ever start to a Premier League season: no points and no goals in their first seven matches.

HONOURS
First Division champions 1994
Division 2 champions 1979
Division 3 (South) champions 1921

DEATHS

The first recorded death as a direct result of a football match came in 1889 when William Cropper of Derbyshire side Staveley FC died of a ruptured bowel sustained in a collision with an opponent.

• **In 1931 Celtic's brilliant young international goalkeeper John Thompson died in hospital after fracturing his skull in a collision with Rangers forward Sam English. Some 40,000 fans attended his funeral, many of them walking the 55 miles from Glasgow to Thompson's home village in Fife. In the same decade two other goalkeepers, Jimmy Utterson of Wolves and Sunderland's Jimmy Thorpe, also died from injuries sustained on the pitch. Their deaths led the Football Association to change the rules so that goalkeepers could not be tackled while they had the ball in their hands.**

• Nine months after scoring for his country against Germany in April 1938, Austria's star striker Matthias Sindelar was found dead in his flat in Vienna alongside his girlfriend. The official cause of death was given as carbon monoxide poisoning, but many believe the pair were murdered by the Nazis.

• **In a tragic incident in October 2014 Indian player Peter Biaksangzuala died after injuring his spine while** performing a somersault to celebrate a goal he had scored for his club, Bethlehem Vengthlang.

• In May 2018 Luyanda Ntshangase, a defensive midfielder with South African Premier Division club Maritzburg United, was struck by lightning during a friendly match and died three days later.

• **In April 2017 Amilcar Henriquez, a 33-year-old Panama international with 85 caps, was shot dead in a drive-by shooting while playing dominoes in Nueva Colon.**

• On 11th November 1923 Aston Villa centre-half Tommy Ball was shot dead by his neighbour, becoming the first and last Football League player to be murdered. Ball's killer, George Stagg, was sentenced to life imprisonment and later declared to be insane.

DEBUTS

Aston Villa striker Howard Vaughton enjoyed the best England debut ever, scoring five goals in a 13-0 rout of Ireland in 1882. The last England player to score a hat-trick on his debut was Luther Blissett, who smashed three past Luxembourg in a 9-0 win at Wembley in 1982.

• **The worst ever international debut was by American Samoa goalkeeper Nicky Salapu against Fiji in 2001. He conceded 13 goals in that game, and then another 44 within a week in three matches against Samoa, Tonga and Australia.**

• Freddy Eastwood scored the fastest goal on debut, netting after just seven seconds for Southend against Swansea in 2004.

• **The fastest goal by an England player on debut was by future Tottenham boss Bill Nicholson after just 19 seconds against Portugal at Goodison Park in 1951.**

• Italian striker Fabrizio Ravanelli is the only player to score a hat-trick on his Premier League debut, striking three times for Middlesbrough in a 3-3 draw against Liverpool on the opening day of the 1996/97 season.

• Arsenal Ladies striker Danielle Carter enjoyed a fantastic debut for England Women in September 2015, scoring a hat-trick in an 8-0 hammering of Estonia in September 2015. For good measure, she hit another treble against the same opposition in her second international appearance the following year.

TROY DEENEY

Born: Birmingham, 29th June 1988
Position: Striker
Club career:
2006-10 Walsall 123 (27)
2006-07 Halesowen Town (loan) 10 (8)
2010- Watford 309 (105)

Fiery and abrasive Watford skipper Troy Deeney is the Hornets' all-time leading scorer in the Premier League with 28 goals, and is only the fifth player to pass a century of goals for the club.

• **However, Deeney's career almost went completely off the rails in 2012**

It doesn't take much to get Troy Deeney fired up

IS THAT A FACT?

In October 2017 Choirul Huda, a goalkeeper with top-flight Indonesian side Persela Lamongan, sadly died after sustaining severe head injuries in a collision with one of his own defenders in a match against Semen Padang.

Derby matches don't get much bigger than Liverpool v Everton

when he was sentenced to 10 months' imprisonment for his part in a brawl outside a Birmingham nightclub. After serving almost three months he was released, and returned to Watford to score 20 goals in the Championship in the 2012/13 season.

• The bustling and aggressive Deeney was equally prolific in the following two campaigns to become the first Watford player ever to score 20 or more goals in three consecutive seasons. His hot scoring streak helped Watford gain promotion to the Premier League in 2015 and earned Deeney a place in in the PFA Championship Team of the Year.

• Deeney started out at Walsall, where he was named the club's Player of the Year in 2010, shortly before joining Watford in a bargain £250,000 (rising to £500,000) deal.

DERBIES

So called because they matched the popularity of the Epsom Derby horse race, 'derby' matches between local sides provoke intense passions among fans and players alike.

• Celtic v Rangers is the most played derby in world football – the two teams having met an incredible 412 times since their first encounter in the Scottish Cup in September 1890. In the 2010/11 season the two teams met a record seven times, the clashes provoking so many violent incidents

in Glasgow that the chairman of the Scottish Police Federation called for future Old Firm matches to be banned.

• The biggest win in a derby match in England was Nottingham Forest's 12-0 thrashing of east Midland rivals Leicester City in the old First Division in 1909. In the Premier League era Chelsea recorded the most emphatic derby win when they smashed Arsenal 6-0 at Stamford Bridge in March 2014.

• Chelsea enjoyed the longest unbeaten run in an English derby, 26 matches against Tottenham in all competitions between 1990 and 2002. In Scotland, Hearts were unbeaten in 22 Edinburgh derbies with Hibs between 1989 and 1994.

• Arsenal's Thierry Henry scored a record 43 goals in 59 Premier League London derbies between 1999 and 2007.

DERBY COUNTY

Year founded: 1884
Ground: Pride Park (33,597)
Nickname: The Rams
Biggest win: 12-0 v Finn Harps (1976)
Heaviest defeat: 2-11 v Everton (1890)

Derby were formed in 1884 as an offshoot of Derbyshire Cricket Club and originally wore an amber, chocolate and blue strip based on the cricket club's colours. Perhaps wisely, they changed to their traditional black-and-white colours in the 1890s.

• The club were founder members of the Football League in 1888 and seven years later moved from the ground they shared with the cricketers to the Baseball Ground (so named because baseball was regularly played there in the 1890s). Derby had to oust a band of gypsies before they could move in, one of whom is said to have laid a curse on the place as he left. No doubt, then, the club was pleased to leave the Baseball Ground for Pride Park in 1997... although when Derby's first game at the new stadium had to be abandoned due to floodlight failure, there were fears that the curse had followed them!

• Runners-up in the FA Cup final in 1898, 1899 and 1903, Derby reached their last final in 1946. Before the match the club's captain, Jack Nicholas, visited a gypsy encampment and paid for the old curse to be lifted. It worked, as Derby beat Charlton 4-1 after extra-time.

• Under charismatic manager Brian Clough, Derby took the top flight by storm after winning promotion to the First Division in 1969. Three years later they won the league in one of the closest title races ever. Having played all their fixtures ahead of their title contenders, Derby's players were actually sitting on a beach in Majorca when they heard news of their victory. The following season Derby reached the semi-finals of the European Cup and, in 1975 under the management of former skipper Dave Mackay, they won the championship again.

• The Rams' last season in the top flight in 2007/08 was an utter disaster as they managed just one win in the whole campaign, equalling a Football League record set by Loughborough in 1900. Even worse, between September 2007 and September 2008 Derby went a record 36 league games without a win, including a record 32 games in the Premier League and another four in the Championship.

• **Derby striker Deon Burton played in a club record 42 internationals for Jamaica between 1997 and 2002.**

• Derby's best ever goalscorer was one of the true greats of the game in the late 19th and early 20th centuries, Steve Bloomer. He netted an incredible 332 goals in two spells at the club between 1892 and 1914, and in 1899 became the first and only Derby player to score a double hat-trick in a match against Sheffield Wednesday.

• **Appointed Derby boss in May 2018, Frank Lampard is the joint-third highest-capped England player to manage in the Football League behind Peter Shilton (Plymouth Argyle) and Bobby Moore (Southend United).**

HONOURS
Division 1 champions 1972, 1975
Division 2 champions 1912, 1915, 1969, 1987
FA Cup 1946

ERIC DIER

Born: Cheltenham, 15th January 1994
Position: Defender/midfielder
Club career:
2012-14 Sporting Lisbon B 16 (2)
2012-14 Sporting Lisbon 27 (1)
2014- Tottenham Hotspur 135 (7)
International record:
2015- England 32 (3)

When Eric Dier fired past Colombia goalkeeper David Ospina in the last 16 of the 2018 World Cup in Russia he became the first ever English player to score a winning penalty in a shoot-out at the

Eric Dier provides a calm presence in midfield for both club and country

tournament, sparking wild celebrations across the country.

• **Born in Cheltenham, Dier moved to Portugal with his parents aged seven and came through the ranks of the Sporting Lisbon academy while also spending 18 months on loan at Everton as a teenager. After breaking into the Sporting first team in 2012 he moved on to Tottenham in a £4 million deal two years later.**

• A disciplined and versatile player who is normally employed as a defensive midfielder but is equally effective at right-back or at centre-back, Dier scored the winner on his Spurs debut in a 1-0 victory at West Ham on the opening day of the 2014/15 campaign. Later that season he played in the League Cup final at Wembley, which Spurs lost 2-0 to London rivals Chelsea.

• Capped by England at all age groups from Under-18s onwards, Dier made his full international debut as a sub in a 2-0 friendly defeat against Spain in November 2015. Four months later he scored his first England goal, heading the winner in a famous 3-2 friendly victory away to Germany, and in November 2017 he captained his country for the same time in a friendly against the same opposition at Wembley.

DISCIPLINE

Yellow and red cards were introduced into English league football on 2nd October 1976, and on the same day Blackburn's David Wagstaffe received the first red card during his side's match with Leyton Orient. Five years later cards were

"Yellow card... and if you don't shut it, you'll get a red next!"

DONCASTER ROVERS

Year founded: 1879
Ground: Keepmoat Stadium (15,231)
Nickname: The Rovers
Biggest win: 10-0 v Darlington (1964)
Heaviest defeat: 0-12 v Small Heath (1903)

Founded in 1879 by Albert Jenkins, a fitter at Doncaster's Great Northern Railway works, Doncaster turned professional in 1885 and joined the Second Division of the Football League in 1901.

• Remarkably, Doncaster hold the record for the most wins in a league season (33 in 1946/47) and for the most defeats (34 in 1997/98).

• Midfield stalwart James Coppinger has played in a club record 506 league games since signing from Exeter City in 2004. Rovers all-time top scorer is Tom Keetley, with 180 league goals in the 1920s, including a club record six in a 7-4 win at Ashington in February 1929.

• In 1946 Doncaster were involved in the longest ever football match, a Third Division (North) cup tie against Stockport County at Edgeley Park which the referee ruled could extend beyond extra-time in an attempt to find a winner. Eventually, the game was abandoned after 203 minutes due to poor light.

• Doncaster have won the third tier a record four times, most recently winning the League One title in 2013.

• Hotshot striker Clarrie Jordan scored in a club record 10 consecutive league games in the 1946/47 season.

HONOURS

League One champions 2013
Division 3 (North) champions 1935, 1947, 1950
Third Division champions 2004
Division 4 champions 1966, 1969
Football League Trophy 2007

DOUBLES

The first club to win the Double of league championship and FA Cup were Preston North End, in the very first season of the Football League in 1888/89. The Lancashire side achieved this feat in fine style, remaining undefeated in the league

---

withdrawn by the Football Association as referees were getting 'too flashy', but the system was re-introduced in 1987.

• A stormy last 16 match between the Netherlands and Portugal in 2006 was the most ill-disciplined in the history of the World Cup. Russian referee Valentin Ivanov was the busiest man on the pitch as he pulled out his yellow card 16 times and his red one four times, with the match ending as a nine-a-side affair. In total, a record 28 players were sent off during the 2006 tournament.

• West Brom midfielder Gareth Barry has been shown a record 123 yellow cards in the Premier League, while Wayne Rooney's total of 102 yellows puts him second on the list of shame. Richard Dunne, Duncan Ferguson and Patrick Vieira share the record for receiving the most red cards in Premier League matches, with eight each.

• Former Colombian international Gerardo Bedoya was sent off a record 46 times in his playing career. In March 2016 in his first match as a coach with Independiente Santa Fe, the man dubbed 'the world's dirtiest footballer' was shown a red card in the first half.

• A record nine Sunderland players were sent off in the 2009/10 season, a total equalled by QPR in 2011/12. Sunderland also hold the record for the most yellow cards in a single campaign, with 94 in 2014/15.

• When a mass brawl erupted in the middle of the pitch during a match between Argentinian sides Victoriano Arenas and Claypole on 26th February 2011, referee Damian Rubino showed red cards to all 22 players and 14 substitutes as well as coaches and technical staff. The total of 36 players sent off set a new world record, smashing the previous 'best' of 20!

• In a bizarre incident in October 2017 Salford City goalkeeper Max Crocombe was sent off for urinating at the side of the pitch during his side's 2-1 win at Bradford Park Avenue in the National League North.

TOP 10

TOTAL PREMIER LEAGUE RED CARDS

1.	Everton	89
2.	Arsenal	86
3.	Newcastle United	80
4.	Chelsea	78
5.	Blackburn Rovers	77
6.	West Ham United	71
7.	Manchester City	65
8.	Manchester United	62
	Sunderland	62
10.	Tottenham Hotspur	61

and keeping a clean sheet in all their matches in the FA Cup.

• Arsenal and Manchester United have both won the Double a record three times. The Red Devils' trio of successes all came within a five-year period in the 1990s (1994, 1996 and 1999), with the last of their Doubles comprising two-thirds of a legendary Treble which also included the Champions League. Arsenal first won the Double in 1971, and since then the Gunners have twice repeated the feat under then manager Arsène Wenger in 1998 and 2002.

• The other English clubs to win the Double are Aston Villa (1897), Tottenham (1961), Liverpool (1986) and Chelsea (2010). Villa's success was especially notable as they won both competitions on the same day, beating Everton 3-2 in the FA Cup final and then learning that title rivals Derby County had lost 1-0 at Bury to hand the Villans the league championship too.

• Linfield have won a world record 24 Doubles, the most recent coming in 2017. The Northern Ireland outfit are followed by Hong Kong's South China (22) and Rangers (18).

DRAWS

Preston North End have drawn more league matches than any other club, having finished on level terms 1,262 times. Bootle FC have drawn the fewest league matches, just three in their single season in the Second Division in 1892/93.

• The highest-scoring draw in the top division of English football was 6-6, in a match between Leicester City and Arsenal in 1930. In an incredible match in the fourth qualifying round of the FA Cup in November 1929, Dulwich Hamlet and Wealdstone drew 7-7 before Dulwich won the replay 2-1.

• The 2018 World Cup featured just one 0-0 draw (between France and Denmark), the lowest number at the tournament since there were no goalless stalemates in 1954.

• Manchester City (1993/94), Sheffield United (1993/94) and Southampton (1994/95) jointly hold the record for the most draws in a Premier League season, with 18. At the other end of the scale, Chelsea drew just three games in both 1997/98 and 2016/17.

• Everton have drawn a record 1,126 top-flight matches, including a record 287 Premier League games.

• The highest-scoring ever recorded in a professional match saw German lower league sides Manzur and DJK Sparta Burgel tie 9-9 in May 2015.

TONI DUGGAN

Toni Duggan is famed for her 'standing on the ball' trick

In July 2017 Toni Duggan became the first English player since Gary Lineker in 1986 to sign for Barcelona when she joined the Catalan giants' women's team from Manchester City.

• Like many top female footballers, Duggan started out playing in a boys' team, Jellytots in Liverpool. She went on to play for Everton Ladies, being named the FA Women's Young Player of the Year in 2009. The following year she helped Everton win the FA Women's Cup, after a 3-2 triumph against Arsenal in the final at the Ricoh Arena, Coventry. In 2013 she moved on to Manchester City, adding the Women's Super League title (2016) and another FA Cup (2017) to her list of honours.

• A lively and energetic striker, Duggan first represented England at Under-17 level. On her 18th birthday she scored in the final of the 2009 UEFA Women's Under-19 championship, which England won against Sweden. She won her first full England cap against Croatia in September 2012, and the following year scored her first international hat-trick in a clinical 8-0 demolition of Turkey at Fratton Park.

• In April 2015 Duggan was criticised by Manchester City fans after posting a picture of herself on social media smiling with then Manchester United manager Louis van Gaal only hours

Tottenham proudly show off their league and FA Cup Double in 1961

after City had lost 4-2 to United in the Premier League. However, she maintained her online presence and the following year became the first female England player to reach 100,000 followers on Twitter.

DUNDEE

Year founded: 1893
Ground: Dens Park (11,506)
Nickname: The Dee
Biggest win: 10-0 v Alloa (1947), v Dunfermline (1947) and v Queen of the South (1962)
Heaviest defeat: 0-11 v Celtic (1895)

Dundee were founded in 1893 after the merger of two local clubs, Dundee Our Boys and Dundee East End.

• **The club's greatest ever moment was in 1962 when the Dee won the Scottish title under the managership of Bob Shankly, brother of the legendary Bill. The following season Dundee reached the semi-finals of the European Cup, before bowing out to eventual winners AC Milan.**

• In April 2010 Dundee goalkeeper Bobby Geddes became the oldest man ever to appear in a Scottish league game when he came on as a first-half substitute during a 1-0 defeat against Raith Rovers in the First Division just four months short of his 50th birthday.

• **Alan Gilzean scored a club record 113 league goals for the Dee between 1957 and 1964, including a season's best 52 in 1963/64, before going**

TOP 10

CLOSEST BRITISH FOOTBALL STADIUMS

1.	Dundee/Dundee United	0.2 miles
2.	Notts County/Notts Forest	0.7 miles
3.	Everton/Liverpool	0.8 miles
4.	Chelsea/Fulham	1.9 miles
6.	Aston Villa/Birmingham City	3.5 miles
7.	Sheff Utd/Sheff Wed	3.8 miles
8.	Millwall/Charlton	3.9 miles
9.	Aston Villa/West Brom	4 miles
	Arsenal/Spurs	4 miles

on to enjoy even more goalscoring exploits with Tottenham.

• Dundee striker Dave Halliday topped the Scottish goalscoring charts with 38 goals in 1923/24 and five years later was the top scorer in England with Sunderland – one of just two players to achieve this particular 'Double' along with Celtic and Aston Villa forward John Campbell.

• **Dundee's Dens Park is situated just a few hundred yards from Dundee United's Tannadice Park, making the two clubs the closest neighbours in British football.**

HONOURS

Division 1 champions 1962
Championship champions 2014
First Division champions 1979, 1992
Division 2 champions 1947
Scottish Cup 1910
Scottish League Cup 1952, 1953, 1974

DUNDEE UNITED

Year founded: 1909
Ground: Tannadice Park (14,223)
Previous name: Dundee Hibernian
Nickname: The Terrors
Biggest win: 14-0 v Nithsdale Wanderers (1931)
Heaviest defeat: 1-12 v Motherwell (1954)

Originally founded as Dundee Hibernian by members of the city's Irish community in 1909, the club changed to its present name in 1923 to attract support from a wider population.

• **The club emerged from relative obscurity to become one of the leading clubs in Scotland under long-serving manager Jim McLean in the 1970s and 1980s, winning the Scottish Premier Division in 1983. The club's success, allied to that of Aberdeen, led to talk of a 'New Firm' capable of challenging the 'Old Firm' of Rangers and Celtic for major honours.**

• United reached the semi-finals of the European Cup in 1984 and the final of the UEFA Cup in 1987, where they lost 2-1 on aggregate to Swedish side Gothenburg. The club's European exploits also include four victories over Barcelona – a 100 per cent record

Dundee are currently top dogs in the Jute City

against the Catalan powerhouse which no other British team can match.

• **After being losing finalists on six previous occasions, Dundee United finally won the Scottish Cup in 1994 when they beat Rangers 1-0 in the final. They won the trophy for a second time in 2010, following a comfortable 3-0 win against shock finalists Ross County, but went down in the 2014 final to surprise winners St Johnstone.**

• Maurice Malpas turned out in a club record 617 league games for the Terrors between 1981 and 2000. The Terrors' record scorer is Peter McKay with 158 league goals between 1947 and 1954.

• **In the 1964/65 season Danish striker Finn Dossing scored in 13 consecutive league games – just one short of the British record set by Falkirk's Evelyn Morrison in 1928/29.**

HONOURS

Premier League champions 1983
Division 2 champions 1925, 1929
Scottish Cup 1994, 2010
Scottish League Cup 1980, 1981

EDERSON

Born: Osasco, Brazil, 17th August 1993
Position: Goalkeeper
Club career:
2011-12 Ribeirao 29
2012-15 Rio Ave 37
2015 Benfica B 4
2015-17 Benfica 37
2017- Manchester City 36
International record:
2017- Brazil 1

Heavily-tattooed Brazil international Ederson became the most expensive goalkeeper in Britain at the time when he joined Manchester City from Benfica for £35 million in June 2017.

• A nimble goalkeeper who distributes the ball superbly with his feet, Ederson paid back much of that fee by helping the Citizens win the 2018 Premier League title with a record 100 points. His total of 16 clean sheets was only bettered by Golden Glove winner David de Gea.

• Ederson started out with Portuguese second-tier outfit Ribeirao before earning a move to the Primeira Liga with Rio Ave. His excellent performances soon caught the eye of Benfica who he joined in 2015, and two years later he won the domestic Double with the Portuguese giants.

• **In May 2018 Ederson gained an entry in the** *Guinness Book of Records* **after setting a world record in training for the longest-ever drop kick, an impressive 75.3 metres.**

UNAI EMERY

Born: Hondarribia, Spain, 3rd November 1971
Managerial career:
2004-06 Lorca Deportivo
2006-08 Almeria
2008-12 Valencia
2012 Spartak Moscow
2013-16 Sevilla
2016-18 Paris Saint-Germain
2018- Arsenal

Appointed Arsenal head coach on a two-year contract in May 2018, Unai Emery is the only manager to have won the Europa League three times. The Spaniard achieved this feat with Sevilla between 2014 and 2016, the last of those triumphs coming thanks to a 3-1 defeat of Liverpool in Basel.

• **After a playing career spent mostly in the Spanish second tier, Emery started out in management with Lorca Deportivo, leading the club to their first ever promotion to the Second Division in 2005. He soon moved on to Almeria, taking the southern Spanish outfit into the top flight for the first time in their history in 2007. The following year he joined Valencia, guiding 'Los Ches' to three consecutive third-place finishes between 2010 and 2012.**

• After a brief and unsuccessful spell with Spartak Moscow, Emery returned to Spain with Sevilla, where he enjoyed three memorable years and was voted European Coach of the Season in 2014.

• **In 2016 Emery took over as manager of Paris Saint-Germain. He led the French giants to two French Cup triumphs and the Ligue 1 title in 2018 before succeeding the long-serving Arsene Wenger at the Emirates.**

TOP 10

ENGLAND GOALSCORERS

1. Wayne Rooney (2003-16)		53
2. Bobby Charlton (1958-70)		49
3. Gary Lineker (1984-92)		48
4. Jimmy Greaves (1959-67)		44
5. Michael Owen (1998-2008)		40
6. Tom Finney (1946-58)		30
Nat Lofthouse (1950-58)		30
Alan Shearer (1992-2000)		30
9. Vivian Woodward (1903-11)		29
Frank Lampard (1999-2014)		29

ENGLAND

First international: Scotland 0 England 0, 1872
Most capped player: Peter Shilton, 125 caps (1971-90)
Leading goalscorer: Wayne Rooney, 53 goals (2003-16)
First World Cup appearance: England 2 Chile 0, 1950
Biggest win: England 13 Ireland 0, 1882
Heaviest defeat: Hungary 7 England 1, 1954

England, along with their first opponents Scotland, are the oldest international team in world football. The two countries met in the first official international in Glasgow in 1872, with honours being shared after a 0-0 draw. The following year, William Kenyon-Slaney of Wanderers FC scored England's first ever goal in a 4-2 victory over Scotland at the Kennington Oval.

• **With a team entirely composed of players from England, Great Britain won the first Olympic Games football tournament in 1908 and again in 1912.**

"Quick, grab the ball and chuck it in the net before the ref turns around"

At last, the Three Lions are roaring again!

• There were many heroes in that 1966 team, including goalkeeper Gordon Banks, skipper Bobby Moore and striker Geoff Hurst, who scored a hat-trick in the 4-2 victory over West Germany in the final at Wembley. Ramsey, too, was hailed for his part in the success and was knighted soon afterwards.

• Since then, however, England fans have experienced more than their fair share of disappointment. Many believed the World Cup was 'coming home' when England reached the semi-final of the tournament in 2018, but Gareth Southgate's team were beaten 2-1 by Croatia after extra-time in Moscow despite taking an early lead thanks to a magnificent Kieran Trippier free kick. England also made it through to the last four in 1990 but, agonisingly, Bobby Robson's team lost on penalties in the semi-final to the eventual winners, West Germany.

• In 1996 England hosted the European Championships and were again knocked out on penalties by Germany at the semi-final stage, with Gareth Southgate the unfortunate player to miss the decisive spot-kick.

• Defender Billy Wright, the first man in the world to win 100 international caps, and Bobby Moore both captained England a record 90 times. Wright also played in a record 70 consecutive England matches between 1951 and 1959.

• Legendary winger Stanley Matthews holds the record for the longest England career – an incredible 22 years and 228 days from 1934 to 1957.

• Gary Lineker is England's top scorer at the World Cup, with a total of 10 goals in 1986 and 1990. Lineker won the Golden Boot at the first of these tournaments, a feat matched by Three Lions skipper Harry Kane in 2018.

• A record six players scored for England at the 2018 World Cup: Harry Kane (six goals), John Stones (two goals), Jesse Lingard, Harry Maguire, Dele Alli and Kieran Trippier.

• Tottenham have provided England with a record 78 players, starting with winger Vivian Woodward in 1903.

• England did not lose a match on home soil against a team from outside the British Isles until 1953 when they were thrashed 6-3 by Hungary at Wembley. The following year England went down to their worst ever defeat to the same opposition, crashing 7-1 in Budapest.

• Although Walter Winterbottom was appointed as England's first full-time manager in 1946, the squad was picked by a committee until Alf Ramsey took over in 1963. Three years later England hosted and won the World Cup – the greatest moment in the country's football history by some considerable margin.

HONOURS
World Cup winners 1966
World Cup Record
1930 Did not enter
1934 Did not enter
1938 Did not enter
1950 Round 1
1954 Quarter-finals
1958 Round 1
1962 Quarter-finals
1966 Winners
1970 Quarter-finals
1974 Did not qualify
1978 Did not qualify
1982 Round 2
1986 Quarter-finals
1990 Fourth place
1994 Did not qualify
1998 Round 2
2002 Quarter-finals
2006 Quarter-finals
2010 Round 2
2014 Round 1
2018 Fourth place

ENGLAND WOMEN

First international: Scotland 2 England 3, 1972
Most capped player: Fara Williams, 168 caps (2001-)
Leading goalscorer: Kelly Smith, 46 goals (1995-2014)
First World Cup appearance: England 3 Canada 2, 1995
Biggest win: England 13 Hungary 0, 2005
Heaviest defeat: Norway 8 England 0, 2000

The England women's team played their first international against Scotland at Greenock on 18th November 1972. Midfielder Sylvia Gore scored the Lionesses' first ever goal in a 3-2 victory.

• Although England have never won a major trophy they have reached two finals of the European Championships, losing on penalties to Sweden in 1984 and going down 6-2 to Germany in 2009. The Lionesses' best ever showing at the World Cup was in 2015 when they came third after a Fara Williams penalty clinched a nail-biting 1-0 win against Germany in the third/fourth play-off.

England's women have had plenty to smile about in recent years

• Williams is England's most decorated player, with a total of 168 caps since making her debut in 2001. The Lionesses' all-time top scorer is ex-Arsenal Ladies striker Kelly Smith who banged in 46 goals between 1995 and 2014.

• Former Arsenal Ladies defender Faye White is England's longest-serving captain, skippering her country for 10 years between 2002 and 2012, and wearing the armband for the vast majority of her 90 caps.

• Hope Powell, a former England international herself, managed the Lionesses for a record 15 years between 1998 and 2013.

World Cup Record
1991 Did not qualify
1995 Quarter-finals
1999 Did not qualify
2003 Did not qualify
2007 Quarter-finals
2011 Quarter-finals
2015 Third place

CHRISTIAN ERIKSEN

Born: Middelfart, Denmark, 14th February 1992
Position: Midfielder
Club career:
2010-13 Ajax 113 (25)
2013- Tottenham Hotspur 171 (41)
International record:
2010- Denmark 82 (23)

Silky Tottenham Hotspur midfielder is the highest-scoring Danish player in Premier League history with 41 goals, passing the previous benchmark set by Arsenal striker Nicklas Bendtner when

he scored in a 3-2 win at West Ham in September 2017. Later in the same campaign, Eriksen scored the third fastest goal in Premier League history, shooting past Manchester United goalkeeper David de Gea after just 11 seconds in Tottenham's 2-0 win at Wembley.

• **As a youth player with Odense Boldklub, Eriksen was a transfer target for numerous top European clubs, but after trials with Chelsea, Manchester United, Barcelona and Real Madrid, he decided to join Ajax as a 16-year-old in 2008. It proved to be an extremely wise move, as the youngster soon cemented a place in the Dutch giants' side and went on to win three league**

Tottenham's Great Dane Christian Eriksen

titles before joining Spurs for £11 million in 2013.

• When he made his international debut in 2010 against Austria, aged 18, Eriksen became the fourth youngest Danish player ever to appear for the national team. He then became the youngest Danish player ever to score in a European Championship qualifier when he netted in a 2-0 win against Iceland the following year. His total of 11 goals in the 2018 World Cup qualifying campaign was only bettered by Cristiano Ronaldo and Robert Lewandowski in Europe.

• **Voted into the Premier League Team of the Year for the first time in 2018, Eriksen is only the second player (after the legendary Brian Laudrup) to be named Danish Footballer of the Year four times, collecting the award in 2013, 2104, 2015 and 2017.**

EUROPA LEAGUE

Since European football's second-tier competition was rebranded as the Europa League in 2010, two clubs have won the trophy three times: Sevilla in 2014, 2015 and 2016, and Atletico Madrid in 2010, 2012 and 2018, when they beat Marseille 3-0 in Lyon in the final. Thanks to Sevilla's two previous triumphs in the UEFA Cup, the forerunner of the Europa League, the team from southern Spain are the most successful club in the history of the competition.

• **In 2011 Porto beat Braga 1-0 in Dublin in the first ever all-Portuguese European final. Porto's match-winner was Colombian striker Radamel Falcao, whose goal in the final was his 17th in the competition that season – a record for the tournament.**

• The competition is now in its third incarnation, having previously been known as the Fairs Cup (1955-71) and the UEFA Cup (1971-2009). The tournament was originally established in 1955 as a competition between cities, rather than clubs. The first winners were Barcelona, who beat London 8-2 on aggregate in a final which, bizarrely, did not take place until 1958!

• **The first team to win the newly named UEFA Cup were Tottenham Hotspur in 1972, who beat Wolves 3-2 on aggregate in the only all-English final. Following Manchester United's triumph in the 2017 Europa League final against Ajax, English clubs have won the competition 12 times. Spanish teams lead the way with 17 victories.**

Portugal's 47-man team proved unstoppable at Euro 2016

UEFA EURO 2016

• Swedish striker Henrik Larsson is the leading scorer in the history of the UEFA Cup with 40 goals for Feyenoord, Celtic and Helsingborg between 1993 and 2009.
• **Liverpool are the most successful English club in the competition, with three victories in the UEFA Cup in 1973, 1976 and 2001, the last of these triumphs coming courtesy of a thrilling 5-4 victory over Alaves – the most goal-packed of all the one-off finals.**

EUROPEAN CHAMPIONSHIPS

Originally called the European Nations Cup, the idea for the European Championships came from Henri Delaunay, the then secretary of the French FA. The first championships in 1960 featured just 17 countries (the four British nations, Italy and West Germany were among those who declined to take part). The first winners of the tournament were the Soviet Union, who beat Yugoslavia 2-1 in the final in Paris.
• **Germany have the best record in the tournament, having won the trophy three times (in 1972, 1980 and 1996) and been runners-up on a further three occasions. Spain have also won the championships three times (1964, 2008 and 2012) and are the only country to retain the trophy following a 4-0 demolition of Italy in the final at Euro 2012 – the biggest win in any European Championships or World Cup final.**
• Germany have scored the most goals at the finals, 72, but also have the worst defensive record, conceding 48.
• **French legend Michel Platini and Portugal's Cristiano Ronaldo are the** leading scorers in the finals of the European Championships with nine goals each. Platini's goals all came in 1984, setting a record for a single tournament.
• Including qualifying matches, Cristiano Ronaldo is the leading scorer in the competition with 29 goals and is the only player to have scored at four finals (2004, 2008, 2012 and 2016). Ronaldo has also made a record 21 appearances at the finals.
• **Italy have featured in a record five penalty shoot-outs at the finals, winning two and losing three.**
• The 2016 finals in France produced a record 108 goals but as a record number of matches were played, 51, the average number of goals per game was an underwhelming 2.12.

European Championships finals
1960 USSR 2 Yugoslavia 1 (Paris)
1964 Spain 2 USSR 1 (Madrid)
1968 Italy 2 Yugoslavia 0 • (Rome)
1972 West Germany 3 USSR 0 (Brussels)
1976 Czechoslovakia 2 *
West Germany 2 (Belgrade)
1980 West Germany 2 Belgium 1 (Rome)
1984 France 2 Spain 0 (Paris)
1988 Netherlands 2 USSR 0 (Munich)
1992 Denmark 2 Germany 0 (Gothenburg)
1996 Germany 2 Czech Republic 1 (London)
2000 France 2 Italy 1 (Rotterdam)
2004 Greece 1 Portugal 0 (Lisbon)
2008 Spain 1 Germany 0 (Vienna)
2012 Spain 4 Italy 0 (Kiev)
2016 Portugal 1 France 0 (Paris)
• After 1-1 draw   * Won on penalties

EURO 2020

Euro 2020 will be the first European Championships to be held in multiple countries, as a special one-off event to mark the 60th anniversary of the first tournament in 1960.
• **The 12 countries which will host matches are Azerbaijan, Denmark, England, Germany, Hungary, Italy, the Netherlands, Republic of Ireland, Romania, Russia, Scotland and Spain. Wembley Stadium will host both semi-finals and the final in July 2020.**
• Unlike previous tournaments, no country will qualify automatically as hosts. Instead 20 countries will come through the usual qualifying process, with the remaining four qualifying via the new UEFA Nations League.

EUROPEAN GOLDEN SHOE

Formerly known as the European Golden Boot, the European Golden Shoe has been awarded since 1968 to the leading scorer in league matches in the top division of every European league. Since 1997 the award has been based on a points system which gives greater weight to goals scored in the leading European leagues.
• **Barcelona star Lionel Messi has won the award five times – once more than his fierce rival Cristiano Ronaldo – and most recently topped the charts in 2017/18 with 34 goals. Messi also holds the record for the most goals scored by a Golden Shoe winner, with an incredible 50 in 2011/12.**
• The first British winner of the award was Liverpool's Ian Rush in 1984, and the most recent was Sunderland's Kevin Phillips in 2000. Since then, Arsenal's Thierry Henry (in 2004 and 2005), Manchester United's Cristiano Ronaldo (in 2008) and Liverpool's Luis Suarez (jointly with Cristiano Ronaldo in 2014) have won the Golden Shoe after topping both the Premier League and European goalscoring charts. When Ronaldo first won the Golden Shoe with Real Madrid in 2011, he became the first player to win the award in two different countries.
• **Players based in the Spanish league have won the award a record 14 times.**

EUROPEAN SUPER CUP

Founded in 1972 as a two-legged final between the winners of the European Cup and the European Cup Winners' Cup, the European Super Cup trophy is

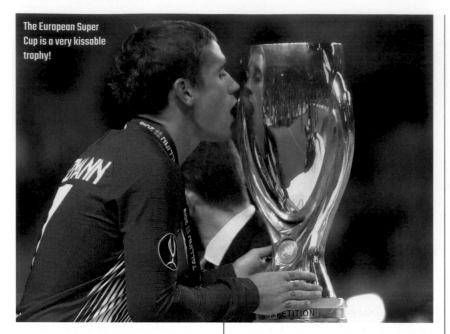

The European Super Cup is a very kissable trophy!

now awarded to the winners of a one-off match between the Champions League and Europa League holders.

• **AC Milan and Barcelona have won the trophy a record five times each. Liverpool are the most successful English club in the competition with three victories (in 1977, 2001 and 2005).**

• Modern-day footballing icons Paolo Maldini (AC Milan) and Dani Alves (Sevilla and Barcelona) have both won the trophy a record four times each.

• **Monaco's Stade Louis II has hosted the final a record 16 times, including for 15 consecutive years between 1998 and 2012.**

• Former Manchester United boss Alex Ferguson coached his team in a record four Super Cup matches, but only finished on the winning side once – in 1991 when United beat Red Star Belgrade 1-0.

EVERTON

Year founded: 1878
Ground: Goodison Park (39,572)
Previous name: St Domingo
Nickname: The Toffees
Biggest win: 11-2 v Derby County (1890)
Heaviest defeat: 0-7 v Sunderland (1934), v Wolves (1939) and v Arsenal (2005)

The club was formed as the church team St Domingo in 1878, adopting the name Everton (after the surrounding area) the following year. In 1888 Everton joined the Football League as founder members, winning the first of nine league titles three years later.

• **One of the most famous names in English football, Everton hold the proud record of spending more seasons, 116, in the top flight than any other club. Relegated only twice, in 1930 and 1951, they have spent just four seasons in total outside the top tier.**

• The club's unusual nickname, the Toffees, stems from a local business called Ye Ancient Everton Toffee House which was situated near Goodison Park. In the early 1930s Everton's precise style of play earned the club the tag 'The School of Science', a nickname which lingers to this day.

• **The club's record goalscorer is the legendary Dixie Dean, who notched an incredible total of 383 goals in all competitions between 1925 and 1937. Dean's best season for the club was in the Toffees' title-winning campaign in 1927/28 when his 60 league goals set a Football League record that is unlikely ever to be beaten. Dean's total of 349 league goals is a record for a player with the same club.**

• Everton's most capped player is long-serving goalkeeper Neville Southall, who made a record 92 appearances for Wales in the 1980s and 1990s. He is also the club's record appearance maker, turning out in 578 league games.

• **In 1931 Everton won the Second Division title, scoring 121 goals in the process. The following season the Toffees banged in 116 goals on their way to lifting the First Division title, becoming the first club to find the net 100 times in consecutive seasons.**

• The club's most successful decade, though, was in the 1980s when, under manager Howard Kendall, they won the league championship (1985 and 1987), FA Cup (1984) and the European Cup Winners' Cup (in 1985, following a 3-1 win over Austria Vienna in the final). Since then Everton have had to play second fiddle to city rivals Liverpool, although the Toffees did manage to

Success has just been out of reach for Everton lately

win the FA Cup for a fifth time in 1995, beating Manchester United in the final thanks to a goal by striker Paul Rideout.

• **The club's record signing is Icelandic midfielder Gylfi Sigurdsson, who moved to Merseyside from Swansea City for £45 million in August 2017. A month earlier the Toffees' Belgian striker Romelu Lukaku joined Manchester United for £75 million in the most expensive transfer deal between two Premier League clubs.**

• In 1893 Everton's Jack Southworth became the first player in Football League history to score six goals in a match when he fired a double hat-trick in a 7-1 victory against West Bromwich Albion.

• **Everton's Louis Saha scored the fastest goal in the FA Cup final, when he netted after 25 seconds against Chelsea at Wembley in 2009. However, the Toffees were unable to hold on to their lead and were eventually beaten 2-1 – one of a record eight times Everton have lost in the final.**

• The oldest ground in the Premier League, Goodison Park is the only stadium in the world to have a church, St Luke the Evangelist, inside its grounds.

• **Everton were the first English club to appear in European competition for five seasons running, achieving this between 1962/63 and 1966/67.**

• Everton have played more games than any other club in the top flight (4,480), drawn more matches (1,126), scored more goals (6,973) and conceded the most (6,209).

HONOURS
Division 1 champions 1891, 1915, 1928, 1932, 1939, 1963, 1970, 1985, 1987
Division 2 champions 1931
FA Cup 1906, 1933, 1966, 1984, 1995
European Cup Winners' Cup 1985

EXETER CITY

Year founded: 1904
Ground: St James Park (8,541)
Nickname: The Grecians
Biggest win: 14-0 v Weymouth (1908)
Heaviest defeat: 0-9 v Notts County (1948) and v Northampton Town (1958)

Exeter City were founded in 1904 following the amalgamation of two local sides, Exeter United and St Sidwell's United. The club were founder members of the Third Division (South) in 1920 and remained in the two lower divisions until they were relegated to the Conference in 2003. Now owned by the Exeter City Supporters' Trust, the club rejoined the Football League in 2008.

• **Club legend Arnie Mitchell played a record 516 games for Exeter between 1952 and 1966. The Grecians' record scorer is Tony Kellow with 129 league goals in three spells at St James Park between 1976 and 1988.**

• On a tour of South America in 1914 Exeter became the first club side to play the Brazilian national team. The Grecians lost 2-0 but the occasion has gone into club folklore, with Exeter fans delighting in taunting their opponents by chanting, "Have you ever, have you ever, have you ever played Brazil?"

• **Beaten by Coventry in the 2018 League Two play-off final, Exeter's longest-serving manager is Paul Tisdale, who was in charge of the Grecians for 12 years from 2006 to 2018 and led City to back-to-back promotions in 2008 and 2009.**

HONOURS
Division 4 champions 1990

EXTRA-TIME

Normally consisting of two halves of 15 minutes each, extra-time has been played to produce a winner in knock-out tournaments since the earliest days of football, although to begin with the playing of the additional time had to be agreed by the two captains. Extra-time was first played in an FA Cup final in 1875, Royal Engineers and the Old Etonians drawing 1-1 (Royal Engineers won the replay 2-0). In all, extra-time has been played in 20 finals, the most recent in 2016 when Manchester United beat Crystal Palace 2-1 despite being reduced to 10 men after Chris Smalling was sent off.

• The first World Cup final to go to extra-time was in 1934, when hosts Italy and Czechoslovakia were

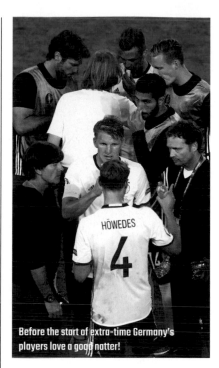

Before the start of extra-time Germany's players love a good natter!

tied 1-1 at the end of 90 minutes. Seven minutes into the additional period, Angelo Schiavio scored the winner for Italy. Since then, six other finals have gone to extra-time, most recently in 2014 when Germany's Mario Gotze scored the winner against Argentina with just seven minutes left to play.

• In an attempt to encourage attacking football and reduce the number of matches settled by penalty shoot-outs, FIFA ruled in 1993 that the first goal scored in extra-time would win the match. The first major tournament to be decided by the so-called 'golden goal' rule was the 1996 European Championships, Germany defeating the Czech Republic in the final thanks to a 94th-minute strike by Oliver Bierhoff. The 2000 final of the same competition was also decided in the same manner, David Trezeguet scoring a stunning winner for France against Italy in the 103rd minute.

• **Concerns that the 'golden goal' put too much pressure on referees led UEFA to replace it with the 'silver goal' in 2002. Under this rule, which was used at Euro 2004 but scrapped afterwards, only the first half of extra-time was played if either team led at the interval.**

IS THAT A FACT?
In June 2018 the EFL decided to scrap extra-time in all League Cup matches apart for the final at Wembley, with drawn matches being decided by penalties after 90 minutes.

FA CUP

The oldest knock-out competition in the world, the FA Cup dates back to 1871 when it was established under the control of the Football Association. The first round of the first FA Cup was played on 11th November 1871, Clapham Rovers' Jarvis Kenrick scoring the very first goal in the competition in a 3-0 win over Upton Park.

• The following year Wanderers beat Royal Engineers at Kennington Oval in the first ever FA Cup final. The only goal of the game was scored by Morton Peto Betts, who played under the pseudonym A.H. Chequer. Uniquely, Wanderers, as holders, were given a bye all the way through to the following year's final, and they took full advantage by beating Oxford University 2-1.

• The FA Challenge Cup – the competition's full title – has always retained the same name despite being sponsored in recent years by Littlewoods (1994-98), AXA (1998-2002), E.ON (2006-11), Budweiser (2011-14) and Emirates (2015-).

• There have, however, been five different trophies. The first trophy – known as the 'little tin idol' – was stolen from a Birmingham shop window in September 1895 where it was on display, having been won by Aston Villa a few months earlier. Sixty years later the thief revealed that the trophy was melted down and turned into counterfeit coins. A second trophy was used until 1910 when it was presented to the FA's long-serving President and former five-time cup winner, Lord Kinnaird. A new, larger trophy was commissioned by the FA from Fattorini and Sons Silversmiths in Bradford – and, by a remarkable coincidence, was won in its first year by Bradford City in 1911. This trophy was used until 1992, when it was replaced with an exact replica. In 2014 a new trophy, with an identical design to the 1911 one, was presented to that year's winners, Arsene Wenger's Arsenal.

• The most successful club in the competition is Arsenal, who won the

cup for a record 13th time in 2017 when they beat Chelsea 2-1 in the final. The only league team to have won the FA Cup in three consecutive years are Blackburn Rovers, who lifted the trophy in 1884, 1885 and 1886. Wanderers also won the cup three years on the trot between 1876 and 1878.

• In 1912 Barnsley needed to play a record 12 matches before they lifted the cup, after a number of their initial ties went to replays. In 1973, though, Bideford played a record 13 matches in the competition and only managed to reach the first round, losing 2-0 to Bristol Rovers.

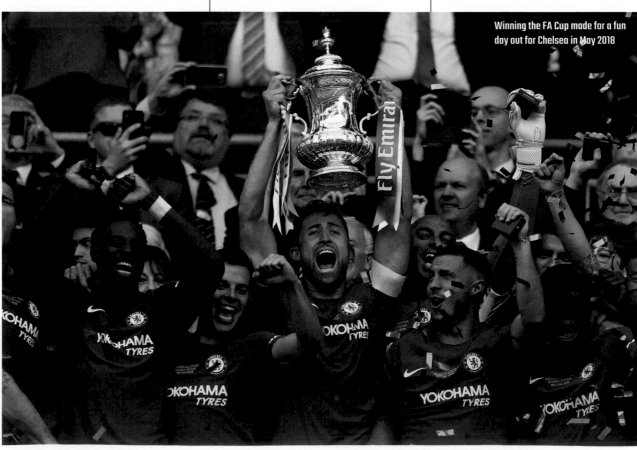

Winning the FA Cup made for a fun day out for Chelsea in May 2018

• The first FA Cup final to be decided by penalties was in 2005, Arsenal beating Manchester United 5-4 following a drab 0-0 draw at the Millennium Stadium, Cardiff. In 2007 the final returned to Wembley, Chelsea becoming the first club to lift the trophy at the new national stadium after a 1-0 victory over Manchester United.

• **Tottenham Hotspur are the only non-league side to win the competition since the formation of the Football League in 1888, lifting the trophy for the first time in 1901 while members of the Southern League. West Ham were the last team from outside the top flight to win the cup, memorably beating Arsenal 1-0 in the 1980 final.**

• The only non-English club to win the FA Cup are Cardiff City, who beat Arsenal 1-0 in 1927. Previously, Scottish club Queen's Park reached the final in 1884 and 1885 but lost on both occasions to Blackburn Rovers.

• **In 1887 Preston North End recorded the biggest win in the history of the competition when they utterly thrashed Hyde 26-0 in a first-round tie. In the same season, Preston's Jimmy Ross scored a record 19 goals in the competition.**

• Former England defender Ashley Cole won the FA Cup a record seven times with Arsenal (in 2002, 2003 and 2005) and Chelsea (in 2007, 2009, 2010 and 2012). Ex-Arsenal boss Arsène Wenger won the cup a record seven times as a manager between 1998 and 2017.

• **The leading scorer in the FA Cup is Notts County's Henry Cursham, who banged in 49 goals between 1877 and 1888. Liverpool's Ian Rush scored a record five goals in three appearances in the final in 1986, 1989 and 1992, but Chelsea's Didier Drogba is the only player to have scored in four finals (2007, 2009, 2010 and 2012).**

• Bournemouth striker Ted MacDougall scored a record nine goals in his club's 11-0 demolition of Margate in the first round of the cup in 1971.

FAMILIES

The first brothers to win the World Cup together were West Germany's Fritz and Ottmar Walter in 1954. England's Bobby and Jack Charlton famously repeated the feat in 1966, when the Three Lions beat West Germany 4-2 in the much-celebrated final at Wembley.

• **The only time two sets of brothers have played in the FA Cup final was in 1876 when the victorious Wanderers side included Frank and Hubert Heron, while losers Old Etonians' line-up featured Alfred and Edward Lyttelton.**

• When he made his debut for Spain against Argentina in March 2018 Chelsea wing-back Marcos Alonso followed in the footsteps of his father and grandfather, both of whom had also played for 'La Roja', in an extremely rare case of a 'third generation international'.

• **The first time a father and son both played in the same international match was in 1996 when 17-year-old Eidur Gudjohnsen came on for his father Arnor, 34, in Iceland's 3-0 win over Estonia. At the 2010 World Cup, brothers opposed each other in an international for the first time when Jerome Boateng (Germany) lined up against Kevin-Prince Boateng (Ghana).**

• The last time three brothers played on the same side in the English top flight was on 9th September 1989 when the trio of Danny, Ray and Rod Wallace featured in Southampton's 4-4 draw at Norwich City.

• **On 24th October 2015 Jordan Ayew (Aston Villa) and Andre Ayew (Swansea City) became the first brothers to score for different sides in the same Premier League match.**

Andre ended up the happier, though, as the Swans won 2-1 at Villa Park.

FIFA

FIFA, the Federation Internationale de Football Association, is the most important administrative body in world football. It is responsible for the organisation of major international tournaments, notably the World Cup, and enacts law changes in the game.

• **Founded in Paris in 1904, FIFA is now based in Zurich and has 211 members, 18 more than the United Nations. The President is Gianni Infantino, who was elected in February 2016 after his long-serving predecessor, Sepp Blatter, was banned from any role in FIFA for six years for making unauthorised payments to then UEFA President Michel Platini. Infantino has since taken steps to clean up an organisation whose reputation has been badly damaged in recent years by allegations that high-ranking FIFA officials have been involved in serious criminal activity, including racketeering and money laundering.**

• Changes that FIFA have introduced into the World Cup include the use of substitutes (1970), penalty shoot-outs to settle drawn games (1982), three points for a group-stage win (1994) and the use of video assistant referees (2018).

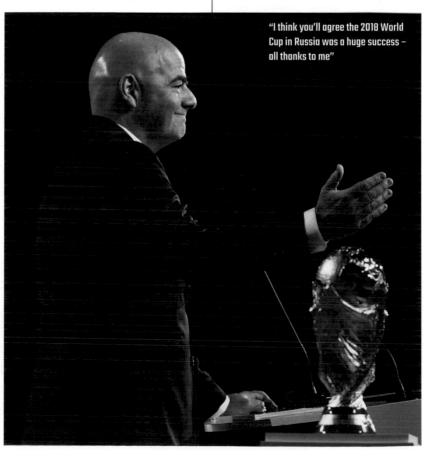

"I think you'll agree the 2018 World Cup in Russia was a huge success – all thanks to me"

- The British football associations have twice pulled out of FIFA. First, in 1918 when they were opposed to playing matches against Germany after the end of the First World War, and in 1928 over the issue of payments to amateurs. This second dispute meant that none of the British teams were represented at the first ever World Cup in 1930.
- In 1992 FIFA decided to introduce a ranking index for all its member countries. As of September 2018 the top-ranked nation was France, followed by Belgium and Brazil.

ROBERTO FIRMINO

Born: Maceio, Brazil, 2nd October 1991
Position: Midfielder/striker
Club career:
2009-10 Figueirense 38 (8)
2010-15 1899 Hoffenheim 140 (35)
2015- Liverpool 103 (36)
International record:
2014- Brazil 25 (7)

Roberto Firmino enjoyed his most prolific season to date for Liverpool in 2017/18, scoring an impressive total of 27 goals in all

Roberto Firmino is always on the look-out for a goalscoring chance

competitions. No fewer than 11 of these came in the Champions League to set a new club record, shared with his team-mate Mohamed Salah.

- An attacking midfielder who is often used as a centre forward for his pressing ability, Firmino also possesses good vision, technical skills and an eye for goal. He joined his first club, Figueirense, as a youngster after being spotted by a local football-loving dentist, and he helped Figueirense gain promotion from the Brazilian second tier in 2010, before moving to Hoffenheim in January 2011.
- After taking a while to settle in Germany, Firmino enjoyed a sensational campaign in 2013/14 when he was named the Bundesliga's 'Breakthrough Player' after scoring 16 league goals – a total only bettered by three other players. The following year he joined Liverpool for £29 million.
- His fine form saw him earn a first cap for Brazil in November 2014 and later that month he scored his first international goal in a friendly against Austria. At the 2018 World Cup in Russia he scored in Brazil's 2-0 defeat of Mexico in the last 16.

FLEETWOOD TOWN

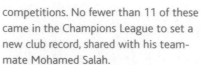

Year founded: 1997
Ground: Highbury Stadium (5,327)
Previous names: Fleetwood Wanderers, Fleetwood Freeport
Nickname: The Trawlermen
Biggest win: 13-0 v Oldham Town (1998)
Heaviest defeat: 0-9 v Bradford City (1949)

Established in 1997 as the third incarnation of a club which dates back to 1908, Fleetwood Town have enjoyed a remarkable rise in recent years. In 2012 the Trawlermen were promoted to the Football League as Conference champions, and just two years later they went up to the third tier after beating Burton Albion 1-0 in the League Two play-off final. Another promotion beckoned in 2017, until Fleetwood were narrowly beaten by Bradford City in the League One play-off semi-final.

- The Trawlermen's highest capped international is right-back Conor McLaughlin, who won 25 caps for Northern Ireland between 2012-17.
- In May 2012 Fleetwood sold prolific striker Jamie Vardy to Leicester City for £1 million – a record fee for a non-league club.
- After making his debut for Fleetwood in the North West Counties Football League Division One in 2003, defender Nathan Pond played for the Trawlermen in seven different divisions – a world record for a player at the same club. His grand total of 460 appearances is also a club record.
- Fleetwood's average home attendance of 3,139 in the 2017/18 season was the lowest in League One.

HONOURS
Conference champions 2012

FLOODLIGHTS

The first ever floodlit match was played at Bramall Lane between two representative Sheffield sides on 14th October 1876 in front of a crowd of 10,000 people (around 8,000 of whom used the cover of darkness to get in without paying). The pitch was illuminated by four lamps, powered by dynamos driven by engines located behind the goals.

- The first game in England played under 'permanent' floodlights was between South Liverpool and a touring Nigerian XI on 28th September 1949. Watched by a record crowd of 13,007 at Holly Park, the match ended in a 2-2 draw.
- For many years the Football Association banned floodlit football, so the first league match played under lights did not take place until 1956, when Newcastle beat Portsmouth 2-0 at Fratton Park. It

IS THAT A FACT?
On 16th December 2017 Stoke's home Premier League match with West Ham was delayed for an hour after two generators failed, leaving the Britannia Stadium floodlights without power.

Brentford's floodlights illuminate a dark night in west London

wasn't the most auspicious of occasions, though, as floodlight failure meant the kick-off was delayed for 30 minutes.

• Arsenal became the first top-flight club in England to install floodlights in 1951 – some 20 years after legendary Gunners manager Herbert Chapman had advocated their use. Chesterfield were the last Football League club to install floodlights, finally putting up a set in 1967.

• In the winter of 1997 two Premier League games, at West Ham and Wimbledon, were abandoned because of floodlight failure. What seemed to be an unfortunate coincidence was eventually revealed to be the work of a shadowy Far Eastern betting syndicate, four members of whom were eventually arrested and sentenced to three years each in prison.

• The first international game at Wembley under floodlights was between England and Spain on 30th November 1955, the home side winning 4-1.

FOOTBALL ASSOCIATION

Founded in 1863 at a meeting at the Freemasons' Tavern in central London, the Football Association is the oldest football organisation in the world and the only national association with no mention of the country in its name.

• The first secretary of the FA was Ebenezer Cobb Morley of Barnes

FC, nicknamed 'The Father of Football', who went on to draft the first set of laws of the game. The most controversial of the 14 laws he suggested outlawed kicking an opponent, known as 'hacking'. The first match to be played under the new laws was between Barnes and Richmond in 1863.

• In 1871 the then secretary of the FA, Charles Alcock, suggested playing a national knock-out tournament similar to the competition he had enjoyed as a schoolboy at Harrow School. The idea was accepted by the FA and the competition, named the FA Challenge Cup, has been running ever since. The FA Cup, as it is usually called, has long been the most famous national club competition in world football.

• Since 1992, the FA has run the English game's top division, the Premier League, which was formed when the old First Division broke away from the then four-division Football League.

• The FA is also responsible for the appointment of the management of the England men's and women's football teams. The FA's main asset is Wembley Stadium, which it owns via its subsidiary, Wembley National Stadium Limited. However, in April 2018 the FA received an offer of £900 for the stadium from Fulham owner Shahid Khan, and may decide to sell in the near future.

• Among the innovations the FA has fought against before finally accepting are the formation of an international tournament, the use of substitutes and the use of floodlights.

FOOTBALL LEAGUE

The Football League was founded at a meeting at the Royal Hotel, Piccadilly, Manchester in April 1888. The prime mover behind the new body was Aston Villa director William McGregor, who became the league's first President.

• The 12 founder members were Accrington, Aston Villa, Blackburn Rovers, Bolton Wanderers, Burnley, Derby County, Everton, Notts County, Preston North End, Stoke City, West Bromwich Albion and Wolverhampton Wanderers. At the end of the inaugural 1888/89 season, Preston were crowned champions.

• In 1892 a new Second Division, absorbing clubs from the rival Football Alliance, was added to the league and by 1905 the two divisions were made up of a total of 40 clubs. After the First World War, the league was expanded again to include a Third Division (later split between North and South sections).

• A further expansion after 1945 took the number of clubs playing in the league to its long-time total of 92. The formation of the Premier League in 1992 reduced the Football League to three divisions – now known as the Championship, League One and League Two.

• As well as being the governing body for the three divisions, the Football League also organises two knock-out competitions: the League Cup (now the EFL Cup) and the Football League Trophy (now the EFL Trophy).

• **Before the formation of the Premier League Liverpool won the First Division a record 18 times, while interestingly Leicester City were Second Division champions a record six times.**

FOOTBALL LEAGUE TROPHY

Rebranded as the EFL Trophy in 2016 and known as the Checkatrade Trophy for sponsorship reasons, the Football League Trophy was first established in 1983 as a knock-out competition for the 48 League One and League Two clubs.

• **The most successful team in the competition are Bristol City with three victories in the final, against Bolton in 1986, Carlisle United in 2003 and Walsall in 2015, while Carlisle have appeared in a record six finals.**

• The competition was expanded in the 2016/17 season to include 16 Premier League and Championship academy teams. The following season Chelsea became the first academy side to reach the semi-finals but lost on penalties to eventual winners Lincoln City.

• **However, the new format has not greatly appealed to fans with an all-time competition low attendance of just 248 turning out for the match between Grimsby Town and Sunderland academy at Blundell Park in November 2017. Meanwhile, a record crowd of 80,841 watched the 1988 final between Wolves and Burnley at Wembley.**

FOOTBALLER OF THE YEAR

Confusingly, there are two Footballer of the Year awards in England and Scotland. The Football Writers' Association award was inaugurated in 1948, and the first winner was England winger Stanley Matthews. In 1974 the Professional Footballers' Association (PFA) set up their own award, Leeds hard man Norman 'Bites Yer Legs' Hunter being the first to be honoured by his peers.

• **Liverpool midfielder Terry McDermott was the first player to win both awards in the same season after helping Liverpool retain the title in 1980. A total of 19 different players have won both Footballer of the Year awards in the same season, most recently Liverpool Mohamed Salah in 202018. Former Arsenal striker Thierry Henry won a record five awards, landing the 'double' in both 2003 and 2004, and also carrying off the Football Writers' award in 2006.**

• Liverpool players have won the Football Writers' Association award a record 13 times, while Manchester United lead the way in the PFA category with 12 wins.

Football Writers' Player of the Year (Premier League era)
1993 Chris Waddle (Sheffield Wednesday)
1994 Alan Shearer (Blackburn Rovers)
1995 Jurgen Klinsmann (Tottenham)
1996 Eric Cantona (Manchester Utd)
1997 Gianfranco Zola (Chelsea)
1998 Dennis Bergkamp (Arsenal)
1999 David Ginola (Tottenham)
2000 Roy Keane (Manchester Utd)
2001 Teddy Sheringham (Manchester Utd)
2002 Robert Pires (Arsenal)
2003 Thierry Henry (Arsenal)
2004 Thierry Henry (Arsenal)
2005 Frank Lampard (Chelsea)
2006 Thierry Henry (Arsenal)
2007 Cristiano Ronaldo (Manchester Utd)
2008 Cristiano Ronaldo (Manchester Utd)
2009 Steven Gerrard (Liverpool)
2010 Wayne Rooney (Manchester Utd)
2011 Scott Parker (West Ham Utd)
2012 Robin van Persie (Arsenal)
2013 Gareth Bale (Tottenham)
2014 Luis Suarez (Liverpool)
2015 Eden Hazard (Chelsea)
2016 Jamie Vardy (Leicester City)
2017 N'Golo Kante (Chelsea)
2018 Mohamed Salah (Liverpool)

Who says the EFL Trophy isn't a major honour? Just look at the size of it!

PFA Footballer of the Year (Premier League era)

1993 Paul McGrath (Aston Villa)
1994 Eric Cantona (Manchester Utd)
1995 Alan Shearer (Blackburn Rovers)
1996 Les Ferdinand (Newcastle Utd)
1997 Alan Shearer (Newcastle Utd)
1998 Dennis Bergkamp (Arsenal)
1999 David Ginola (Tottenham)
2000 Roy Keane (Manchester Utd)
2001 Teddy Sheringham (Manchester Utd)
2002 Ruud van Nistelrooy (Manchester Utd)
2003 Thierry Henry (Arsenal)
2004 Thierry Henry (Arsenal)
2005 John Terry (Chelsea)
2006 Steven Gerrard (Liverpool)
2007 Cristiano Ronaldo (Manchester Utd)
2008 Cristiano Ronaldo (Manchester Utd)
2009 Ryan Giggs (Manchester Utd)
2010 Wayne Rooney (Manchester Utd)
2011 Gareth Bale (Tottenham)
2012 Robin van Persie (Arsenal)
2013 Gareth Bale (Tottenham)
2014 Luis Suarez (Liverpool)
2015 Eden Hazard (Chelsea)
2016 Riyad Mahrez (Leicester City)
2017 N'Golo Kante (Chelsea)
2018 Mohamed Salah (Liverpool)

FOREST GREEN ROVERS

Year founded: 1889
Ground: The New Lawn (5,141)
Previous names: Forest Green, Nailsworth & Forest Green United, Stroud FC
Nickname: Rovers
Biggest win: 8-0 v Hyde (2013)
Heaviest defeat: 0-10 v Gloucester (1900)

Now owned by green energy tycoon Dale Vince, Forest Green Rovers were founded in Nailsworth, Gloucestershire by a local church minister in 1889 and five years later were founder members of the mid-Gloucestershire league. During more than a century in the non-league wilderness the club was briefly renamed Nailsworth & Forest Green United (1911) and Stroud FC (1989).

• Rovers were finally promoted to the Football League following a 3-1 win against Tranmere Rovers in the 2017 National League play-off final at Wembley. The following season they just about preserved their new-found status, finishing one point clear of the drop zone.

• In 2009 Rovers reached the third round of the FA Cup for the first time in their history, losing 4-3 to Championship side Derby County in front of a record crowd of 4,836 at their New Lawn stadium.

• Powered by renewable energy, Forest Green Rovers were named as the world's very first carbon neutral football club by the United Nations in July 2018.

• With a population of just 5,794 Nailsworth is the smallest place ever to have a Football League club.

FRANCE

First international: Belgium 3 France 3, 1904
Most capped player: Lilian Thuram, 142 caps (1994-2008)
Leading goalscorer: Thierry Henry, 51 goals (1997-2010)
First World Cup appearance: France 4 Mexico 1, 1930
Biggest win: France 10 Azerbaijan 0, 1995
Heaviest defeat: France 1 Denmark 17, 1908

It literally rained gold when France won the 2018 World Cup

The third most successful European football nation ever, France have won both the World Cup and the European championships twice. The most recent of those triumphs came in 2018 when a French side including Premier League stars like Paul Pogba, N'Golo Kante and skipper Hugo Lloris beat Croatia 4-2 in the World Cup final in the Luzhniki stadium, Moscow.

• **Twenty years earlier, France won the World Cup for the first time on home soil in 1998 with a stunning 3-0 victory over Brazil in the final in Paris. Midfield genius Zinedine Zidane was the star of the show, scoring two headed goals. The team also included Didier Deschamps, France's manager in 2018 and one of just three men (along with Brazil's Mario Zagallo and West Germany's Franz Beckenbauer) to win the World Cup as both a player and a coach.**

• In 2000 France became the first World Cup holders to go on to win the European Championships when they overcame Italy in the final in Rotterdam. This, though, was a much closer affair with the French requiring a 'golden goal' by striker David Trezeguet in extra-time to claim the trophy.

• **France had won the European Championships once before, in 1984. Inspired by the legendary Michel Platini, who scored a record nine goals** in the tournament, Les Bleus beat Spain 2-0 in the final in Paris. In 2016 France had another chance to win the trophy on home soil but surprisingly lost 1-0 in the final to Portugal after extra-time.

• French striker Just Fontaine scored an all-time record 13 goals at the 1958 World Cup finals in Sweden. His remarkable strike rate helped his country finish third in the tournament.

• **Former Bordeaux defender Franck Jurietti set a record for the shortest international career ever when he came on for the last five seconds of France's 4-0 win over Cyprus in October 2005 and never played for his country again.**

HONOURS
World Cup winners *1998, 2018*
European Championships winners *1984, 2000*
Confederations Cup winners *2001, 2003*
World Cup Record
1930 Round 1
1934 Round 1
1938 Round 2
1950 Did not qualify
1954 Round 1
1958 Third place
1962 Did not qualify
1966 Round 1

1970 Did not qualify
1974 Did not qualify
1978 Round 1
1982 Fourth place
1986 Third place
1990 Did not qualify
1994 Did not qualify
1998 Winners
2002 Round 1
2006 Runners-up
2010 Round 1
2014 Quarter-finals
2018 Winners

FREE KICKS

A method for restarting the game after an infringement, free kicks may either be direct (meaning a goal can be scored directly) or indirect (in which case a second player must touch the ball before a goal can be scored).

• **Brazilian midfielder Juninho Pernambucano holds the world record for the most goals scored direct from a free kick with 76, most of them coming during his time at French club Lyon between 2001 and 2009. Incredibly, the record for the most free kicks scored by a player for just one club is held by a goalkeeper, Rogerio Ceni of Sao Paulo with 61.**

• David Beckham holds the record for the most Premier League goals direct from

A free-kick to Barcelona, taken by Lionel Messi. Wonder what happens next?

free kicks with 15 for Manchester United between 1993 and 2003 and his total of 65 goals from dead balls outside the box is a record for a British player. Manchester United's Cristiano Ronaldo (2007/08) and Manchester City's Yaya Toure (2013/14) jointly hold the record for the most goals from free kicks in a single Premier League campaign, with four each.

• Tottenham goalkeeper Paul Robinson scored the longest-range free kick in Premier League history when he walloped one in from an incredible 96 yards against Watford on 17th March 2007.

• The last player to score direct from a free kick in the FA Cup final was Arsenal's Santi Cazorla with a 25-yard stunner against Hull City in 2014.

• Vanishing spray from an aerosol can to mark the 10 yards defenders must retreat from an attacking free kick was introduced to the Premier League at the start of the 2014/15 season. The spray was first used at an international tournament in the 2011 Copa America and made its debut at the World Cup in Brazil in 2014.

FRIENDLIES

The first official international friendly took place on 30th November 1872 between Scotland and England at the West of Scotland Cricket Ground, Partick, Glasgow. The Scottish side for the match, which ended in a 0-0 draw, was made up entirely of players from the country's leading club, Queen's Park.

• England's first ever friendly against continental opposition was on 6th June 1908 against Austria in Vienna. England won that match 6-1 and went on to win a record 12 friendlies on the trot before drawing 2-2 with Belgium in 1923.

• On 6th February 2007 London played host to a record four international friendlies on the same night – and England weren't even one of the eight teams in action! At the Emirates Stadium Portugal beat Brazil 2-0, Ghana thrashed Nigeria 4-1 at Brentford's Griffin Park, South Korea beat European champions Greece 1-0 at Craven Cottage, while at Loftus Road Denmark were 3-1 winners over Australia.

• Then England manager Sven-Goran Eriksson became the first Three Lions boss to substitute all 11 starters in a 2-1 friendly defeat to Italy in 2002. However, two years later FIFA ruled that the maximum number of substitutes that could be used in an international friendly would be limited to six per team.

FULHAM

Year founded: 1879
Ground: Craven Cottage (25,700)
Previous name: Fulham St Andrew's
Nickname: The Cottagers
Biggest win: 10-1 v Ipswich Town (1963)
Heaviest defeat: 0-10 v Liverpool (1986)

London's oldest club, Fulham were founded in 1879 by two clergymen. Originally known as Fulham St Andrew's, the club adopted its present name nine years later. After winning the Southern League in two consecutive seasons Fulham were elected to the Football League in 1907.

• Before moving to Craven Cottage in 1896, Fulham had played at no fewer than 11 different grounds. Including a stay at Loftus Road from 2002-04 while the Cottage was being redeveloped, Fulham have played at 13 venues, a total only exceeded by QPR.

• The proudest moment in the club's history came in May 2010 when Fulham met Atletico Madrid in Hamburg in the first Europa League final. Sadly for their fans, the Cottagers lost 2-1 in extra-time despite putting up a spirited fight.

• In 1975 Fulham reached the FA Cup final for the first (and so far only) time, losing 2-0 to West Ham. The Cottagers have appeared in the semi-final six times, including a forgettable occasion in 1908 when they were hammered 6-0 by Newcastle, to this day the biggest ever winning margin at that stage of the competition.

• Midfield legend Johnny Haynes holds the club's appearance record, turning out in 594 league games between 1952 and 1970. 'The Maestro', as he was known to Fulham fans, is also the club's most honoured player at international level, with 56 England caps. Welsh international striker Gordon Davies is Fulham's top scorer with 159 league goals in two spells at the club between 1978 and 1991.

• Fulham made their record signing when they bought Cameroon international midfielder Andre Anguissa from Marseille for £30 million in August 2018, taking the Cottagers' spending in the summer transfer window past £100 million – a record for a newly-promoted club.

• Fulham's biggest ever win, 10-1 against Ipswich on Boxing Day 1963, was the last time a team scored double figures in the English top flight.

• In 2014/15 Fulham used a Premier League record 39 different players, although their large squad didn't do them much good as they were relegated to the Championship at the end of the season. However, to the delight of their fans, the Cottagers bounced back to the top flight via the play-offs in 2018 following a 1-0 victory against Aston Villa in the final at Wembley.

• In the same year talented Fulham winger Ryan Sessegnon became the first Championship player ever to be nominated for the PFA Young Player of the Year.

HONOURS
First Division champions 2001
Division 2 champions 1949
Second Division champions 1999
Division 3 (South) champions 1932

Ryan Sessegnon on the move for Fulham

DAVID DE GEA

Born: Madrid, 7th November 1990
Position: Goalkeeper
Club career:
2008-09 Atletico Madrid B 35
2009-11 Atletico Madrid 57
2011- Manchester United 237
International record:
2014- Spain 33

Manchester United's David de Gea has been voted into the PFA Team of the Year five times, most recently at the end of the 2017/18 season, to set a record for the Premier League era (although he has some way to go to match Peter Shilton's 10 selections in the 1970s and 1980s).

• **After coming through the youth ranks at Atletico Madrid, De Gea enjoyed a great first season with** Atleti, helping them win the Europa League in 2010 following a 2-1 victory against Fulham in the final in Hamburg. The next summer he moved on to Manchester United for around £18 million, then a record fee for a goalkeeper in the British game.

• Following some unconvincing early performances for United De Gea was dropped to the bench, but after winning his place back his form soon improved. In 2013 he helped United win the Premier League title and he has since added the FA Cup (2016) and League Cup (2017) to his list of honours. In 2018 he won the Golden Glove award after keeping 18 clean sheets in the Premier League.

• **De Gea has won the BBC's 'Save of the Season' an incredible five times since it was introduced in 2013, most recently topping the poll for a brilliant double block against Arsenal in the 2017/18 season. Manchester United's Player of the Year in 2014, 2015, 2016 and 2018, De Gea is the only player in the club's history to win this award three times on the trot.**

• De Gea made his first appearance for Spain in a 2-0 friendly win against El Salvador in June 2014. He started all of Spain's four games at the 2018 World Cup but didn't enjoy the best of tournaments, conceding six goals from just seven shots on target.

GERMANY

First international: Switzerland 5 Germany 3, 1908
Most capped player: Lothar Matthaus, 150 caps (1980-2000)
Leading goalscorer: Miroslav Klose, 71 goals (2001-14)
First World Cup appearance: Germany 5 Belgium 2, 1934
Biggest win: Germany 16 Russian Empire 0, 1912
Heaviest defeat: Austria 6 Germany 0, 1931

Germany (formerly West Germany) have the joint second best record in the World Cup behind Brazil, having won the tournament four times and reached the final on a record eight occasions. They have also won the European Championships a joint-record three times and been losing finalists on another three occasions.

• **The Germans recorded their fourth World Cup triumph in Brazil in 2014, when they beat Argentina 1-0 in the final thanks to Mario Gotze's extra-time goal. Perhaps more remarkable, though, was their performance in the**

David de Gea's 'scorpion kick' save didn't quite go as planned

Exit stage left. Germany bowed out of the 2018 World Cup at the group stage

semi-final when they massacred the hosts 7-1 – the biggest ever win at that late stage of the competition and one of the most amazing World Cup scorelines ever. Germany's other victories came in 1954 (against Hungary), on home soil in 1974 (against the Netherlands) and at Italia 90 (against Argentina).

• Lothar Matthaus, a powerhouse in the German midfield for two decades, played in a record 25 matches at the World Cup in five tournaments between 1982 and 1998. His total of 150 caps for Germany is also a national record.

• Germany striker Miroslav Klose is the all-time leading scorer at the World Cup with a total of 16 goals, one ahead of Brazil's Ronaldo and two better than fellow German Gerd 'the Bomber' Muller.

• Between 10th July 2010 and 22nd June 2012 Germany won a world record 15 competitive matches on the trot – a run which ended when they lost 2-1 to Italy in the semi-final of Euro 2012.

• Germany hold the record for both the biggest win in the European Championship qualifiers (13-0 against San Marino in 2006) and the UEFA section of the World Cup qualifiers (a resounding 12-0 against Cyprus in 1969).

TOP 10

GERMANY GOALSCORERS

1.	Miroslav Klose (2001-14)	71
2.	Gerd Muller (1966-74)	68
3.	Lukas Podolski (2004-17)	49
4.	Rudi Voller (1982-94)	47
	Jurgen Klinsmann (1987-98)	47
6.	Karl-Heinz Rummenigge (1976-86)	45
7.	Uwe Seeler (1954-70)	43
8.	Michael Ballack (1999-2010)	42
9.	Thomas Muller (2010-)	38
10.	Oliver Bierhoff (1996-2002)	37

HONOURS
World Cup winners 1954, 1974, 1990, 2014
European Championships winners 1972, 1980, 1996
Confederations Cup winners 2017
World Cup Record
1930 Did not enter
1934 Third place
1938 Round 1
1950 Did not enter
1954 Winners
1958 Fourth place
1962 Quarter-finals
1966 Runners-up
1970 Third place
1974 Winners
1978 Round 2
1982 Runners-up
1986 Runners-up
1990 Winners
1994 Quarter-finals
1998 Quarter-finals
2002 Runners-up
2006 Third place
2010 Third place
2014 Winners
2018 Round 1

STEVEN GERRARD

Born: Whiston, 30th May 1980
Managerial career:
2018- Rangers

Appointed Rangers manager in June 2018 after an 18-month spell as Liverpool youth team coach, Anfield legend Steven Gerrard is only the second Englishman (after Mark Warburton) to occupy the Ibrox hotseat.

• Famed for his surging runs and thunderous shooting, Gerrard is the only player to have scored in the FA Cup final, the League Cup final, the UEFA Cup final and the Champions League final. He achieved this feat between 2001 and 2006

How long now before Stevie G's hair turns grey?

while winning all four competitions with the Reds (and, indeed, earning winner's medals in the FA Cup and League Cup on two occasions).

• By the time he decided to move on to LA Galaxy in 2015 he had made more than 500 Premier League appearances for the Reds, one of just three players (along with Ryan Giggs and former team-mate Jamie Carragher) to reach that milestone with one club.

• In the 2006 FA Cup final Gerrard scored two stunning goals against West Ham, including a last-minute equaliser which many rate as the best ever goal in the final. Liverpool went on to win the match on penalties and Gerrard's heroics were rewarded with the 2006 PFA Player of the Year award. Three years later he was voted Footballer of the Year by the football writers. Then, in 2014, he was voted into the PFA Team of the Year for a Premier League-era record eighth time.

• Gerrard made his international debut for England against Ukraine in 2000 and scored his first goal for his country with a superb 20-yarder in the famous 5-1 thrashing of Germany in Berlin in 2001. He captained England at the 2010 and 2014 World Cups and at the 2012 European Championships. With 114 caps, Gerrard is fourth on the list of England's all-time appearance makers behind Peter Shilton, David Beckham and fellow Liverpudlian Wayne Rooney.

GIANT-KILLING

Many of the most remarkable instances of giant-killing have occurred in the FA Cup, with teams from lower down the football pyramid beating supposedly superior opposition. The first shock of this type occurred in 1888 when non-league Warwick County beat First Division Stoke City 2-1 in the first qualifying round of the competition.

• **Only two non-league teams have beaten Premier League outfits in the FA Cup, Luton Town sensationally beating Norwich City 1-0 in the fourth round in 2013 and Lincoln City surprising Burnley by the same score in the fifth round in 2017.**

• In their non-league days Yeovil Town beat a record 20 league teams in the FA Cup. The Glovers' most famous win came in the fourth round in 1949 against First Division Sunderland, who they defeated 2-1 on their notorious sloping pitch at Huish Park.

• **Giant-killing was all the rage in 2009 with a record eight non-league clubs reaching the third round of the FA Cup. Conversely, no non-league teams made it to the third round in 2018 – the first time this had happened for 67 years.**

• Giant-killings also happen at international level. Among the shocks at the World Cup, for example, are North Korea defeating Italy 1-0 in 1966, holders France going down 1-0 to Senegal in 2002 and reigning champions Germany memorably losing 2-0 to South Korea in 2018.

RYAN GIGGS

Born: Cardiff, 29th November 1973
Managerial career:
2014 Manchester United (caretaker)
2018- Wales

Appointed Wales manager in January 2018, Ryan Giggs got off to the best ever start of any Dragons boss when his side annihilated China 6-0 in his first match in charge.

• **In a glorious career with Manchester United, Ryan Giggs became the most decorated player in English football history. Between 1991 and 2014, when he announced** his retirement from the game, he won 22 major honours: a record 13 Premier League titles, four FA Cups, three League Cups and two Champions League trophies. In addition, in 2009 he was voted PFA Player of the Year by his fellow professionals.

• A one-club man who briefly filled in as caretaker manager in 2014, Giggs made a record 963 appearances for United in all competitions – 205 more than the previous record holder, Sir Bobby Charlton. His total of 632 Premier League appearances is only bettered by Gareth Barry.

• **Giggs enjoyed his best ever year in 1999 when he won the Premiership, FA Cup and Champions League with United. His goal against Arsenal in that season's FA Cup semi-final, when he dribbled past four defenders before smashing the ball into the roof of the net from a tight angle, was voted the best of the past 50 years by** *Match of the Day* **viewers in 2015.**

• Once Wales' youngest ever player, Giggs previously played for England Schoolboys under the name Ryan Wilson (the surname being that of his father, a former Welsh rugby league player). However, having no English grandparents, Giggs was ineligible to play for the England national team and was proud to represent Wales on 64 occasions before retiring from international football in 2007.

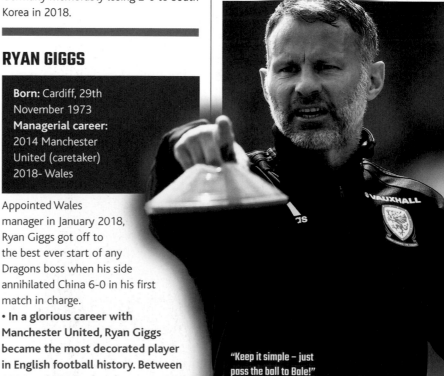

"Keep it simple – just pass the ball to Bale!"

GILLINGHAM

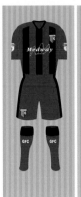

Year founded: 1893
Ground: Priestfield Stadium (11,582)
Previous name: New Brompton
Nickname: The Gills
Biggest win: 12-1 v Gloucester City (1946)
Heaviest defeat: 2-9 v Nottingham Forest (1950)

Founded by a group of local businessmen as New Brompton in 1893, the club changed to its present name in 1913. Seven years later Gillingham joined the new Third Division but in 1938 were voted out of the league in favour of Ipswich Town. They eventually returned in 1950.

• Goalkeeper John Simpson played in a record 571 league games for the Gills between 1957 and 1972, while his team-mate Brian Yeo scored a club record 136 goals.

• Gillingham have reached the FA Cup sixth round just once, going down 5-0 to eventual winners Chelsea in 2000.

• **In their 1995/96 promotion campaign Gillingham only conceded** 20 goals – a record for a 46-game season in the Football League.

• Winger Luke Freeman became the youngest ever player in the FA Cup proper when he came on as a sub for Gillingham against Barnet in 2007 aged just 15 years and 233 days.

HONOURS
League Two champions 2013
Division 4 champions 1964

OLIVIER GIROUD

Born: Chambery, France, 30th September 1986
Position: Striker
Club career:
2005-08 Grenoble 23 (2)
2007-08 Istres (loan) 33 (14)
2008-10 Tours 44 (24)
2010-12 Montpellier 73 (33)
2010 Tours (loan) 17 (6)
2012-18 Arsenal 180 (73)
2018- Chelsea 13 (3)
International record:
2011- France 81 (31)

When Olivier Giroud helped Chelsea win the 2018 FA Cup final following a 1-0 defeat of Manchester United he became only the third outfield foreign player – after ex-Blues strikers Didier Drogba and Salomon Kalou – to lift the cup four times, the Frenchman having previously enjoyed success in the competition with his former club Arsenal in 2014, 2015 and 2017.

• **A tall, powerful striker who finishes well on the ground and in the air, Giroud first came to the fore when he was top scorer in the French second division with Tours in 2009/10, his goalscoring feats also earning him the Ligue 2 Player of the Year award.**

• A move to Montpellier followed, and in only his second season with the club Giroud helped the southern French side win the league for the first time in their history. The striker's 21 goals during the campaign made him the league's joint-top scorer and were instrumental in Montpellier's surprise success.

• **Later that summer he joined Arsenal for £9.6 million and he went on to hit double figures in all five of his complete seasons with the Gunners before joining Chelsea for £18 million in January 2018.**

• Giroud won his first cap for France in a 1-0 friendly win over the USA in 2011. In June 2017 he became the first player to score a hat-trick for his country for 17 years when he hit a treble in a 5-0 demolition of Paraguay and the following year Giroud was part of the France team that won the World Cup after a 4-2 win against Croatia in the final in Moscow.

GOAL CELEBRATIONS

Elaborate and sometimes spectacular goal celebrations have been a feature of English football since the mid-1990s when the Premier League started opening its doors to large numbers of overseas players. Middlesbrough striker Fabrizio Ravanelli, for instance, was famed for pulling his shirt over his head after scoring, and soon players were removing their shirts altogether, sometimes to reveal personal, political or religious messages written on a t-shirt.

• **In 2003 FIFA decided that things had got out of hand and ruled that any player removing his shirt would be booked. The first player to be sent off after falling foul of this new law was Everton's Tim Cahill, who was shown a second yellow against Manchester City in 2004.**

• In 2013 West Brom striker Nicolas Anelka was fined a record £80,000 by

You can see why defenders find Olivier Giroud scary!

the FA and banned for five matches after celebrating a goal at West Ham by placing his arm across his chest in a gesture known as the 'quenelle' which, especially in Anelka's native France, carries anti-semitic connotations. The former France star was subsequently sacked by his club for gross misconduct.

• Denmark striker Nicklas Bendtner was fined £80,000 by UEFA at Euro 2012 after celebrating a goal against Portugal by lowering his shorts and revealing the logo of gambling company Paddy Power on his underpants.

• In September 2014 Cameroonian striker Joel of Brazilian side Coritiba celebrated a goal against Sao Paulo by jumping over an advertising hoarding – only to fall down a hole leading to an underground stairwell. "I've made a fool of myself," he reflected afterwards.

• PSG striker Neymar is famed for his unusual goal celebrations. In 2011, while playing for Santos, he was sent off after donning a mask of himself thrown onto the pitch by a fan, and in January 2018 he celebrated a penalty against Amiens by balancing one of his boots on his head.

Fabrizio Ravanelli's ghost impression was a hit at parties in the 1990s

• Bristol City caused on online storm in the 2017/18 season by celebrating every goal they scored during the campaign with a bizarre 'gif', with examples including a player swinging around a fire extinguisher, ironing a City shirt or pouring a pint of milk over his head.

GOAL OF THE SEASON

The Goal of the Season award has been awarded by the BBC's flagship football programme *Match of the Day* since 1971 (apart from the years 2001-04 when, for broadcasting rights reasons, the award was given by ITV). The 2018 winner was Leicester striker Jamie Vardy, who topped the poll with a stunning left-foot volley against West Brom.

• Manchester United striker Wayne Rooney is the only player to win the award three times, most recently in 2011 for an acrobatic overhead kick against local rivals Manchester City. Liverpool's John Aldridge (in 1988 and 1989) and Arsenal's Jack Wilshere (in 2014 and 2015) are the only two players to have won the award in consecutive seasons.

• Incredibly, in 1988 all 10 shortlisted goals were scored by players from Liverpool, that season's league champions. The award was won by John Aldridge for his volley in the FA Cup semi-final against Nottingham Forest.

• The first player from outside the British Isles to win the award was Leeds and Ghana striker Tony Yeboah, for a thunderous drive against Wimbledon in the 1995/96 season.

GOALKEEPERS

• On 27th March 2011 Sao Paulo's Rogerio Ceni became the first goalkeeper in the history of football to score 100 career goals when he netted with a free kick in a 2-1 win against Corinthians. His unlikely century was made up of 56 free kicks and 44 penalties. By the time he retired in 2015 Ceni had taken his career goals total to 131 – better than countless outfield players!

• Just five goalkeepers have scored in the Premier League: Peter Schmeichel (Aston Villa), Brad Friedel (Blackburn Rovers), Paul Robinson (Tottenham), Tim Howard (Everton) and Asmir Begovic (Stoke City). Begovic's goal after just 13 seconds against Southampton in November 2013 is the fastest ever by a goalkeeper in English football history and was scored at a greater distance (91.9 metres) than any goal ever.

• Iker Casillas (formerly of Real Madrid) and Juventus' Gianluigi Buffon have both been voted World Goalkeeper of the Year a record five times.

• In a long career for Derby County and Bradford Park Avenue between 1907 and 1925, Ernie Scattergood scored eight penalties – a record number of goals for a goalkeeper in the Football League.

• The most-capped goalkeeper in history is Mohamed Al-Deayea, who turned out 178 times for Saudi Arabia between 1993 and 2006. In the women's game, Gemma Fay played a record 203 times in goal for Scotland between 1998 and 2017.

IS THAT A FACT?
Liverpool striker Roberto Firmino has been booked a record eight times for 'excessive goal celebrations' – either taking his shirt off or running into the crowd – since the start of the 2012/13 season.

TOP 10

PREMIER LEAGUE GOALSCORERS

1.	Alan Shearer (1992-2006)	260
2.	Wayne Rooney (2002-18)	208
3.	Andy Cole (1993-2008)	187
4.	Frank Lampard (1996-2015)	177
5.	Thierry Henry (1999-2012)	175
6.	Robbie Fowler (1993-2008)	163
7.	Jermain Defoe (2000-)	162
8.	Michael Owen (1997-2013)	150
9.	Les Ferdinand (1992-2005)	149
10.	Teddy Sheringham (1992-2007)	146

GOALS

Manchester City scored a Premier League record 106 goals on their way to the title in the 2017/18 season. Altogether less impressively, Derby County managed just 20 goals during the 2007/08 Premier League season. Swindon Town hold the unwanted record for the most goals conceded in a Premier League campaign, with 100 in 1993/94.

• Peterborough United hold the record for the most league goals in a season, banging in 134 in 1960/61 on their way to claiming the Fourth Division title. In 1937/38 Raith Rovers scored an incredible 142 goals in just 34 games in the Scottish Second Division to set a British record which still stands to this day.

• Aston Villa hold the top-flight record, with 128 goals in 1930/31. Despite their prolific attack, the Villans were pipped to the First Division title by Arsenal (amazingly, the Gunners managed 127 goals themselves).

• Arthur Rowley scored a record 434 Football League goals between 1946 and 1965, notching four for West Brom, 27 for Fulham, 251 for Leicester City and 152 for Shrewsbury. Former Republic of Ireland international John Aldridge is the overall leading scorer in post-war English football, with an impressive total of 476 goals in all competitions for Newport County, Oxford United, Liverpool and Tranmere between 1979 and 1998.

• Joe Payne set an English Football League record for goals in a game by scoring 10 times for Luton against Bristol Rovers on 13th April 1936. Earlier in the decade, Sheffield United striker Jimmy Dunne scored in a record 12 consecutive top-flight league games in the 1931/32 season. The Premier League record is

held by Leicester City star Jamie Vardy, who scored in 11 games on the trot in 2015/16.

• In 1998 AIK Stockholm won the Swedish title despite being the lowest-scoring team in the league with a paltry 25 goals in 26 games. Incredibly, Ghana outfit Aduana Stars matched this feat in 2010, scoring just 19 goals in 30 matches.

• The biggest win in international football saw Vanuatu hammer Micronesia 46-0 in an Olympic qualifier in July 2015.

• Brazil have scored a record 229 goals at the World Cup while Germany have conceded the most goals, 125.

ANTOINE GRIEZMANN

Born: Macon, France, 21st March 1991
Position: Forward
Club career:
2009-14 Real Sociedad 179 (46)
2014- Atletico Madrid 143 (79)
International record:
2014- France 61 (24)

Antoine Griezmann became the first player to score a goal in the World Cup final with the help of the video assistant referee when he converted a penalty which was eventually awarded to France

in the 2018 showpiece against Croatia. After France's 4-2 win Griezmann was named 'Man of the Match' and he also picked up the Bronze Ball for the third best player at the tournament.

• Just two months earlier, Griezmann scored twice in the Europa League final as Atleti beat Marseille 3-0 in Lyon to become only the second club to win the competition three times in its rebranded format.

• Griezmann's total of six goals at Euro 2016 helped him win the Player of the Tournament award and was the best return for a player since fellow Frenchman Michel Platini hit a record nine goals at the 1984 tournament.

• However, the nippy forward had to be satisfied with a runners-up medal after the hosts lost in the final to Portugal, and he also finished on the losing side in the 2016 Champions League final after his club, Atletico Madrid, lost on penalties to city rivals Real – a match in which Griezmann missed from the spot in normal time. The Frenchman thus became only the second player (after Michael Ballack in 2008) to lose in both finals in the same season.

• After being rejected by a number of clubs in his native France for being too small, Griezmann began his career with

Antoine Griezmann's boy band audition seemed to go well...

Real Sociedad, helping the Basque outfit win the Segunda Division in his debut campaign in 2009/10. A £24 million move to Atletico Madrid followed in 2014, and in his first season in the Spanish capital Griezmann was voted into the Team of the Year after scoring 22 league goals – a record for a French player in a single La Liga campaign. Following another fine season in 2015/16 he came third in the inaugural Best FIFA Men's Player award.

GRIMSBY TOWN

Year founded: 1878
Ground: Blundell Park (9,027)
Previous name: Grimsby Pelham
Nickname: The Mariners
Biggest win: 8-0 v Darlington (1885) and v Tranmere Rovers (1925)
Heaviest defeat: 1-9 v Phoenix Bessemer (1882) and v Arsenal (1931)

The club was founded at the Wellington Arms in 1878 as Grimsby Pelham (the Pelhams being a local landowning family), becoming plain Grimsby Town a year later and joining the Second Division as founder members in 1892. After losing their Football League place in 2010, the Mariners returned to League Two in 2016 after beating Forest Green Rovers 3-1 in the National League play-off final at Wembley.
• **Grimsby enjoyed a glorious decade in the 1930s, when they were promoted to the top flight and** reached two FA Cup semi-finals, losing to Arsenal in 1936 and Wolves three years later.
• In 1909 Grimsby's Walter Scott became the first goalkeeper to save three penalties in a match. However, his heroics were in vain as the Mariners still lost 2-0 to Burnley.
• **Stalwart defender and loyal one-club man John McDermott played in a record 647 league games for the Mariners between 1987 and 2007.**

> HONOURS
> *Division 2 champions* 1901, 1934
> *Division 3 champions* 1980
> *Division 3 (North) champions* 1926, 1956
> *Division 4 champions* 1972
> *Football League Trophy* 1998

PEP GUARDIOLA

> **Born:** Santpedor, Spain, 18th January 1971
> **Managerial career:**
> 2007-08 Barcelona B
> 2008-12 Barcelona
> 2013-16 Bayern Munich
> 2016- Manchester City

In 2018 Manchester City boss Pep Guardiola became the first Spanish manager to win the Premier League. He was rewarded with the Manager of the Season award and also picked up a record four consecutive Manager of the Month awards between September and December 2017.
• **Previously, with Barcelona, Guardiola became the only coach to lead a club to six trophies in a calendar year, claiming an amazing Sextuple in 2009 when his former charges won the Spanish title, the Copa del Rey, the Champions League, the Spanish Super Cup, the UEFA Super Cup and, finally, the FIFA Club World Cup.**
• After winning 14 trophies in four years – an impressive haul unmatched by any other Barcelona manager – Guardiola quit the Catalan club in 2012, citing "tiredness" as the main reason for his decision. A year later he took over the reins at Bayern Munich and in his first season with the German giants in 2013/14 won the league and cup Double, the FIFA Club World Cup and the European Super Cup.
• **He claimed two more Bundesliga titles with Bayern before moving to Manchester in July 2016. In his first season at the Etihad he guided City to Champions League qualification, but also endured the worst ever run of his managerial career when his new team went six games without a win in the autumn of 2016.**
• A defensive midfielder in his playing days for Barcelona and Spain, Guardiola was a key member of Johan Cruyff's attack-minded 'Dream Team' which won the Catalans' first European Cup in 1992 and four La Liga titles in the early 1990s.

"I must tell my old mate Jose Mourinho to try this body-surfing lark – it might help him lighten up"

HAMILTON ACADEMICAL

Year founded: 1874
Ground: SuperSeal
Stadium (5,510)
Nickname: The Accies
Biggest win: 11-1 v
Chryston (1885)
Heaviest defeat: 1-11
v Hibernian (1965)

Founded in 1874 by the Rector and
pupils of Hamilton Academy, Hamilton
Academical is the only professional
club in Britain to have originated from
a school team. Shortly after the start of
the 1897/98 season, the Accies joined the
Scottish League in place of Renton, who
were forced to resign for financial reasons.
• Hamilton fans have had little to
cheer over the years, but the club did
reach the Scottish Cup final in 1911
(losing to Celtic after a replay) and
again in 1935 (losing to Rangers).
• English striker David Wilson scored
a club record 246 goals for the Accies
between 1928 and 1939, including a
seasonal best of 34 in 1936/37.
• With a capacity of just 5,510,
Hamilton's ground (now known as the
SuperSeal stadium for sponsorship
reasons) is the smallest in the Scottish
Premiership. It is also one of just
two in the top flight, along with
Kilmarnock's Rugby Park, to have an
artificial pitch.
• Rugged defender Colin Miller won a
club record 29 caps for Canada in his first
of two spells at Hamilton between 1988
and 1993.

HONOURS
First Division champions 1986, 1988,
2008
Division 2 champions 1904
Third Division champions 2001

HAT-TRICKS

Geoff Hurst is the only player to have
scored a hat-trick in a World Cup final,
hitting three goals in England's 4-2 defeat
of West Germany at Wembley in 1966.
• **Eighteen-year-old Tony Ross scored
the fastest hat-trick in football
history in 1964, taking just 90
seconds to complete a treble for Ross
County in a Highland League match
against Nairn County.**
• In 2004 Bournemouth's James Hayter
scored the fastest hat-trick in Football
League history, finding the net three
times against Wrexham in just two
minutes and 20 seconds. Sadio Mane
holds the record for the fastest hat-
trick in Premier League history, hitting a
quick-fire treble for Southampton in a
6-1 rout of Aston Villa on 16th May 2015
in just two minutes and 56 seconds.
• **The legendary Dixie Dean scored
a record 37 hat-tricks during his
career, while his contemporary
George Camsell scored a record nine
hat-tricks for Middlesbrough in the
1925/26 season.**
• Japanese international Masashi
Nakayama of Jubilo Iwata scored a world
record four consecutive hat-tricks in the
J League in April 1998.
• Argentinian striker Gabriel Batistuta
is the only player to have scored hat-
tricks at two World Cups, firing trebles
past Greece in 1994 and Jamaica four
years later.
• Players from Germany (including
West Germany) have scored a record
seven hat-tricks at the World Cup finals.
England's total is just three: Hurst (1966),
Gary Lineker (against Poland, 1986) and
Harry Kane (against Panama, 2018).
• **Alan Shearer scored a record 11
Premier League hat-tricks for Blackburn
and Newcastle. The unfortunate Matt
Le Tissier of Southampton is the only
player to twice finish on the losing side**

IS THAT A FACT?
A record 19 hat-tricks were
scored in the Premier League in
the 1993/94 and 2011/12 seasons,
while a measly three were
registered in the whole of the
2006/07 campaign.

The great Dixie Dean
scored a record 37
hat-tricks

despite scoring a Premier League hat-
trick, in defeats against Norwich City
(5-4 in 1994) and Nottingham Forest
(4-3 in 1995).

EDEN HAZARD

Born: Louviere, Belgium, 7th January
1991
Position: Midfielder
Club career:
2007-12 Lille 147 (36)
2012- Chelsea 208 (69)
International record:
2008- Belgium 92 (25)

A creative midfielder who possesses
wonderful dribbling skills, Eden Hazard
added the FA Cup to his list of honours
with Chelsea after scoring the winner
from the penalty spot in the 2018 final
against Manchester United at Wembley.
The Belgian wizard had previously won
the Premier League title with the Blues
in 2015 and 2017, topping both the PFA
and Football Writers' Player of the Year
polls in the first of these years.
• **The son of footballers – his father
played in the Belgian second tier,
while his mother was a striker in the
women's league – Hazard joined Lille
when he was 14, making his debut for
the first team just two years later.
In his first full season, 2008/09, he
became the first non-French player
to win the Young Player of the Year
award. He scooped the award again
the following season to become the
first player to win it twice.**

Eden Hazard's slick footwork can often leave defenders looking foolish

• In 2011, after completing a league and cup Double with Lille, Hazard was voted Player of the Year – aged 20, he was the youngest player to win the award. The following year he became only the second player to retain the trophy.

• After signing for Chelsea for £32 million in May 2012, Hazard's eye-catching performances in his first season at Stamford Bridge helped power the Blues to Europa League glory. However, his temperament was questioned by some pundits after he was stupidly sent off in the League Cup semi-final against Swansea for kicking the ball from underneath the body of a time-wasting ball boy. The following year, though, saw him up his game another notch and he was voted PFA Young Player of the Year and second behind Liverpool's Luis Suarez in the main poll.

• Hazard was first capped by Belgium, aged 17, against Luxembourg in 2008 and has gone on to win over 90 caps. He captained his country at Euro 2016 and the 2018 World Cup,

where he was awarded the Silver Ball as the tournament's second best player behind Croatia's Luka Modric.

HEADERS

In September 2011 Jone Samuelsen of Odd Grenland scored with a header from 58.13 metres in a Norwegian top-flight match against Tromso to set a record for the longest distance headed goal. He was helped, though, by the fact that the Tromso goalkeeper had gone upfield for a corner, leaving his goal unguarded.

• Huddersfield striker Jordan Rhodes scored the fastest headed hat-trick in Football League history in 2009, nodding in three goals against Exeter City in eight minutes and 23 seconds to smash a record previously held by Everton legend Dixie Dean.

• Giraffe-like striker Peter Crouch holds the record for the most headed goals in Premier League history, with 53.

• Just two players have scored a hat-trick of headers at

the World Cup: Tomas Skuhravy for Czechoslovakia against Costa Rica in 1990, and Miroslav Klose for Germany against Saudi Arabia in 2002.

• Only two players have scored headed hat-tricks in the Premier League: Duncan Ferguson for Everton against Bolton in 1997, and Salomon Rondon for West Brom against Swansea in 2016.

It's probably fair to say Duncan Ferguson was good with his head...

IS THAT A FACT?
Chelsea's Alvaro Morata was the most effective performer in the air in the 2017/18 Premier League season with seven headed goals, just one short of the record set by Blackburn's Roque Santa Cruz in 2007/08 and matched by Swansea's Fernando Llorente in 2016/17.

HEART OF MIDLOTHIAN

Year founded: 1874
Ground: Tynecastle (20,099)
Nickname: Hearts
Biggest win: 21-0 v Anchor (1880)
Heaviest defeat: 1-8 v Vale of Leven (1883)

Hearts were founded in 1874, taking their unusual and romantic-sounding name from a popular local dance hall which, in turn, was named after the famous novel *The Heart of the Midlothian* by Sir Walter Scott. The club were founder members of the Scottish League in 1890, winning their first title just five years later.

• The club enjoyed a golden era in the late 1950s and early 1960s, when they won two league championships and five cups. In the first of those title triumphs in 1958 Hearts scored 132 goals, many of them coming from the so-called 'Terrible Trio' of Alfie Conn, Willie Bauld and Jimmy Wardhaugh. The total is still a record for the top flight in Scotland. In the same year Hearts conceded just 29 goals, giving them the best ever goal difference in British football, an incredible +103.

• In 1965 Hearts came agonisingly close to winning the championship again when they were pipped by Kilmarnock on goal average after losing 2-0 at home to their title rivals on the last day of the season. Twenty-one years later they suffered a similar fate, losing the title on goal difference to Celtic after a surprise last-day defeat against Dundee. Annoyingly for their fans, on both occasions Hearts would have won the title if the alternative method for separating teams level on points had been in use.

• The club's record goalscorer is John Robertson with 214 goals between 1983 and 1998. Midfielder Gary Mackay made a record 640 appearances for Hearts between 1980 and 1997.

• Hearts won the Scottish Cup in 2012, thrashing local rivals Hibs 5-1 in the final at Hampden Park – the biggest victory in the final since Hearts themselves were tonked by the same score by Rangers in 1996. It was the eighth time that Hearts had won the Scottish Cup, making them the fourth most successful club in the competition after Celtic, Rangers and Queen's Park.

• Hearts made their record signing in 2006 when Racing Genk winger Mirsad Beslija moved to Edinburgh for £850,000. The following year Craig Gordon left the club for Sunderland for £9 million, then a record fee for a British goalkeeper and a record sale for Hearts.

• Relegated from the Premiership in 2014, Hearts bounced back by winning the Championship in fine style the following season with a second-tier record 91 points.

> HONOURS
> **Division 1 champions** 1895, 1897, 1958, 1960
> **Championship champions** 2015
> **First Division champions** 1980
> **Scottish Cup** 1891, 1896, 1901, 1906, 1956, 1998, 2006, 2012
> **League Cup** 1955, 1959, 1960, 1963

JORDAN HENDERSON

Born: Sunderland, 17th June 1990
Position: Midfielder
Club career:
2008-11 Sunderland 71 (4)
2009 Coventry City (loan) 10 (1)
2011- Liverpool 207 (21)
International record:
2010- England 44 (0)

A dynamic and hardworking midfielder who can also score the occasional spectacular goal from the edge of the box, Liverpool skipper Jordan Henderson led his club to the 2018 Champions League final but finished on the losing side after a 3-1 defeat to Real Madrid in Kiev.

• A product of the Black Cats' academy, Henderson was twice voted Sunderland Young Player of the Year after making his debut for his hometown club in a forgettable 5-0 defeat at Chelsea in November 2008. He joined Liverpool for around £20 million in 2011.

• Henderson helped Liverpool win the League Cup in 2012, although he was substituted before the Reds' penalty shoot-out victory over Cardiff City in the final, and later that year played in Liverpool's 2-1 defeat by Chelsea in the FA Cup final.

After being made Liverpool captain in 2015, he led the Reds to the League Cup final the following year, but they lost on penalties to Manchester City.

• First capped by England in 2010, Henderson was named his country's Under-21 Player of the Year in 2012. He has since represented his country at four major tournaments, earning particular praise for his performances at the 2018 World Cup. However, despite accumulating 44 caps, Henderson is yet to register his first international goal – among England midfielders none has played more often for their country without once finding the net.

"Watch the ball... watch the ball... watch the... zzzzzzzz"

HIBERNIAN

Year founded: 1875
Ground: Easter Road (20,421)
Previous name: Hibernians
Nickname: Hibs
Biggest win: 22-1 v 42nd Highlanders (1881)
Heaviest defeat: 0-10 v Rangers (1898)

Founded in 1875 by Irish immigrants, the club took its name from the Roman word for Ireland, Hibernia. After losing many players to Celtic the club disbanded in 1891, but reformed and joined the Scottish League two years later.

• Hibs won the Scottish Cup for the first time in 1887 and lifted the same trophy again in 1902. However, they then had to wait 114 years before winning the cup again, beating Rangers 3-2 in a thrilling final in 2016 – the first ever between two clubs from outside the top flight. The following season Hibs returned to the big time after topping the Scottish Championship table.

• The club enjoyed a golden era after the Second World War, winning the league championship in three out of five seasons between 1948 and 1952 with a side managed by Hugh Shaw that included the 'Famous Five' forward line of Bobby Johnstone, Willie Ormond, Lawrie Reilly, Gordon Smith and Willie Turnbull. All of the Famous Five went on to score 100 league goals for Hibs, a feat only achieved for the club since by Joe Baker.

• In 1955 Hibs became the first British side to enter the European Cup, having been invited to participate in the new competition partly because their Easter Road ground had floodlights. They did Scotland proud, reaching the semi-finals of the competition before falling 3-0 on aggregate to French side Reims.

• Hibs hold the British record for the biggest away win, thrashing Airdrie 11-1 on their own patch on 24th October 1959. As if to prove that the astonishing result was no fluke, they also hit double figures at Partick later that season, winning 10-2.

• When Joe Baker made his international debut against Northern Ireland in 1959 he became the first man to represent England while playing for a Scottish club. In the same season Baker scored an incredible 42 goals in just 33 league games to set a club record.

• Winger Arthur Duncan played in a club record record 446 league games for Hibs between 1969 and 1984.

Enjoying a second spell at Easter Road, Steven Whittaker is fronting up for Hibernian at full-back in 2018/19

HONOURS
Division 1 champions 1903, 1948, 1951, 1952
Championship champions 2017
First Division champions 1981, 1999
Division 2 champions 1894, 1895, 1933
Scottish Cup 1887, 1902, 2016
League Cup 1972, 1991, 2007

HOME AND AWAY

Brentford hold the all-time record for home wins in a season. In 1929/30 the Bees won all 21 of their home games at Griffin Park in Division Three (South). However, their away form was so poor that they missed out on promotion to champions Plymouth.

• **The highest number of straight home wins is 25, a record set by Bradford Park Avenue in the Third Division (North) in 1926/27. Meanwhile, Manchester City won a record 20 home Premier League games on the trot between March 2011 and March 2012.**

• Stockport's 13-0 win over Halifax in 1934 is the biggest home win in Football League history (equalled by Newcastle against Newport in 1946). Sheffield United hold the record for the most emphatic away win, thrashing Port Vale 10-0 way back in 1892.

• **On their way to winning the title in 2009/10, Chelsea scored a record 68 Premier League goals at home. Liverpool hold the away record with an impressive 48 in 2013/14.**

• Chelsea won a record 18 home games in the Premier League in 2005/06, a tally matched by Manchester United in 2010/11 and Manchester City the following season. City, though, are out on their own on their travels, racking up an impressive 16 away wins in 2017/18.

TOP 10

TOP-FLIGHT HOME WINS

1.	Liverpool	1,227
2.	Everton	1,223
3.	Arsenal	1,185
4.	Manchester United	1,121
5.	Aston Villa	1,106
6.	Manchester City	976
7.	Newcastle United	914
8.	Tottenham Hotspur	902
9.	Sunderland	867
10.	Chelsea	865

Manchester City captain Steph Houghton loves a physical tussle... her opponents are probably less keen, though!

STEPH HOUGHTON

Born: Durham, 23rd April 1988
Position: Defender
Club career:
2002-07 Sunderland Women
2007-10 Leeds United Ladies 45 (9)
2010-13 Arsenal Ladies 74 (11)
2014- Manchester City 63 (7)
International record:
2007- England 96 (11)

A central defender who carries a big threat at set pieces, Steph Houghton has been captain of the England Women's team since 2014.

• She started out with Sunderland Women, initially as a striker and then a midfielder before moving into defence, and was voted the Women's FA Young Player of the Year in 2007. In the same year she signed for Leeds United Ladies, with whom she won the FA Women's Premier League Cup in 2010.

• Greater success followed with Arsenal Ladies, including two Women's Super League titles and the Women's FA Cup in 2011 and 2013, Houghton scoring in the latter final after just two minutes in a 3-0 win against Bristol Academy.

• In 2014 she joined Manchester City, leading them to the league title in 2016 and the Women's FA Cup the following year.

• The first woman ever to appear on the cover of *Shoot* magazine, Houghton has played for England since 2007 and also represented Great Britain at the 2012 London Olympic Games where she scored three goals in four games, including winners against both New Zealand and Brazil.

HUDDERSFIELD TOWN

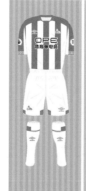

Year founded: 1908
Ground: John Smith's Stadium (24,500)
Nickname: The Terriers
Biggest win: 11-0 v Heckmondwike (1909)
Heaviest defeat: 1-10 v Manchester City (1987)

Huddersfield Town were founded in 1908 following a meeting held at the local Imperial Hotel some two years earlier – it took the club that long to find a ground to play at! The club were elected to the Second Division of the Football League two years later.

• The Terriers enjoyed a golden era in the 1920s when, under the shrewd management of the legendary Herbert Chapman, they won three consecutive league titles between 1924 and 1926 – no other club had matched this feat at the time and only three have done so since. The Terriers also won the FA Cup in 1922, beating Preston 1-0 at Stamford Bridge.

• Huddersfield won the first of their league titles in 1924 by pipping Cardiff City on goal average, the first time ever the champions had been decided by this method.

• After 45 years outside the top flight Huddersfield finally returned to the big time when they beat Reading in the 2017 Championship play-off final. It was a close run thing, though, with the Terriers triumphing 4-3 on penalties after a tense 0-0 draw. Huddersfield's unlikely promotion to the Premier League meant that they became only the second club (after Blackpool) to win three different divisional play-offs.

• In 1932 prolific striker Dave Mangnall scored in 11 consecutive games for Huddersfield – just one game short of the top-flight record set by Sheffield United legend Jimmy Dunne the previous season.

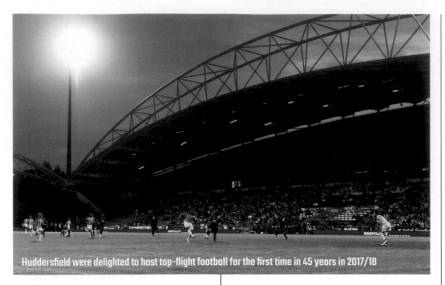

Huddersfield were delighted to host top-flight football for the first time in 45 years in 2017/18

• Outside left Billy Smith made a record 521 appearances, scoring 114 goals, for Huddersfield between 1913 and 1934. Smith and his son, Conway, who started out with the Terriers before playing for QPR and Halifax, were the first father and son combination to both hit a century of goals in league football.

• However, Huddersfield's record scorer is England international George Brown, who notched 159 goals in all competitions between 1921 and 1929.

• The Terriers smashed their transfer record in June 2018 when they paid Monaco £17.5 million for Dutch defender Terence Kongolo, following a successful loan spell in Yorkshire. The club's coffers were boosted by a record £8 million in 2012 when prolific Scottish striker Jordan Rhodes joined Blackburn.

HONOURS
Division 1 champions 1924, 1925, 1926
Division 2 champions 1970
Division 4 champions 1980
FA Cup 1922

HULL CITY

Year founded: 1904
Ground: KC Stadium (24,450)
Nickname: The Tigers
Biggest win: 11-1 v Carlisle United (1939)
Heaviest defeat: 0-8 v Wolves (1911)

Hull City were formed in 1904, originally sharing a ground with the local rugby league club. The Tigers joined the Football League in 1905 but failed to achieve promotion to the top flight until 2008.

• Hull enjoyed their best ever moment when they reached their first ever FA Cup final in 2014. The Tigers roared into a shock 2-0 lead against runaway favourites Arsenal at Wembley, but unfortunately eventually went down 3-2 after extra-time.

• In 2008 Hull first made it into the top flight thanks to a play-off final victory over Bristol City, with local boy Dean Windass scoring the vital goal. The triumph meant that the Tigers had climbed from the bottom tier to the top in just five seasons – a meteoric rise only bettered in the past by Fulham, Swansea City and Wimbledon.

• The club's record goalscorer is Chris Chilton, who banged in 193 league goals in the 1960s and 1970s. His sometime team-mate Andy Davidson has pulled on a Hull shirt more than any other player at the club, making 520 league appearances between 1952 and 1968.

• In his first spell at Hull between 1991 and 1996, goalkeeper Alan Fettis played a number of games as a striker during an injury crisis. He did pretty well too, scoring two goals!

• In August 2016 Hull splashed a club record £13 million on Spurs midfielder Ryan Mason. The Tigers received a club record £17 million when central defender Harry Maguire moved to Leicester City in June 2017.

• Hull were the first team in the world to lose in a penalty shoot-out, Manchester United beating them 4-3 on spot-kicks in the semi-final of the Watney Cup in 1970.

HONOURS
Division 3 champions 1966
Division 3 (North) champions 1933, 1949

"Ok, lads, remember we're tigers – not pussy cats"

ZLATAN IBRAHIMOVIC

Born: Malmo, Sweden, 3rd October 1981
Position: Striker
Club career:
1999-2001 Malmo 40 (16)
2001-04 Ajax 74 (35)
2004-06 Juventus 70 (23)
2006-09 Inter Milan 88 (57)
2009-11 Barcelona 29 (16)
2010-11 AC Milan (loan) 29 (14)
2011-12 AC Milan 32 (28)
2012-16 Paris Saint-Germain 122 (113)
2016-18 Manchester United 33 (17)
2018- LA Galaxy 18 (15)
International record:
2001-16 Sweden 116 (62)

A tremendously gifted striker with a uniquely individualistic style of play, LA Galaxy superstar Zlatan Ibrahimovic is the only player to have won league titles with six different European clubs.

• His incredible run began with Ajax, who he had joined from his first club

Malmo in 2001, when the Amsterdam giants won the Dutch league in 2004. Ibrahimovic's golden touch continued with his next club, Juventus, where he won back-to-back Serie A titles, although these were later scrubbed from the record books following Juve's involvement in a match-fixing scandal.

• At his next club, Inter Milan, Ibrahimovic fared even better, helping the Nerazzuri win a hat-trick of titles in 2007, 2008 and 2009. He then moved to Barcelona and, despite failing to see eye-to-eye with boss Pep Guardiola, won a La Liga title medal in 2010. Returning to Italy, his astonishing run of success continued with AC Milan, who were crowned Serie A champions in 2011.

• In the summer of 2012 Ibrahimovic was transferred to newly moneyed Paris Saint-Germain for £31 million, taking his combined transfer fee up to a then world record £150 million. In four years with PSG, he won four league titles, two French cups, was voted Ligue 1 Player of the Year three times, topped the Ligue 1 scoring charts three times and became the club's all-time leading scorer after banging in 156 goals in all competitions, including a season's best 50 in 2015/16.

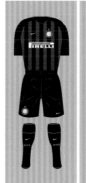

IS THAT A FACT?
Sweden's all-time top scorer, Zlatan Ibrahimovic is the only player to score four goals in a match against England, achieving this feat in a 4-2 friendly defeat of the Three Lions in Stockholm in November 2012.

• Ibrahimovic enjoyed yet more success with Manchester United in 2016/17. He scored twice in the Red Devils' 3-2 defeat of Southampton in the League Cup final and helped his new club reach the Europa League final, although he sadly missed their win over Ajax through injury.

INTER MILAN

Year founded: 1908
Ground: San Siro (80,018)
Nickname: Nerazzurri (The black and blues)
League titles: 18
Domestic cups: 7
European cups: 6
International cups: 3

Founded in 1908 as a breakaway club from AC Milan, Internazionale (as they are known locally) are the only Italian team never to have been relegated from Serie A and have spent more seasons in the top flight, 87, than any other club.

• Inter were the first Italian club to win the European Cup twice, beating the mighty Real Madrid 3-1 in the 1964 final before recording a 1-0 defeat of Benfica the following year. They had to wait 45 years, though, before making it a hat-trick with a 2-0 defeat of Bayern Munich in Madrid in 2010 – a victory that, with the domestic league and cup already in the bag, secured Inter the first ever Treble by an Italian club.

• Under legendary manager Helenio Herrera, Inter introduced the 'catenaccio' defensive system to world football in the 1960s. Playing with a sweeper behind two man-markers, Inter conceded very few goals as they powered to three league titles between 1963 and 1966.

• The club endured a barren period domestically until they were awarded their first Serie A title for 17 years in 2006 after Juventus and AC Milan, who had both finished above them in the league table, had points deducted

The Incredible Hulk on the warpath? No, it's just yet another goal for Zlatan!

Inter Milan are proud never to have been relegated from Serie A

for their roles in a match-fixing scandal. Inter went on to win the championship in more conventional style in the following four years – the last two of these triumphs coming under Jose Mourinho – winning an Italian record 17 consecutive league games in 2006/07.

• Inter's San Siro stadium, which they share with city rivals AC Milan, is the largest in Italy, with a capacity of over 80,000. The stadium has hosted the European Cup/Champions League final on four occasions, a record only surpassed by Wembley.

HONOURS
Italian champions 1910, 1920, 1930, 1938, 1940, 1953, 1954, 1963, 1965, 1966, 1971, 1980, 1989, 2006, 2007, 2008, 2009, 2010
Italian Cup 1939, 1978, 1982, 2005, 2006, 2010, 2011
European Cup/Champions League 1964, 1965, 2010
UEFA Cup 1991, 1994, 1998
Intercontinental Cup/Club World Cup 1964, 1965, 2010

IPSWICH TOWN

Year founded: 1878
Ground: Portman Road (30,311)
Nickname: The Blues, The Tractor Boys
Biggest win: 10-0 v Floriana (1962)
Heaviest defeat: 1-10 v Fulham (1963)

The club was founded at a meeting at the town hall in 1878 but did not join the Football League until 1938, two years after turning professional.

• **Ipswich were the last of just four clubs to win the old Second and First Division titles in consecutive seasons, pulling off this remarkable feat in 1962 under future England manager Sir Alf Ramsey. The team's success owed much to the strike partnership of Ray Crawford and Ted Phillips, who together scored 61 of the club's 93 goals during the title-winning campaign.**

• Two years after that title win, though, Ipswich were relegated after conceding 121 goals – only Blackpool in 1930/31 (125 goals against) have had a worse defensive record in the top flight. The Blues' worst defeat in a season to forget was a 10-1 hammering at Fulham, the last time a team has conceded double figures in a top-flight match.

• **However, the club enjoyed more success under their longest serving boss Bobby Robson, another man who went on to manage England, in the following two decades. In 1978 Ipswich won the FA Cup, beating favourites Arsenal 1-0 in the final at Wembley, and three years later they won the UEFA Cup with midfielder John Wark contributing a then record 14 goals during the club's continental campaign.**

• Ipswich have the best home record in European competition of any club, remaining undefeated at Portman Road in 31 games (25 wins and six draws) since making their debut in the European Cup in 1962 with a 10-0 hammering of Maltese side Floriana – the Blues' biggest win in their history.

• **With 203 goals for the Tractor Boys between 1958 and 1969, Ray Crawford is the club's record goalscorer. Mick Mills is the club's record appearance maker, turning out 591 times between 1966 and 1982.**

• Defender Allan Hunter is Ipswich's most-capped player, turning out 47 times for Northern Ireland while based at Portman Road between 1971 and 1982.

HONOURS
Division 1 champions 1962
Division 2 champions 1961
Division 3 (South) champions 1954, 1957
FA Cup 1978
UEFA Cup 1981

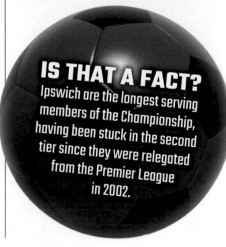
IS THAT A FACT?
Ipswich are the longest serving members of the Championship, having been stuck in the second tier since they were relegated from the Premier League in 2002.

ISCO

Born: Benalmadena, Spain, 21st April 1992
Position: Midfielder
Club career:
2009-11 Valencia B 52 (16)
2010-11 Valencia 4 (0)
2011-13 Malaga 69 (14)
2013- Real Madrid 157 (32)
International record:
2013- Spain 32 (11)

With his superb close control and dazzling dribbling skills, attacking midfielder Isco has been an instrumental figure in the Real Madrid side which has won the Champions League four times since 2014.

• Born Francisco Roman Alarcon Suarez in 1992, Isco got his big break with Valencia before moving to Malaga in 2011. The following year his eye-catching performances earned him the Golden Boy award, given to the most impressive footballer in Europe aged under 21, and helped propel Malaga into the Champions League for the first time in their history.

• In June 2013 Isco signed for Real Madrid for around £25 million and immediately endeared himself to fans at the Bernabeu by scoring a late winner on his debut in a 2-1 home victory against Real Betis.

• Isco played for Spain at every age level from Under-16 upwards to make his senior debut in a 3-1 friendly win against Uruguay in February 2013. Later that year he played in the European Under-21 Championship final, scoring from the spot in Spain's 4-2 victory over Italy in Jerusalem. At the World Cup in Russia in 2018 he scored for Spain in the 2-2 draw with Morocco that took his country through to the knock-out stage.

ITALY

First international: Italy 6 France 2, 1910
Most capped player: Gianluigi Buffon, 176 caps (1997-2018)
Leading goalscorer: Luigi Riva, 35 goals (1965-74)
First World Cup appearance: Italy 7 USA 1, 1934
Biggest win: Italy 11 Egypt 3, 1928
Heaviest defeat: Hungary 7 Italy 1, 1924

Italy have the joint best record of any European nation at the World Cup, having won the tournament four times (in 1934, 1938, 1982 and 2006). Only Brazil, with five wins, have done better in the competition.

• The Azzurri, as they are known to their passionate fans, are the only country to have been involved in two World Cup final penalty shoot-outs. In 1994 they lost out to Brazil, but in 2006 they beat France on penalties after a 1-1 draw in the final in Berlin.

• Italy goalkeeper Dino Zoff is the oldest man to play in a World Cup final, helping the Azzurri win in 1982 against West Germany when aged 40 and 133 days.

• The most humiliating moment in Italy's sporting history came in 1966 when they lost 1-0 to minnows North Korea at the World Cup in England. The Italians had a remarkably similar embarrassment at the 2002 tournament when they were knocked out by hosts South Korea after a 2-1 defeat. More woe followed when Italy failed even to qualify for the 2018 World Cup in Russia – missing out on the party for the first time since 1958 – when they lost 1-0 on aggregate to Sweden in the play-offs.

• With 176 appearances for Italy before he retired from international football in 2018, goalkeeper Gianluigi Buffon is the highest-capped European player ever and the fourth highest in football history.

• Italy have won the European Championships just once, beating Yugoslavia 2-0 in a replayed final in Rome in 1968 after a 1-1 draw. They reached the final again in 2000 but lost 2-1 to France on the 'golden goal' rule in Rotterdam, and endured more disappointment in 2012 when they were hammered 4-0 by Spain in the final in Kiev.

HONOURS
World Cup winners 1934, 1938, 1982, 2006
European Championships winners 1968
World Cup Record
1930 Did not enter
1934 Winners
1938 Winners
1950 Round 1
1954 Round 1
1958 Did not qualify
1962 Round 1
1966 Round 1
1970 Runners-up
1974 Round 1
1978 Fourth place
1982 Winners
1986 Round 2
1990 Third place
1994 Runners-up
1998 Quarter-finals
2002 Round 2
2006 Winners
2010 Round 1
2014 Round 1
2018 Did not qualify

Spanish superstar Isco's stud control is truly sublime

GABRIEL JESUS

Born: Sao Paulo, Brazil, 3rd April 1997
Position: Striker
Club career:
2015-17 Palmeiras 47 (16)
2017- Manchester City 39 (20)
International record:
2016- Brazil 22 (10)

On the last day of the 2017/18 Premier League season livewire striker Gabriel Jesus scored a late winner for Manchester City at Southampton which meant that the champions became the first club ever to reach 100 points in the English top flight.

• Jesus started out with Palmeiras, one of the biggest clubs in his home city of Sao Paulo. In 2015 he was voted best newcomer in the Brazilian league and the following year he picked up the Player of the Season award as Palmeiras won their first national league for 22 years. In January 2017 he joined City for £27 million.

• Jesus was part of the Brazil side which lost to Serbia in the final of the 2015 Under-20 World Cup and the following year he helped Brazil win Gold at the Rio Olympics after the South Americans beat Germany on penalties in the final.

• He was top scorer for his country in the 2018 World Cup qualifiers with seven goals, but failed to register a single goal during the actual tournament in Russia.

JUVENTUS

Year founded: 1897
Ground: Juventus Stadium (41,254)
Nickname: The Zebras
League titles: 34
Domestic cups: 13
European cups: 8
International cups: 2

The most famous and successful club in Italy, Juventus were founded in 1897 by pupils at a school in Turin – hence the team's name, which means 'youth' in Latin. Six years later the club binned their original pink shirts and adopted their distinctive black-and-white-striped kit after an English member of the team had a set of Notts County shirts shipped out to Italy.

• Juventus emerged as the dominant force in Italian football in the 1930s when they won a best ever five titles in a row. They have a record 34 titles to their name and are the only team in Italy allowed to wear two gold stars on their shirts, signifying 20 Serie A victories. In 2017/18 Juve became the first Italian club to win the Serie A title seven times on the trot and the first ever to win four consecutive Doubles.

• When, thanks to a single goal by their star player, French playmaker Michel Platini, Juventus beat Liverpool in the European Cup final in 1985 they became the first ever club to win all three European trophies. However, their triumph at the Heysel Stadium in Brussels was overshadowed by the death of 39 of their fans, who were crushed to death as they tried to flee from crowd trouble before the kick-off.

• Juventus won the trophy again in 1996, beating Ajax on penalties in Rome, but since then have lost five Champions League finals, most recently going down 4-1 to Real Madrid in Cardiff in 2017. The club's total of seven defeats in the final is a record for the competition.

• Juventus have won the Coppa Italia a record 13 times, most recently beating AC Milan 4-0 in the 2018 final to claim the trophy for a record fourth consecutive time.

• In 2014 Juventus won the Serie A title with a record 102 points, winning a record 33 league games including all 19 of their home matches.

HONOURS
Italian champions 1905, 1926, 1931, 1932, 1933, 1934, 1935, 1950, 1952, 1958, 1960, 1961, 1967, 1972, 1973, 1975, 1977, 1978, 1981, 1982, 1984, 1986, 1995, 1997, 1998, 2002, 2003, 2012, 2013, 2014, 2015, 2016, 2017, 2018
Italian Cup 1938, 1942, 1959, 1960, 1965, 1979, 1983, 1990, 1995, 2015, 2016, 2017, 2018
European Cup/Champions League 1985, 1996
UEFA Cup 1977, 1990, 1993
European Cup Winners' Cup 1984
European Super Cup 1984, 1996
Club World Cup 1985, 1996

"What a goal by me! Next on my to-do list, turning water into wine!"

HARRY KANE

Born: Chingford, 28th July 1993
Position: Striker
Club career:
2011- Tottenham Hotspur 150 (108)
2011 Leyton Orient (loan) 18 (5)
2012 Millwall (loan) 22 (7)
2012-13 Norwich City (loan) 3 (0)
2013 Leicester City (loan) 13 (2)
International record:
2015- England 30 (19)

With 39 Premier League goals in 2017, England captain Harry Kane holds the record for the most goals in the competition in a calendar year. His total of 56 goals in all competitions was also the best in the whole of Europe, breaking the seven-year domination of La Liga's Cristiano Ronaldo and Lionel Messi.

• Despite scoring a career best 30 goals in the 2017/18 season, Kane was pipped to the Golden Boot by Liverpool's Mohamed Salah, who deprived him of a third consecutive award. However, he was voted into the PFA Team of the Year for a fourth year on the trot.

• A clever player who can create as well as score goals, Kane came through the Tottenham youth system and spent time on loan with Leyton Orient, Millwall, Norwich and Leicester before finally establishing himself in the Spurs first team in 2014. The following year his fine form saw him voted PFA Young Player of the Year.

• An England international at Under-17, Under-19, Under-20 and Under-21 level, Kane made his senior debut against Lithuania in a Euro 2016 qualifier at Wembley in March 2015. His international career got off to a dream start, too, as he came off the bench to score with a header after just 78 seconds – the third fastest goal by an England player on debut.

• After a disappointing Euro 2016, Kane showed his best form at the 2018 World Cup in Russia. His total of six goals at the tournament won him the Golden Boot – only the second Englishman (after Gary Lineker in 1986) to win the award – and he was also voted into the FIFA World Cup Dream Team.

A rare shot of an almost stationary N'Golo Kante

N'GOLO KANTE

Born: Paris, France, 29th March 1991
Position: Midfielder
Club career:
2011-13 Boulogne 38 (3)
2013-15 Caen 75 (4)
2015-16 Leicester City 37 (1)
2016- Chelsea 69 (2)
International record:
2016- France 31 (1)

After helping Chelsea win the Premier League title in 2017, N'Golo Kante became the first outfield player to lift the trophy in consecutive seasons with two different clubs, having starred in the Leicester City team which surprisingly claimed the top spot the previous year. Kante's unstinting efforts for the Blues also saw him win both the PFA Player of the Year award and the Footballer of the Year gong. At the end of 2017 he finished eighth in the voting for the ballon d'Or, the highest-ranked Premier League player in the list.

• A tenacious midfielder who loves to make surging forward runs from deep, Kante started out with Boulogne in the third tier of French football, before moving to Caen in 2013. In his first season with his new club he played in every match as Caen won promotion to Ligue 1.

• After a £5.6 million transfer to Leicester in the summer of 2015, Kante was soon gaining plaudits for his hard-working, unselfish style of play which helped propel the Foxes to the top of the table. His excellent campaign, which saw him make a season best 175 tackles, ended with him being nominated for the PFA Player of the Year award and

"Wow, I'm the top scorer at the World Cup!"

KANTE

named in the PFA Team of the Year before he moved to Stamford Bridge for £32 million, then a record for a player leaving the King Power Stadium.

• Kante was rewarded with his first French cap in March 2016, coming on as a half-time sub in a 3-2 win against the Netherlands in Amsterdam. Later that month he made his first start for Les Bleus, scoring in a 4-2 win against Russia in Paris. In 2018 he was part of the France side which won the World Cup, starting all seven of his country's matches.

KICK-OFF

Scottish club Queen's Park claim to have been the first to adopt the traditional kick-off time of 3pm on a Saturday, which allowed those people who worked in the morning time to get to the match.

• The fastest ever goal from a kick-off was scored in just two seconds by Nawaf Al Abed, a 21-year-old striker for Saudi Arabian side Al Hilal in a cup match against Al Shoalah in 2009. After a team-mate tapped the ball to him, Al Abed struck a fierce left-foot shot from the halfway line which sailed over the opposition keeper and into the net.

• Ledley King scored the fastest goal in Premier League history, striking just 9.9

IS THAT A FACT?
The fastest ever goal in British football was scored after 2.1 seconds straight from the kick-off by Maryhill midfielder Gareth Stokes against Clydebank in the West of Scotland Super League First Division in April 2017.

seconds after the kick-off for Tottenham Hotspur against Bradford City on 9th December 2000.

• The fastest goal in the FA Cup was scored by Gareth Morris for Ashton United, who struck from 60 yards just four seconds after the kick-off against Skelmersdale United in the first qualifying round of the competition in September 2001.

• The first ever league match to be played on a Sunday kicked-off at 11.30am on 20th January 1974, a London derby between Millwall and Fulham. To get around the law at the time, admission to The Den was by 'programme only' – the cost of a programme cunningly being the same as a match ticket.

KILMARNOCK

Year founded: 1869
Ground: Rugby Park (17,889)
Nickname: Killie
Biggest win: 13-2 v Saltcoats Victoria (1896)
Heaviest defeat: 1-9 v Celtic (1938)

The oldest professional club in Scotland, Kilmarnock were founded in 1869 by a group of local cricketers who were keen to play another sport during the winter months. Originally, the club played rugby (hence the name of Kilmarnock's stadium, Rugby Park) before switching to football in 1873.

• That same year Kilmarnock entered the inaugural Scottish Cup and on 18th October 1873 the club took part in the first ever match in the competition, losing 2-0 in the first round to Renton.

• Kilmarnock's greatest moment was back in 1965 when they travelled to championship rivals Hearts on the last day of the season requiring a two-goal win to pip the Edinburgh side to the title on goal average. To the joy of their travelling fans, Killie won 2-0 to claim the title by 0.04 of a goal.

• Two years later Kilmarnock had their best ever run in Europe, when they reached the semi-finals of the Fairs Cup before losing 4-2 on aggregate to Leeds United.

• Alan Robertson played in a club record 607 games for Kilmarnock between 1972 and 1989. Killie's top scorer is Willie Culley, who notched 149 goals between 1911 and 1923.

• Kilmarnock have won the Scottish Cup three times, most recently defeating Falkirk 1-0 in the 1997 final. The club won the League Cup for the first time in 2012, after a 1-0 win against Celtic in the final.

• The club's longest serving manager was Hugh Spence, who was in charge for 807 games between 1919 and 1937.

HONOURS
Division 1 champions 1965
Division 2 champions 1898, 1899
Scottish Cup 1920, 1929, 1997
Scottish League Cup 2012

Raheem Sterling fancied a quick game of 'He's Behind You' but Dele Alli clearly wasn't interested

FRAN KIRBY

Born: Reading, 19th June 1993
Position: Striker
Club career:
2012-15 Reading Women 42 (67)
2015- Chelsea Women 34 (23)
International record:
2014- England 30 (10)

Fran Kirby, the 2018 PFA Women's Player of the Year

Nippy Chelsea Women striker Fran Kirby became the most expensive female player in Britain when she joined the Blues from Reading for £60,000 in July 2015, shortly after being dubbed 'the mini Messi' by then England boss Mark Sampson for her impressive performances at the Women's World Cup in Canada.

• In 2018 Kirby was named the PFA Player of the Year and the Football Writers' Women's Footballer of the Year following a great season with the Blues, which culminated in her scoring with a delightfully placed curling shot in the 3-1 defeat of Arsenal Ladies in the Women's FA Cup final at Wembley.

After losing six consecutive cup finals, Jurgen Klopp was starting to get a bit tetchy

• After joining Reading as a seven-year-old and progressing through the Royals' youth system, Kirby became the first woman to be offered a professional contract by the club. A prolific goal poacher, she was top scorer in the Women's Super League 2 in 2014 with 24 goals in just 16 appearances.
• Kirby made her England debut in August 2014, scoring in a 4-0 thrashing of Sweden at Victoria Park, Hartlepool.

KIT DEALS

In May 2016 Barcelona signed the biggest ever kit deal in football history with American company Nike. The deal, which started at the beginning of the 2018/19 campaign, sees Barcelona being paid £1 billion over 10 seasons in return for wearing Nike supplied training and playing kit. Real Madrid's 10-year deal with Adidas signed in 2015 is not far behind, being worth around £850 million.
• Manchester United's £75 million per year kit deal with Adidas is the most lucrative in the Premier League, followed by Chelsea's £60 million per year deal with Nike.
• Adidas were the most popular kit suppliers at the 2018 World Cup in Russia, providing home and away strips for 12 of the 32 countries. However, Nike were the kit suppliers for both finalists, winners France and runners-up Croatia.

JURGEN KLOPP

Born: Stuttgart, Germany, 16th June 1967
Managerial career:
2001-08 Mainz 05
2008-15 Borussia Dortmund
2015- Liverpool

After replacing Brendan Rodgers as Liverpool manager in October 2015, Jurgen Klopp has made steady progress with the Reds, culminating in leading the club to the final of the Champions League in 2018, which they lost 3-1 to Real Madrid in Kiev. Two years earlier he took his side to the League Cup final and the Europa League final. However, Klopp's men lost both matches, meaning that the unfortunate German has been beaten in his last six cup finals.
• Klopp took his first steps in management in 2001 with Mainz 05, the club he had previously turned out for more than 300 times as a striker-turned-defender. By the time he left Mainz in 2008 he was the club's longest serving manager.
• An engaging character who is rarely seen without a big smile on his face, Klopp made his reputation with Borussia Dortmund, who he led to consecutive Bundesliga titles in 2011 and 2012. In the second of those years Dortmund also claimed their first ever domestic Double after thrashing Bayern Munich 5-2 in the final of the German Cup.

• The following year Klopp took Dortmund to the final of the Champions League after they overcame Jose Mourinho's Real Madrid in the semi-finals. Again, their opponents in the final were Bayern, but this time the Bavarian side exacted revenge with a 2-1 victory at Wembley. Klopp then endured more agony when Dortmund lost the 2014 and 2015 German Cup finals to Bayern and Wolfsburg, respectively.

• Klopp was named German Manager of the Year in 2011 and 2012, the first man ever to win this award in two consecutive years.

VINCENT KOMPANY

Born: Uccle, Belgium, 10th April 1986
Position: Defender
Club career:
2003-06 Anderlecht 73 (5)
2006-08 Hamburg 29 (1)
2008- Manchester City 246 (17)
International record:
2004- Belgium 82 (4)

Vincent Kompany is the most successful captain in Manchester City's history, leading the Citizens to three Premier League titles, the most recent coming in 2018 when they amassed a record 100 points. He has also lifted the League Cup on three occasions in 2014, 2016 and 2018, scoring in the last of these finals in a 3-0 defeat of Arsenal at Wembley.

• In 2011 Kompany became the first City captain since Tony Book in 1969 to raise the FA Cup, when the Mancunians beat Stoke City 1-0 in the final at Wembley. His consistent performances earned him a place in the PFA Team of the Season, an accolade he has since achieved twice more.

• Kompany began his career with Anderlecht, with whom he won the Belgian league in both 2004 and 2006. He moved on to Hamburg after that second triumph, before joining City for around £6 million in 2008.

• Aged just 17 when he made his debut for Belgium against France in 2004, Kompany is one of the youngest players ever to represent his country. He was appointed captain of the Red Devils in 2011 and led Belgium to the last eight at the 2014 World Cup before a 1-0 defeat to Argentina ended their hopes. Injury ruled him out of Euro 2016 but he returned for the 2018 World Cup, helping Belgium come a best ever third.

Toni Kroos, Real Madrid's in-house German 'Professor'

TONI KROOS

Born: Greifswald, East Germany, 4th January 1990
Position: Midfielder
Club career:
2007-08 Bayern Munich II 13 (4)
2007-14 Bayern Munich 130 (13)
2009-10 Bayer Leverkusen (loan) 43 (10)
2014- Real Madrid 124 (11)
International record:
2010- Germany 86 (13)

A key figure in midfield for both club and country, Toni Kroos is the only German player to have won the Champions League four times, achieving this feat after successes with Bayern Munich (2013) and Real Madrid (2016, 2017 and 2018).

• Nicknamed 'the Professor', Kroos is an intelligent playmaker who creates numerous chances for his team-mates, as he demonstrated at the 2014 World Cup when he topped the assists ratings with four. Die Mannschaft's triumph in Brazil meant that Kroos became the first ever player born in the now defunct East Germany to win the competition.

• Kroos began his career with Bayern Munich, helping them win three Bundesliga titles, two German Cups and the FIFA Club World Cup before joining Real Madrid in 2014. He added the La Liga title to his list of honours in 2016.

• After starring for Germany at various youth levels, Kroos won his first senior cap against Argentina in 2010. Four years later his impressive displays in South America saw him named in the FIFA World Cup All-Star Team but, along with the rest of his colleagues, he failed to hit the same heights in Russia in 2018.

Insert your own 'two is Kompany, three is where you finish at the World Cup' joke here...

ALEXANDRE LACAZETTE

Born: Lyon, France, 28th May 1991
Position: Striker
Club career:
2008-11 Lyon B 53 (23)
2010-17 Lyon 203 (100)
2017- Arsenal 32 (14)
International record:
2013- France 16 (3)

After signing from Lyon for a then club record £41.5 million, Alexandre Lacazette enjoyed a good first season with Arsenal in 2017/18 hitting 17 goals in all competitions. He got off to a great start, scoring after just 94 seconds of his Premier League debut against Leicester City and found the net in his first three home league games – the first Arsenal player to achieve this feat for 24 years.
• **A lively two-footed striker who possesses pace and dribbling ability, Lacazette came through the academy of his hometown club, Lyon, making** his senior debut aged 19. In 2012 he helped Lyon win the French cup, thanks to a 1-0 win against third-tier semi-professional Quevilly in the final at the Stade de France.
• His best season with Lyon was in 2014/15 when he was voted Ligue 1 PLayer of the Year after topping the division's goalscoring charts with an impressive 27 goals.
• Lacazette has represented France from Under-16 level onwards, and in 2010 scored the winning goal in the European Under-19 Championship final when hosts France beat Spain 2-1. He made his senior debut in June 2013 in a 1-0 friendly loss to Uruguay in Montevideo but missed the cut for the 2018 World Cup.

LAWS

Thirteen original laws of association football were adopted at a meeting of the Football Association in 1863, although these had their roots in the eponymous 'Cambridge Rules' established at Cambridge University as far back as 1848.
• **No copy of those 1848 rules now exist, but they are thought to have included laws relating to throw-ins, goal-kicks, fouls and offside. They even allowed for a length of string to be used as a crossbar.**
• Perhaps the most significant rule change occurred in 1925 when the offside law was altered so that an attacking player receiving the ball would need to be behind two opponents, rather than three. The effect of this rule change was dramatic, with the average number of goals per game in the Football League rising from 2.55 in 1924/25 to 3.44 in 1925/26.
• **The laws of the game are governed by the International Football Association Board, which was founded in 1886 by the four football associations of the United Kingdom. Each of these associations still has one vote on the IFAB, with FIFA having four votes. Any changes to the laws of the game require a minimum of six votes.**
• In recent years important changes to the laws of the game include the introduction of the 'back pass' rule in 1992, which prevented goalkeepers from handling passes from their own team-mates; goals being permitted direct from the kick off (1997); and the introduction of goal-line technology (2012) and video assistant referees (2018).

LEAGUE CUP

With eight wins to their name, Liverpool are the most successful club in League Cup history. The Reds have also appeared in a record number of finals, 12. However, Manchester City have dominated the competition in recent years with three triumphs in the last five seasons, most recently crushing Arsenal 3-0 in the 2018 final – one of a record six defeats suffered by the Gunners in the final.
• **The competition has been known by more names than any other in British football. Originally called the Football League Cup (1960-81), it has subsequently been rebranded through sponsorship deals as the Milk Cup (1981-86), Littlewoods Cup (1986-90), Rumbelows Cup (1990-92), Coca-Cola Cup (1992-98), Worthington Cup (1998-2003), Carling Cup (2003-12), the Capital One Cup (2012-16) and the Carabao Cup (from 2017).**
• Ian Rush won a record five winner's medals in the competition with Liverpool (1981-84 and 1995) and, along with Geoff Hurst, is also the leading scorer in the history of the League Cup with 49 goals. In the 1986/87 season Tottenham's Clive Allen scored a record 12 goals in the competition.
• **Oldham's Frankie Bunn scored a record six goals in a League Cup match when Oldham thrashed Scarborough 7-0 on 25th October 1989.**

A striker should be hungry for goals, but Alexandre Lacazette is perhaps taking it too far

- Liverpool won the competition a record four times in a row between 1981 and 1984, going undefeated for an unprecedented 25 League Cup matches.
- **In 1983 West Ham walloped Bury 10-0 to record the biggest ever victory in the history of the League Cup. Three years later Liverpool equalled the Hammers' tally with an identical thrashing of Fulham.**
- In 1985 Barry Venison became the youngest ever player to captain a team in a Wembley final when he skippered Sunderland in the League Cup final against Norwich aged 20 and 220 days. However, he finished on the losing side after the Canaries won 1-0.
- **Swansea City recorded the biggest ever win in the final, thrashing Bradford City 5-0 in 2013, although the Bantams were the first side from the fourth tier of English football to reach a major Wembley final.**
- The first League Cup final to be played at Wembley was between West Brom and QPR in 1967. QPR were then a Third Division side and pulled off a major shock by winning 3-2. Prior to 1967, the final was played two legs.
- **On two occasions a League Cup match has featured a record 12 goals: Arsenal's 7-5 win at Reading in**

Sergio Aguero just loves the League Cup

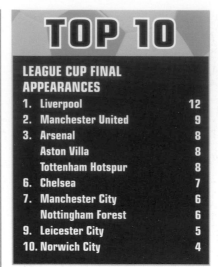

TOP 10

LEAGUE CUP FINAL APPEARANCES

1.	Liverpool	12
2.	Manchester United	9
3.	Arsenal	8
	Aston Villa	8
	Tottenham Hotspur	8
6.	Chelsea	7
7.	Manchester City	6
	Nottingham Forest	6
9.	Leicester City	5
10.	Norwich City	4

2012, and Dagenham's 6-6 draw with Brentford two years later.
- A competition record 32 penalties were taken when Derby County beat Carlisle United 14-13 in a first round shoot-out in August 2016.

LEEDS UNITED

Year founded: 1919
Ground: Elland Road (37,890)
Nickname: United
Biggest win: 10-0 v Lyn Oslo (1969)
Heaviest defeat: 1-8 v Stoke City (1934)

Leeds United were formed in 1919 as successors to Leeds City, who had been expelled from the Football League after making illegal payments to their players. United initially joined the Midland League before being elected to the Second Division in 1920.
- Leeds' greatest years were comfortably in the 1960s and early 1970s under legendary manager Don Revie. The club were struggling in the Second Division when he arrived at Elland Road in 1961 but, building his side around the likes of Jack Charlton, Billy Bremner and Johnny Giles, Revie soon turned Leeds into a formidable force.
- During the Revie years Leeds won two league titles in 1969 and 1974, the FA Cup in 1972, the League Cup in 1968, and two Fairs Cup in 1968 and 1971. In the last of those triumphs Leeds became the first ever club to win a European trophy on the away goals rule after they drew 2-2 on aggregate with Italian giants Juventus.
- **Leeds also reached the final of the European Cup in 1975, losing 2-0 to Bayern Munich. Sadly, rioting by the club's fans resulted in Leeds becoming the first English club to be suspended from European competition. The ban lasted three years.**
- Peter Lorimer, another Revie-era stalwart, is the club's leading scorer, hitting 168 league goals in two spells at Elland Road (1962-79 and 1983-86). England World Cup winner Jack Charlton holds the club appearance record, turning out in 773 games in total between 1952 and 1973.
- **In 1992 Leeds pipped Manchester United to the title to make history as the last club to win the old First Division before it became the Premiership. Ironically, Leeds' star player at the time, Eric Cantona, joined the Red Devils the following season. The club remained a force over the next decade, even reaching the Champions League semi-final in 2001, but financial mismanagement saw them plummet to League One in 2007 – a season in which Leeds used a club record 44 players – before they climbed back into the Championship three years later.**
- Central defender Lucas Radebe won a club record 61 caps for South Africa while at Elland Road between 1994 and 2003.
- **After Crystal Palace's Roy Hodgson, Leeds boss Marcelo Bielsa is the most experienced international manager currently in English football, having previously been in charge of both Argentina and Chile.**

HONOURS
Division 1 champions 1969, 1974, 1992
Division 2 champions 1924, 1964, 1990
FA Cup 1972
League Cup 1968
Fairs Cup 1968, 1971

This young Leicester fan has only known good times at the King Power Stadium

LEICESTER CITY

Year founded: 1884
Ground: King Power Stadium (32,315)
Previous name: Leicester Fosse
Nickname: The Foxes
Biggest win: 13-0 v Notts Olympic (1894)
Heaviest defeat: 0-12 v Nottingham Forest (1909)

Founded in 1884 as Leicester Fosse by old boys from Wyggeston School, the club were elected to the Second Division a decade later. In 1919 they changed their name to Leicester City, shortly after Leicester was given city status.

• Leicester enjoyed their greatest success in 2016 when, under the leadership of popular manager Claudio Ranieri, they won the Premier League title in one of the greatest upsets in sporting history. The Foxes were 5,000-1 outsiders at the start of the campaign, but defied the odds thanks in part to the goals of striker Jamie Vardy, who set a new Premier League record by scoring in 11 consecutive matches.

• The following season Leicester enjoyed their best ever European campaign, reaching the quarter-finals of the Champions League before losing 2-1 on aggregate to Atletico Madrid.

• Leicester have won the second-tier championship seven times – a record only matched by Manchester City. On the last of these occasions in 2013/14 the Foxes set a number of significant club records, including highest number of points (102) and most league games won (33).

• In 1909, while still known as Leicester Fosse, the club suffered their worst ever defeat, losing 12-0 to East Midlands neighbours Nottingham Forest – still a record score for a top-flight match. It later emerged that the Leicester players had been celebrating the wedding of a team-mate for two full days before the game, which might have contributed to their pitiful performance!

• Leicester's only cup success has come in the League Cup, the Foxes winning the competition in 1964, 1997 and 2000 – when skipper Matt Elliott scored both goals in a 2-1 defeat of Tranmere Rovers at Wembley.

• Leicester made their record signing in August 2016, when Algerian striker Islam Slimani joined the club

IS THAT A FACT?
Leicester are the only club to have played in four FA Cup finals and lost them all. Beaten in 1949, 1961 and 1963, they were defeated again by Manchester City in 1969 – the same season they were relegated from the top flight. Previously, only Manchester City (in 1926) had suffered this double blow.

from Sporting Lisbon for £30 million. In July 2018 the Foxes received a club record £60 million when winger Riyad Mahrez signed for Manchester City.

• **Arthur Chandler holds the club goalscoring record, netting 259 times between 1923 and 1935, while Arthur Rowley hit a record 44 of Leicester's seasonal best 109 league goals in 1956/57. The club's appearance record is held by defender and ex-Leicestershire county cricketer Graham Cross, who turned out 599 times in all competitions for the Foxes between 1960 and 1976.**

• When, in 2005, Ashley Chambers made his debut for the Foxes in a League Cup tie against Blackpool aged 15 and 203 days, he became the youngest ever player in the history of the competition.

• **Long-serving midfielder Andy King has won a club record 41 caps for Wales since making his international debut in 2009.**

HONOURS
Premier League champions 2016
Championship champions 2014
Division 2 champions 1925, 1937, 1954, 1957, 1971, 1980
League One champions 2009
League Cup 1964, 1997, 2000

ROBERT LEWANDOWSKI

Born: Warsaw, Poland, 21st August 1988
Position: Striker
Club career:
2005 Delta Warsaw 10 (4)
2005-06 Legia Warsaw II 5 (2)
2006-08 Znicz Pruszkow 59 (36)
2008-10 Lech Poznan 58 (32)
2010-14 Borussia Dortmund 131 (74)
2014- Bayern Munich 126 (106)
International record:
2008- Poland 98 (55)

On 22nd September 2015 Robert Lewandowski scored five goals for Bayern Munich against Wolfsburg in just eight minutes and 59 seconds – the fastest five-goal haul ever in any major European league. Incredibly, the pacy Polish striker had begun the match on the bench!

• **After starting out in the Polish lower leagues, Lewandowski made his name at Lech Poznan. In only his second season in the top flight, in 2009/10, he led the scoring charts with 18 goals as Poznan won the title.**

Robert Lewandowski's party-piece is doing the splits mid-match

• In the summer of 2010 Lewandowski moved on to Dortmund for around £4 million. The fee proved to be a bargain as Lewandowski's goals helped his club win two league titles and the German Cup in 2012, the Pole scoring a hat-trick in Dortmund's 5-2 demolition of Bayern Munich in the final. The following season Lewandowski set a new club record when he scored in 12 consecutive league games, and he also became the first player to score four goals in a Champions League semi-final, achieving this record in Dortmund's shock 4-1 defeat of competition heavyweights Real Madrid.

• **After topping the Bundesliga scoring charts in 2013/14 he moved on to Bayern Munich, with whom he has since won four titles. In 2015/16 Lewandowski became the first player for 39 years to score 30 goals in a Bundesliga campaign and the following season he was even more prolific, hitting a career-best 54 goals in total for club and country. In 2017/18 he was the Bundesliga's top scorer for a third time with 29 goals.**

• Lewandowski first played for Poland aged 20 in 2008, coming off the bench to score in a World Cup qualifier against San Marino to become his country's second ever youngest goalscorer on his debut. During the qualifiers for Russia

2018 he scored a European record 16 goals and he is now his country's highest scorer ever with 55 goals.

LINCOLN CITY

Year founded: 1884
Ground: Sincil Bank (10,120)
Nickname: The Imps
Biggest win: 13-0 v Peterborough United (1895)
Heaviest defeat: 3-11 v Manchester City (1895)

Lincoln City were founded in 1884 as the successors to Lincoln Rovers and are the oldest club never to have played in the top flight. The Imps have endured a fair amount of misery over the years, suffering a record five demotions from the Football League but always bouncing back, most recently winning the National League championship in 2017.

• **In the same year Lincoln made headline news when they became the first non-league club since 1914 to reach the quarter-finals of the FA Cup after thrilling wins against**

Championship duo Ipswich and Brighton, and Premier League Burnley. However, with Wembley in their sights the Imps' cup dreams were cruelly crushed by Arsenal, who beat them 5-0 at the Emirates.

• In 1976, under the stewardship of future England boss Graham Taylor, Lincoln won the old Division 4 title with a record 74 points (the highest ever total until 1981/82 when wins earned an additional point).

• **Lincoln made their first ever visit to Wembley in 2018, and it proved to be a memorable one for their fans as they beat Shrewsbury Town 1-0 in the final of the Football League Trophy.**

• Strangely, Lincoln enjoyed their biggest win and suffered their heaviest defeat in the same year, 1895, going down 11-3 to Manchester City in the old Second Division before thrashing Peterborough United 13-0 in the first qualifying round of the FA Cup a few months later.

HONOURS
Division 3 (North) champions 1932, 1948, 1952
Division 4 champions 1976
National League champions 2017
Conference champions 1988
Football League Trophy 2018

JESSE LINGARD

Born: Warrington, 15th December 1992
Position: Midfielder
Club career:
2011- Manchester United 84 (13)
2012-13 Leicester City (loan) 5 (0)
2013-14 Birmingham City (loan) 13 (6)
2014 Brighton and Hove Albion 15 (3)
2015 Derby County (loan) 14 (2)
International record:
2016- England 18 (2)

A lively and enterprising attacking midfielder, Jesse Lingard enjoyed his most prolific season to date with Manchester United in 2017/18, scoring 13 goals in all competitions.

• **However, the most important goal of Lingard's career came in the 2016 FA Cup final when he came off the bench to hit the winner in extra-time against Crystal Palace. The following season he was on target again at Wembley, scoring for United in their hard-earned 3-2 defeat of Southampton in the League Cup final.**

• Lingard joined United as a seven-year-old and graduated through the ranks to help the Red Devils win the FA Youth Cup in 2011, getting on the scoresheet in a 6-3 aggregate win in the final against Sheffield United. He then had a number of loans away from Old Trafford, most notably at Birmingham City where he scored four goals on his debut in August 2013 against Sheffield Wednesday in a 4-1 win at St Andrew's.

• **Lingard made his England debut in a 2-0 victory against Malta at Wembley**

in October 2016, and he notched his first goal for the Three Lions in a 1-0 friendly win away to the Netherlands in March 2018. At the World Cup finals in Russia later that year he scored one of the goals of the tournament with a delicious curler in England's 6-1 rout of Panama.

LIVERPOOL

Year founded: 1892
Ground: Anfield (54,074)
Nickname: The Reds
Biggest win: 11-0 v Stromsgodset (1974)
Heaviest defeat: 1-9 v Birmingham City (1954)

Liverpool were founded as a splinter club from local rivals Everton following a dispute between the Toffees and the landlord of their original ground at Anfield, John Houlding. When the majority of Evertonians decided to decamp to Goodison Park in 1892, Houlding set up Liverpool FC after his attempts to retain the name 'Everton' had failed.

• **With 18 league titles to their name, including the Double in 1986, Liverpool are the second most**

successful club in the history of English football behind deadly rivals Manchester United – although their last championship success came way back in 1990. The Reds' total of 104 seasons in the top flight is only surpassed by Aston Villa (105) and Everton (116).

• Liverpool dominated English football in the 1970s and 1980s after the foundations of the club's success were laid by legendary manager Bill Shankly in the previous decade. Under Shankly's successor, Bob Paisley, the Reds won 13 major trophies – a haul only surpassed by Manchester United's Sir Alex Ferguson.

• **As their fans love to remind their rivals Liverpool are the most successful English side in Europe, having won the European Cup/ Champions League on five occasions. Losing Champions League finalists in 2018, the Reds first won the trophy in 1977, beating Borussia Monchengladbach 3-1 in Rome, and the following year became the first British team to retain the cup (after a 1-0 win in the final against Bruges at Wembley, club legend Kenny Dalglish grabbing the all-important goal). Liverpool have also won the UEFA Cup three times, giving them a total of eight European triumphs.**

• Liverpool have won the League Cup a record eight times, including four times in a row between 1981 and 1984, and are the only club to win the trophy twice on penalties (in 2001 and 2012). Reds striker Ian Rush is the joint-leading scorer in the history of the competition with 49 goals, hitting all but one of these for Liverpool in two spells at the club in the 1980s and 1990s.

"So, Jesse, how many goals have you scored for England now?"

Liverpool's front three rarely miss the chance to have a friendly chat amongst themselves

• Rush also scored a record five goals in three FA Cup finals for Liverpool in 1986, 1989 and 1992 – all of which were won by the Reds. In all, the Merseysiders have won the trophy seven times, most recently in 2006 when they became only the second team (after Arsenal the previous year) to claim the cup on penalties.

• When Liverpool recorded their biggest ever victory, 11-0 against Norwegian no-hopers Stromsgodset in the Cup Winners' Cup in 1974, no fewer than nine different players got on the scoresheet to set a British record for the most scoring players in a competitive match.

• England international striker Roger Hunt is the club's leading scorer in league games, with 245 goals between 1958 and 1969. His team-mate Ian Callaghan holds the Liverpool appearance record, turning out in 640 league games between 1960 and 1978.

• Powerful centre-back Virgil van Dijk is the club's record signing, joining the Reds from Southampton in January 2018 for £75 million, a world record fee for a defender. In the same month hugely popular Brazilian midfielder Philippe Coutinho left Anfield for Barcelona for £142 million, in the most expensive deal ever involving a British club.

• Between 1976 and 1983 Liverpool full-back Phil Neal played in 365 consecutive league games – a record for the top flight of English football.

• Kop legend Steven Gerrard won a club record 114 international caps for England between 2000 and 2014, and scored a British record 41 goals in European competition.

• During the Reds' exciting Champions League campaign in 2017/18, in-form strikers Roberto Firmino and Mohamed Salah both scored a club record 11 goals in the competition.

• **Liverpool utility man James Milner holds the record for scoring in the most Premier League matches, 47, without finishing on the losing side.**

HONOURS
Division 1 champions *1901, 1906, 1922, 1923, 1947, 1964, 1966, 1973, 1976, 1977, 1979, 1980, 1982, 1983, 1984, 1986, 1988, 1990*
Division 2 champions *1894, 1896, 1905, 1962*
FA Cup *1965, 1974, 1986, 1989, 1992, 2001, 2006*
League Cup *1981, 1982, 1983, 1984, 1995, 2001, 2003, 2012*
Double *1986*
European Cup/Champions League *1977, 1978, 1981, 1984, 2005*
UEFA Cup *1973, 1976, 2001*
European Super Cup *1977, 2001, 2005*

LIVINGSTON

Year founded: 1943
Ground: Almondvale Stadium (8,716)
Previous names: Ferranti Thistle, Meadowbank Thistle
Nickname: The Lions
Biggest win: 8-0 v Stranraer (2012)
Heaviest defeat: 0-8 v Hamilton Academical (1974)

Founded in 1943 as the works team Ferranti Thistle, the club changed its name on joining the Scottish League in 1974 to Meadowbank Thistle after moving to the council-owned Meadowbank Stadium in Edinburgh. In 1995 the club moved west to Livingston and adopted the town's name.

• **Livingston's best season in the old SPL was in 2002 when the club finished third in the league behind Celtic and Rangers. After a 12-year absence, the Lions were promoted back to the top flight in 2018 following a 3-1 aggregate win in the play-off final against Partick Thistle.**

• The club's greatest day, though, came in 2004 when they beat Hibs 2-0 in the final of the Scottish League Cup at Hampden Park.

- When Livingston won the League One title in 2017 striker Liam Buchanan scored a club best 27 goals in a single season.
- Livingston received a club record £1 million when Spanish striker David Fernandez joined Celtic in 2002. The Lions' record signing cost an altogether more modest £60,000, when midfielder Barry Wilson signed from Inverness Caledonian Thistle in 2000.

HONOURS
First Division champions 2001
League One champions 2017
Second Division champions 1987, 1999, 2011
Third Division champions 1996, 2010
League Cup 2004

HUGO LLORIS

Born: Nice, France, 26th December 1986
Position: Goalkeeper
Club career:
2004-06 Nice B 20
2005-08 Nice 72
2008-12 Lyon 146
2012- Tottenham Hotspur 206
International record:
2008- France 104

Tottenham's Hugo Lloris has won more caps for France than any other goalkeeper and has also captained his country a record 80 times. His greatest moment for Les Bleus came in 2018 when he led them to victory in the World Cup final against Croatia.

- **After starting out with his hometown club Nice, Lloris made his name with Lyon. During a four-year stint with the French giants, Lloris was voted Ligue 1 Goalkeeper of the Year three times, but only managed to win one piece of silverware – the French Cup in 2012, following a 1-0 victory in the final over third-tier US Quevilly. He joined Tottenham that summer, enjoying his best season with the north Londoners in 2016/17 when he was part of a defence which conceded the fewest goals in the Premier League that campaign, just 26.**

- Famed for his superb reflexes, his fast and accurate distribution and his ability to rush out to the edge of the box to snuff out dangerous opposition attacks, Lloris won the European Under-19 Championship with France in 2005. He was awarded his first senior cap in 2008, keeping a clean sheet in a 0-0 draw with Uruguay, and he skippered his country for the first time in a 2-1 friendly win against England at Wembley in November 2010.

- At Euro 2016 Lloris was in fine form, especially in France's 2-0 win against Germany in the semi-final. However, in the final he was beaten by a low shot from Portugal's Eder in extra-time and finished on the losing side.

RUBEN LOFTUS-CHEEK

Born: Lewisham, 23rd January 1996
Position: Midfielder
Club career:
2014- Chelsea 22 (1)
2017-18 Crystal Palace (loan) 24 (2)
International record:
2017- England 8 (0)

A powerful central midfielder with a deft touch, Ruben Loftus-Cheek was one of the key figures for Crystal Palace as they recovered from a disastrous start to the 2017/18 Premier League season to finish in mid-table.

- **The south Londoner joined Chelsea when aged eight, and progressed through the club's academy to help the Blues win the FA Youth Cup in 2012 and 2014 and the UEFA Youth League in 2015.**

- Loftus-Cheek made his senior bow for Chelsea as a sub in a Champions League match against Sporting Lisbon in December 2014, but found it difficult to

Conceding a goal leaves French international Hugo Lloris spitting with rage cement a first-place at Stamford Bridge before joining Palace on a season-long loan in July 2017.

• Capped by England from Under-16 level onwards, Loftus-Cheek scored in the final against France at the Under-21 Toulon Tournament in 2016 and was named Player of the Tournament. The following year he made his senior debut, putting in a 'Man of the Match' display in a 0-0 draw with Germany at Wembley and he was a surprise selection in Gareth Southgate's squad for the World Cup in Russia.

ROMELU LUKAKU

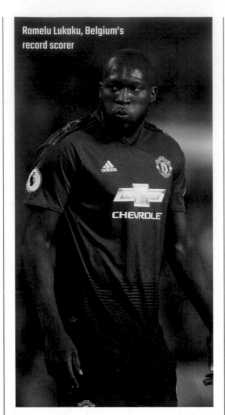

Romelu Lukaku, Belgium's record scorer

Born: Antwerp, Belgium, 13th May 1993
Position: Striker
Club career:
2009-11 Anderlecht 73 (33)
2011-14 Chelsea 10 (0)
2012-13 West Bromwich Albion (loan) 35 (17)
2013-14 Everton (loan) 31 (15)
2014-17 Everton 110 (53)
2017- Manchester United 34 (16)
International record:
2010- Belgium 75 (40)

In July 2017 Romelu Lukaku joined Manchester United from Everton for £75 million (potentially rising to a British record £90 million) in the most expensive ever transfer between two English clubs. He got off to a superb start at Old Trafford, scoring 10 goals in his first nine matches to set a new club record and ending the 2017/18 campaign with 27 goals for the Red Devils in all competitions.

• Lukaku's 25 goals in 2016/17 put him second behind Harry Kane in the race for the Golden Boot and was the best ever haul by an Everton player in the Premier League era – as is his total of 53 league goals for the Toffees. During the campaign Lukaku scored in nine consecutive home games to equal a club record set by the legendary Dixie Dean in 1934.

• Powerfully built, strong, quick and athletic, Lukaku enjoyed a great first season with his original club, Anderlecht, scoring 15 league goals as they won the Belgian championship in 2010. The following campaign he was the top scorer in Belgium with 20 goals across all competitions.

• Chelsea snapped up Lukaku for £10 million in 2011 but he struggled to make an impact at Stamford Bridge and the following season was loaned out to West Brom. The young striker thrived at the Hawthorns, netting 17 goals – the most ever in a single season by a Baggies player in the Premier League era. After another successful loan season at Everton, Lukaku joined the Toffees in a permanent deal for £28 million in July 2014, making him the club's most expensive ever player at the time.

• The son of a former Zaire (now DR Congo) international, Lukaku made his bow for Belgium in March 2010 while still only 16. He is now his country's all-time top scorer and enjoyed a good World Cup in Russia in 2018, scoring four goals to help Belgium finish third.

LUTON TOWN

Year founded: 1885
Ground: Kenilworth Road (10,356)
Nickname: The Hatters
Biggest win: 15-0 v Great Yarmouth Town (1914)
Heaviest defeat: 0-9 v Small Heath (1898)

Founded in 1885 following the merger of two local sides, Luton Town Wanderers and Excelsior, Luton Town became the first professional club in the south of England five years later.

• The club's greatest moment came in 1988 when they beat Arsenal 3-2 in the League Cup final. The Hatters returned to Wembley for the final the following year, but lost to Nottingham Forest – the same club which beat them in their only FA Cup final appearance in 1959.

• In 1936 Luton striker Joe Payne scored a Football League record 10 goals in a Third Division (South) fixture against Bristol Rovers. The Hatters won the match 12-0 to record their biggest ever league victory.

• Midfielder Bob Morton made a record 495 league appearances for the Hatters between 1946 and 1964, while his team-mate Gordon Turner scored a record 243 goals for the club.

• In January 2013, while they were languishing in the Football Conference, Luton became the first non-league team to beat a Premier League outfit in the FA Cup when they won 1-0 at Norwich City in a fourth round tie. The following season the Hatters won the Conference title with a club record 101 points

• 2018 Luton were promoted again to League One after finishing second in League Two behind Accrington Stanley. They attack-minded Hatters were also top scorers in their division with an impressive 94 goals.

HONOURS
Division 2 champions 1982
League One champions 2005
Division 3 (South) champions 1937
Division 4 champions 1968
Conference champions 2014
League Cup 1988
Football League Trophy 2009

ALEX McLEISH

Born: Glasgow, 21st January 1959
Managerial career:
1994-98 Motherwell
1998-2001 Hibernian
2001-06 Rangers
2007 Scotland
2007-11 Birmingham City
2011-12 Aston Villa
2012-13 Nottingham Forest
2014-15 Genk
2016 Zamalek
2018- Scotland

Scotland manager Alex McLeish is only the third man – after Andy Beattie and the legendary Jock Stein – to have filled the role twice, his previous spell in charge of the Tartan Army coming in 2007 when he won an impressive seven out of 10 games in charge.
• In an up-and-down managerial career McLeish enjoyed his best days with Rangers, who he led to the domestic Treble in 2003 and a second SPL title in 2005.
• In four years in charge of Birmingham City McLeish guided the Blues to promotion to the Premier League in 2009 and to an unlikely triumph in the League Cup two years later, following a shock 2-1 win against Arsenal in the final at Wembley. However, Birmingham were relegated on the last day of the 2010/11 season, prompting McLeish to quit the St Andrews hotseat. Subsequent spells in charge of Aston Villa, Nottingham Forest, Belgium giants Genk and Egyptian titans Zamalek did not go especially well for the Scot.
• In a long and trophy-laden playing career with Aberdeen, McLeish made 693 appearances for the Dons – a total only bettered by his team-mate and fellow central defender Willie Miller – while his total of 77 caps for Scotland is only surpassed by Kenny Dalglish, Jim Leighton and Darren Fletcher.

MACCLESFIELD TOWN

Year founded: 1874
Ground: Moss Rose (5,908)
Nickname: The Silkmen
Biggest win: 9-0 v Hartford St Johns (1884)
Heaviest defeat: 1-8 v Davenham (1885)

Previously a rugby union club, Macclesfield switched to football in 1874 but had to wait until 1997 before finally achieving league status. Relegated from League Two in 2012, the Silkmen returned to the big time as National League champions in 2018.
• During Euro '96 eventual champions Germany used Moss Rose as a training base. Coincidentally, one of the stars of that tournament for England, midfielder Paul Ince, later had a spell in charge of Macclesfield.
• Stalwart defender Darren Tinson played in a record 263 Football League games for Macclesfield between 1997 and 2003, while his team-mate Matthew Tipton is the Silkmen's top league scorer with 50 goals between 2002 and 2010.
• The club's most-capped international is defender George Abbey who played 10 times for Nigeria during the tail end of a five year-spell at Moss Rose between 1999-2004.

HONOURS
National League champions 2018
Conference champions 1995, 1997

HARRY MAGUIRE

Born: Sheffield, 5th March 1993
Position: Defender
Club career:
2011-14 Sheffield United 134 (9)
2014-17 Hull City 54 (2)
2015 Wigan Athletic (loan) 16 (1)
2017- Leicester City 38 (2)
International record:
2017- England 12 (1)

A commanding and physically imposing centre-half, Harry Maguire was one of the unsung heroes of England's run to the semi-finals of the 2018 World Cup, thwarting numerous opposition attacks and scoring with a thumping header in the quarter-final win against Sweden.
• Maguire came through the youth system at Sheffield United to make his debut for the Blades against Cardiff City in April 2011. He was voted the club's 'Player of the Year' in 2012, and two years later joined Premier League outfit Hull City for £2.5 million.
• However, he initially struggled to make an impact with the Tigers and was sent on loan to Wigan. He eventually became a regular with Hull in the 2016/17 season at the end of which he was voted the club's 'Player of the Year'. Following Hull's relegation he was he sold to Leicester for £12 million in June 2017 and after a fine debut campaign with the Foxes in which he played every minute of the club's 38 league matches he collected another 'Player of the Year' award.
• Capped just once at Under-21 level in November 2012, Maguire made his debut for England as a starter in a 1-0 defeat of Lithuania in August 2017.

Harry Maguire's forehead has become one of the most famous in football following the 2018 World Cup

RIYAD MAHREZ

Born: Sarcelles, France, 24th September 1991
Position: Winger
Club career:
2009-10 Quimper 27 (1)
2010-13 Le Havre II 60 (24)
2011-14 Le Havre 60 (6)
2014-18 Leicester City 158 (42)
2018- Manchester City
International record:
2014- Algeria 39 (8)

Silky winger Riyad Mahrez became the most expensive African player ever when he moved from Leicester City to table-topping Manchester City for £60 million in July 2018.

• Mahrez was the first Leicester City player and the first African to be named PFA Player of the Year in 2016 after helping the Foxes top the Premier League table in sensational style. Later that year he made it a double when he headed the African Footballer of the Year poll.

• A slender wideman who is blessed with superb ball control, Mahrez was a vital figure in Leicester's unexpected title success, scoring 17 goals – better than any other midfielder that season – and making 11 assists. Considering he cost the Foxes just £250,000 when he signed from Le Havre in January 2014 he

Riyad Mahrez is Manchester City's record signing

has to be rated one of the best bargain buys in English football history.

• First capped by Algeria in 2014, Mahrez enjoyed his best game for his country at the 2017 Africa Cup of Nations in Gabon when he scored twice in a 2-2 draw with Zimbabwe.

MANAGER OF THE SEASON

Former Manchester United boss Sir Alex Ferguson won the FA Premier League Manager of the Season award a record 11 times. He also won the old Manager of the Year award in 1993, giving him a total of 12 triumphs.

• Arsène Wenger (in 1998, 2002 and 2004) and Jose Mourinho (2005, 2006 and 2015) are the only other managers to win the award more than once since it was introduced in the 1993/94 season.

• Just two English managers have won the award: Harry Redknapp (Tottenham Hotspur) in 2010 and Alan Pardew (Newcastle United) in 2012.

• Tony Pulis topped the poll in 2014 despite his club, Crystal Palace, only finishing 11th in the Premier League – the lowest ever placing for a manager collecting the award.

• In 2018 Pep Guardiola became the first Spanish manager to win the award after guiding Manchester City to the Premier League title in record-breaking style.

MANCHESTER CITY

Year founded: 1887
Ground: Etihad Stadium (55,097)
Previous name: Ardwick
Nickname: The Citizens
Biggest win: 12-0 v Liverpool Stanley (1890)
Heaviest defeat: 2-10 v Small Heath (1894)

City have their roots in a church team which was renamed Ardwick in 1887 and became founder members of the Second Division five years later. In 1894, after suffering financial difficulties, the club was reformed under its present name.

• Now owned by Sheikh Mansour of the Abu Dhabi Royal Family, City are one of the

TOP 10

PREMIER LEAGUE GOALS IN A SEASON

1.	Manchester City (2017/18)	106
2.	Chelsea (2009/10)	103
3.	Manchester City (2013/14)	102
4.	Liverpool (2013/14)	101
5.	Manchester United (1999/2000)	97
6.	Manchester City (2011/12)	93
7.	Manchester United (2011/12)	89
8.	Manchester United (2001/02)	87
	Arsenal (2004/05)	87
10.	Manchester United (2009/10)	86
	Manchester United (2012/13)	86
	Tottenham Hotspur (2016/17)	86

richest clubs in the world. In recent years the Sheikh has splashed out big money on stars like Kevin de Bruyne, David Silva, Raheem Sterling and John Stones and he has been rewarded with a stash of silverware, receiving the first return on his huge investment in 2011 when City won the FA Cup. More silverware followed the next season as City won the Premier League, their first league title since 1968, after pipping arch rivals Manchester United on goal difference. In 2014 City won the Premier League for a second time, Chilean boss Manuel Pellegrini becoming the first non-European manager to win the title.

• A third title in seven seasons arrived in 2018 under the guidance of former Barcelona and Bayern Munich boss Pep Guardiola. Playing a slick and inventive brand of attacking football that thrilled fans and bewildered opponents, City smashed numerous Premier League records during a memorable campaign including most points won (100), most goals scored (106), best goal difference (+79), most wins (32), most consecutive wins (18) and biggest title-winning margin (19 points).

• Prior to the modern era, the late 1960s were the most successful period in City's history, a side featuring the likes of Colin Bell, Francis Lee and Mike Summerbee winning the league title (1968), the FA Cup (1969), the League Cup (1970) and the European Cup Winners' Cup (also in 1970), and for a short time usurping Manchester United as the city's premier club.

• City also won the league title in 1937. Incredibly, the following season they

Will Manchester City top their record 100 points tally this season? Benjamin Mendy isn't quite sure

MANCHESTER UNITED

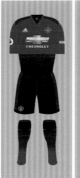

Year founded: 1878
Ground: Old Trafford (74,994)
Previous name: Newton Heath
Nickname: Red Devils
Biggest win: 10-0 v Anderlecht (1956)
Heaviest defeat: 0-7 v Blackburn (1926), Aston Villa (1930) and v Wolverhampton Wanderers (1931)

were relegated to the Second Division despite scoring more goals than any other side in the division. To this day they remain the only league champions to suffer the drop in the following campaign. Almost as bizarrely, City were agonisingly demoted from the top flight in 1983 after spending just the final four minutes of the entire season in the relegation zone.

• Argentinian striker Sergio Aguero, a key figure in City's recent triumphs, is the club's all-time leading goalscorer with 199 goals in all competitions since arriving from Atletico Madrid in 2011. The club's record appearance maker is Alan Oakes, who turned out 564 times in the sky blue shirt between 1958 and 1976.

• The club have won the League Cup five times, most recently beating Arsenal 3-0 in the 2018 final at Wembley. City have also won the FA Cup five times and, in 1926, were the first club to reach the final and be relegated in the same season. A 1-0 defeat by Bolton at Wembley ensured a grim campaign ended on a depressing note.

• In January 1961 Denis Law scored a club record six goals in an FA Cup tie at Luton. Unfortunately, the match was abandoned due to a waterlogged pitch with City leading 6-2, and although Law was again on target when the game was replayed City went down to a 3-1 defeat.

• City have won the title for the second tier of English football a joint-record seven times, most recently in 2002 when they returned to the Premiership under then manager Kevin Keegan. Four years earlier the club experienced their lowest ever moment when they dropped into the third tier of English football for the first and only time in their history – the first European trophy winners to ever sink this low.

• The club's most expensive purchase is skilful Algerian winger Riyad Mahrez, who signed from Leicester City for £60 million in July 2018. In August 2017 City received a club record £25 million when they sold Nigeria international striker Kelechi Iheanacho to Leicester City.

• Mercurial midfielder David Silva is the club's highest capped international, having played 77 times for Spain since he joined the Citizens in 2010.

HONOURS
Premier League champions 2012, 2014, 2018
Division 1 champions 1937, 1968
First Division champions 2002
Division 2 champions 1899, 1903, 1910, 1928, 1947, 1966
FA Cup 1904, 1934, 1956, 1969, 2011
League Cup 1970, 1976, 2014, 2016, 2018
European Cup Winners' Cup 1970

The club was founded in 1878 as Newton Heath, a works team for employees of the Lancashire and Yorkshire Railway. In 1892 Newton Heath (who played in yellow-and-green-halved shirts) were elected to the Football League but a decade later went bankrupt, only to be immediately reformed as Manchester United with the help of a local brewer, John Davies.

• United are the most successful club in the history of English football, having won the league title a record 20 times. The Red Devils have been the dominant force of the Premier League era, winning the title a record 13 times under former manager Sir Alex Ferguson.

• United were the first English club to win the Double on three separate occasions, in 1994, 1996 and 1999. The last of these triumphs was particularly memorable as the club also went on to win the Champions League, famously beating Bayern Munich 2-1 in the final in Barcelona thanks to late goals by Teddy Sheringham and Ole Gunnar Solskjaer, to record English football's first ever Treble.

• Under legendary manager Sir Matt Busby United became the first ever English club to win the European Cup in 1968, when they beat Benfica 4-1 in the final at Wembley. Victory was especially sweet for Sir Matt who, a decade earlier, had narrowly survived the Munich air crash which claimed the lives of eight of his players as the team returned from a European Cup fixture in Belgrade. United also won European football's top club prize in 2008, beating Chelsea in the Champions League final on penalties in Moscow.

• When United won the Europa League in 2017 – after beating Dutch outfit Ajax 2-0 in the final in Stockholm – they

Manchester United midfielder Fred just loves to ride piggy-back on Paul Pogba!

became only the second British club (after Chelsea) to win all three historic European trophies, having previously won the Cup Winners' Cup in 1991.

• United won the FA Cup for the first time in 1909, beating Bristol City 1-0 in the final. Beaten by Chelsea in the 2018 final, the club's total of 12 wins in the competition is only bettered by Arsenal. In 2000 the Red Devils became the first holders not to defend the cup when they played in the first FIFA Club World Cup Championship instead.

• Old Trafford has the highest capacity of any dedicated football ground bar Wembley in Britain but, strangely, when United set an all-time Football League attendance record of 83,260 for their home game against Arsenal on 17th January 1948 they were playing at Maine Road, home of local rivals Manchester

City. This was because Old Trafford was badly damaged by German bombs during the Second World War, forcing United to use their neighbours' ground in the immediate post-war period.

• United's leading appearance maker is Ryan Giggs, who played in an incredible 963 games in all competitions for the club between 1991 and 2014. Winger Steve Coppell played in a club record 206 consecutive league games between 1977 and 1981.

• The club's highest goalscorer is Wayne Rooney, who banged in a total of 253 goals in all competitions between 2004 and 2017. Rooney is also United's most capped international, with 110 appearances for England in his time at Old Trafford.

• United provided a record seven players for the England team for a World Cup qualifier away to Albania in March 2001. David Beckham, Nicky Butt, Andy Cole, Gary Neville and Paul Scholes all started the match, while Wes Brown and Teddy Sheringham came off the bench in England's 3-1 win.

• United hold the record for the biggest ever Premier League victory, thrashing Ipswich Town 9-0 at Old Trafford in March 1995. Andy Cole scored five goals in that game to set a record for the league that was matched by Dimitar Berbatov, against Blackburn in November 2010.

• Known for many years as a big-spending club, United's record signing is French midfielder Paul Pogba,

who cost a then world record £89.3 million when he moved from Juventus in August 2016. The club's most expensive sale is former Old Trafford hero Cristiano Ronaldo, who joined Real Madrid for a then world record £80 million in 2009.

• United hold the record for the most wins in the Premier League era (629), the most goals scored (1,924) and the most points accumulated (2,102).

• With around 90 million followers on Facebook and Twitter, Manchester United have more fans worldwide than any other English club.

HONOURS

Premier League champions 1993, 1994, 1996, 1997, 1999, 2000, 2001, 2003, 2007, 2008, 2009, 2011, 2013
Division 1 champions 1908, 1911, 1952, 1956, 1957, 1965, 1967
Division 2 champions 1936, 1975
FA Cup 1909, 1948, 1963, 1977, 1983, 1985, 1990, 1994, 1996, 1999, 2004, 2016
League Cup 1992, 2006, 2009, 2010, 2017
Double 1994, 1996, 1999
European Cup/Champions League 1968, 1999, 2008
Europa League 2017
European Cup Winners' Cup 1991
European Super Cup 1991
Intercontinental Cup/Club World Cup 1999, 2008

TOP 10

CLUB REVENUES IN 2016/17

1.	Manchester United	£581.2 million
2.	Real Madrid	£579.7 million
3.	Barcelona	£557.1 million
4.	Bayern Munich	£505.1 million
5.	Manchester City	£453.3 million
6.	Arsenal	£419 million
7.	Paris Saint-Germain	£417.8 million
8.	Chelsea	£367.8 million
9.	Liverpool	£364.5 million
10.	Juventus	£348.6 million

Sadio Mane holds the record for the fastest Premier League hat-trick

SADIO MANE

Born: Sedhiou, Senegal, 10th April 1992
Position: Striker/winger
Club career:
2011-12 Metz 22 (2)
2012-14 Red Bull Salzburg 63 (31)
2014-16 Southampton 67 (21)
2016- Liverpool 56 (23)
International record:
2012- Senegal 51 (14)

Senegal international Sadio Mane enjoyed a magnificent season with Liverpool in 2017/18, contributing 20 goals in all competitions including strikes in both legs of the Champions League semi-final against Roma and a poacher's finish against Real Madrid in the final against Real Madrid, which the Reds lost 3-1 in Kiev.

• A speedy attacker who generally finishes with calm confidence, Mane started out with French club Metz before coming to the fore with Red Bull Salzburg, with whom he won the Austrian Double in 2014. In the same year he joined Southampton for £11.8 million.

• In May 2015 Mane made headlines when he hit the fastest Premier League hat-trick ever, scoring three times in a 6-1 rout of Aston Villa in an incredible two minutes and 56 seconds. The following season he was the Saints' top scorer in all competitions with 15 goals and in June 2016 he joined Liverpool for £34 million, then a record fee for an African player.

• Mane made his debut for Senegal in 2012, representing his country at that year's Olympics in London. At the 2018 World Cup in Russia he scored in Senegal's 2-2 draw with Japan but he couldn't prevent the west Africans from being eliminated at the group stage.

MANSFIELD TOWN

One Call INSURANCE

Year founded: 1897
Ground: One Call Stadium (9,186)
Previous names: Mansfield Wesleyans, Mansfield Wesley
Nickname: The Stags
Biggest win: 9-2 v Rotherham United (1932)
Heaviest defeat: 1-7 v Reading (1932), v Peterborough United (1966) and v QPR (1966)

The club was founded as Mansfield Wesleyans, a boys brigade team, in 1897, before becoming Mansfield Town in 1910. The Stags eventually joined the Football League in 1931, remaining there until relegation to the Conference in 2008. Five years later the club bounced back to League Two as Conference champions with a club record 95 points.

• In 1950/51 Mansfield were the first club ever to remain unbeaten at home in a 46-game season, but just missed out on promotion to the old Second Division. The Stags finally reached the second tier in 1977, but were relegated at the end of the campaign.

• Already Sheffield United's all-time top scorer, striker Harry Johnson arrived at Mansfield in 1932 and in just three seasons scored 104 league goals to set a record for the Stags that still stands. Goalkeeper Rod Arnold played in a club record 440 league games for the Stags between 1971 and 1984.

• Mansfield's Field Mill ground (now known as the One Call Stadium for sponsorship purposes) is the oldest in the world hosting professional football, the first match having been played there in 1861.

HONOURS
Division 3 champions 1977
Division 4 champions 1975
Conference champions 2013
Football League Trophy 1987

MARCELO

Born: Rio de Janeiro, Brazil, 12th May 1988
Position: Defender
Club career:
2005-06 Fluminense 30 (6)
2007- Real Madrid 320 (23)
International record:
2006- Brazil 58 (6)

A left-back who is famed for his marauding forward runs and mop of frizzy hair, Marcelo is one of the most successful players in Champions League history with four winners' medals, all won with Real Madrid between 2014 and 2018.

• Born Marcelo Vieira da Silva in Rio de Janeiro, he started out with local club Fluminense before joining the Spanish giants in the January 2007 transfer window. Apart from his European triumphs, Marcelo has also won four La Liga titles and the Copa del Rey on two occasions with the Spanish titans.

• Marcelo made his debut for Brazil in September 2006, scoring with a fierce low drive from outside the box in a comfortable 2-0 friendly win against Wales at White Hart Lane.

• Less happily, he scored Brazil's first ever own goal at the World Cup in a 3-1 defeat of Croatia in 2014. Despite that gaffe, he was voted into the FIFA World Cup Dream Team at the end of the tournament and was selected by the fans again in 2018.

Marta – the greatest woman to have played the game?

UMea IK win the Women's Champions League (then called the Women's Cup) in 2004 after an 8-0 aggregate thrashing of Frankfurt, in which she chipped in with three goals. Her total of 46 goals in the Champions League is only bettered by two other players.

• Fast, talented, creative and tenacious, Marta is Brazil's all-time top scorer with 108 goals while her skills on the pitch have seen her dubbed 'Pele with skirts' by none other than the Brazilian legend himself.

MARTA

Born: Dois Riachos, Brazil, 19th February 1986
Position: Striker
Club career:
2000-02 Vasco da Gama 16 (4)
2002-04 Santa Cruz 38 (16)
2004-08 Umea IK 103 (210)
2009 Los Angeles Sol 19 (10)
2010 FC Gold Pride 24 (19)
2011 Santos 12 (13)
2011 Western New York Flash 14 (10)
2012-14 Tyreso FF 38 (27)
2014-17 FC Rosengard 43 (23)
2017- Orlando Pride 31 (15)
International record:
2002- Brazil 133 (110)

Rated by many as the greatest female player ever, Brazil striker Marta has been voted FIFA Women's Player of the Year a record five times and has also been runner-up on another five occasions.
• **Marta, or Marta Vieira da Silva to give her full name, is all-time leading scorer at the Women's World Cup with 15 goals. She was the top scorer at the 2007 tournament with seven goals, but had to settle for a runners-up medal after Brazil lost 2-0 to Germany in the final in Shanghai.**
• At club level, Marta's greatest achievement was helping Swedish outfit

MASCOTS

In April 2018 Everton skipper Phil Jagielka led out the Toffees for their home match against Newcastle holding the world's first virtual mascot, AV1. The robot was controlled from his home by chronically-ill 14-year-old Everton fan Jack McLinden and allowed him to experience the same viewpoint as if he had been out on the pitch with his heroes.
• **Swansea mascot Cyril the Swan was fined a record £1,000 in 1999 for celebrating a goal against Millwall in the FA Cup by running onto the pitch and pushing the referee. Two years later Cyril was in trouble again when he pulled off the head of Millwall's Zampa the Lion mascot and drop-kicked it into the crowd.**

• After signing a new sponsorship deal with a boiler company in the summer of 2018, West Brom unveiled football's strangest mascot – a man dressed as a combi boiler! Fans reacted positively to 'Boiler Man' on social media, but for the moment at least he is only the club's deputy mascot behind 'Baggie Bird'.
• **Charlton fan Daniel Boylett was jailed for 21 months and banned from attending football matches for six years after attempting to punch Crystal Palace's mascot, a live eagle called Kayla, during the south London rivals' League Cup tie in September 2015. Kayla, though, had the last laugh as the Eagles ran out 4-1 winners.**
• The first World Cup mascot was World Cup Willie, a lion wearing a Union Jack waistcoat created by children's illustrator Reg Hoye for the 1966 tournament in England. Since then notable World Cup mascots include Naranjito (an orange sporting the colours of Spain for the 1982 tournament), Ciao! (a red-white-and green stickman for Italia '90), Footix (a massive blue cockerel for France '98)

Liverpool's Mighty Red mascot takes flight at Anfield

and Zabivaka (a Russian wolf for the 2018 World Cup).

• A young girl mascot became something of an internet sensation in March 2018 when she cheekily flicked a 'V' sign and stuck out her tongue during the Dutch national anthem ahead of the international friendly between the Netherlands and England in Amsterdam.

MATCH-FIXING

The first recorded incidence of match-fixing occurred in 1900 when Jack Hillman, goalkeeper with relegation-threatened Burnley, was alleged to have offered a bribe to the Nottingham Forest captain. Hillman was found guilty of the charges by a joint Football Association and Football League commission and banned for one year.

• Nine players received bans after Manchester United beat Liverpool at Old Trafford in April 1915. A Liverpool player later admitted the result had been fixed in a Manchester pub before the match. For his part in the scandal, United's Enoch West was banned for life – although the punishment was later waived... when West was 62!

• In the mid-1960s English football was rocked by a match-fixing scandal when former Everton player Jimmy Gauld revealed in a newspaper interview that a number of games had been rigged as part of a betting coup. Gauld implicated three Sheffield Wednesday players in the scam, including England internationals Tony Kay and Peter Swan. The trio were later sentenced to four months in prison and banned for life from football. Ringleader Gauld received a four-year prison term.

• In April 2018 Albania's leading club KF Skenderbeu were sensationally banned from all European competition for 10 years and hit with a one million euro fine by UEFA after being accused of fixing more than 50 domestic and continental matches for betting purposes.

• Armando Izzo, a player with Serie B side US Avellino 1912, was banned from football for 18 months and fined 50,000 euros in April 2017 following match-fixing allegations.

• Saudi Arabian referee Fahad Al-Mirdasi was dropped from the 2018 World Cup in Russia after confessing to attempted match-fixing in his home country.

Kylian Mbappe isn't your average 19-year-old... he's already got his hands on the World Cup!

KYLIAN MBAPPE

Born: Paris, France, 20th December 1998
Position: Striker
Club career:
2015-16 Monaco B 12 (4)
2015-18 Monaco 41 (16)
2017-18 Paris St-Germain (loan) 27 (13)
2018- Paris St-Germain
International record:
2017- France 22 (8)

Paris Saint-Germain striker Kylian Mbappe became the second most expensive player in the world when he joined the club from Monaco, initially on a season-long loan, for £166 million in the summer of 2017. He immediately paid back some of that staggering fee by helping PSG win the Double in his first campaign in the French capital.

• A product of the famous Clairefontaine national academy, Mbappe holds the records for Monaco as the club's youngest player and goalscorer -– in both cases passing benchmarks previously set by the legendary Thierry Henry. In 2017 he helped Monaco win their first league title for 17 years, contributing 26 goals in all competitions.

• A devastatingly quick attacker, Mbappe was part of the French Under-19 team which won the European Championships in 2016, scoring five goals in the tournament in total – just one fewer than the top scorer, his team-mate Jean-Kevin Augustin.

• He made his senior debut for France against Luxembourg in March 2017 aged 18, becoming the second youngest ever player to represent his country. The following year Mbappe became the first teenager since the legendary Pele in 1958 to score in the World Cup final, rifling home from the edge of the box in France's 4-2 win against Croatia in Moscow.

LIONEL MESSI

Rated by many as the best player in the world, Lionel Messi is Barcelona's all-time leading scorer with an incredible 552 goals in all competitions. No fewer than 383 of those came in La Liga, making the diminutive Argentinian the competition's leading all-time scorer.

• Life, though, could have been very different for Messi, who suffered from a growth hormone deficiency as a child in Argentina. However, his outrageous talent was such that

"Please, God, don't let Ronaldo win the Champions League again this year"

32Red

Year founded: 1876
Ground: Riverside Stadium (34,000)
Nickname: Boro
Biggest win: 11-0 v Scarborough (1890)
Heaviest defeat: 0-9 v Blackburn Rovers (1954)

Barcelona were prepared to move him and his immediate family to Europe when he was aged just 13 and pay for his medical treatment.

• Putting these problems behind him, he has flourished to the extent that in 2009 he was named both World Player of the Year and European Player of the Year, and in 2010 he was the inaugural winner of the FIFA Ballon d'Or – an award he won a record four times before it was rebranded as the FIFA Men's Best Player.

• A brilliant dribbler, in 2012 Messi became the first player to be top scorer in four consecutive Champions League campaigns (2009-12) and he also set another record for the competition when he struck five goals in a single game against Bayer Leverkusen. In 2015 he helped Barcelona become the first European club to win the Treble of league, cup and Champions League twice, scoring twice in the Copa del Rey final against Athletic Bilbao.

IS THAT A FACT?
Lionel Messi has scored seven hat-tricks in the Champions League, a record matched only by Cristiano Ronaldo.

• Messi scored a world record 91 goals in the calendar year of 2012 for club and country, and the following year became the first player to score against every other La Liga club in consecutive matches. In 2018 he claimed the European Golden Shoe for a record fifth time after netting 34 goals in La Liga.

• **Messi made his international debut in 2005 but it was a forgettable occasion – he was sent off after just 40 seconds for elbowing a Hungarian defender. Happier times followed in 2007 when he was voted Player of the Tournament at the Copa America and in 2008 when he won a gold medal with the Argentine football team at the Beijing Olympics.**

• At the 2014 World Cup he won the Golden Ball as the tournament's outstanding player, but had to be satisfied with a runners-up medal after Argentina's defeat by Germany in the final. The following year he turned down the Player of the Tournament award at the Copa America following Argentina's defeat to hosts Chile in the final and after his country's defeat in the final to the same opposition in 2016 he announced his retirement from international football.

• **However, a huge public campaign calling for him to change his mind was successful, and he marked his return with the winning goal against old foes Uruguay in a World Cup qualifier in September 2016. With 65 goals for his country, Messi is Argentina's all-time top scorer.**

Founded by members of the Middlesbrough Cricket Club at the Albert Park Hotel in 1876, the club turned professional in 1889 before reverting to amateur status three years later. Winners of the FA Amateur Cup in both 1895 and 1898, the club turned pro for a second time in 1899 and was elected to the Football League in the same year.

• **In 1905 Middlesbrough became the first club to sign a player for a four-figure transfer fee when they forked out £1,000 for Sunderland and England striker Alf Common. On his Boro debut Common paid back some of the fee by scoring the winner at Sheffield United... the Teesiders' first away win for two years!**

• The club had to wait over a century before winning a major trophy, but finally broke their duck in 2004 with a 2-1 victory over Bolton in the League Cup final at the Millennium Stadium, Cardiff.

• **Two years later Middlesbrough reached the UEFA Cup final, after twice overturning three-goal deficits earlier in the competition. There was no happy ending, though, as Boro were thrashed 4-0 by Sevilla in the final in Eindhoven.**

• In 1997 the club were deducted three points by the FA for calling off a Premier League fixture at Blackburn at short notice after illness and injury ravaged their squad. The penalty resulted in Boro being relegated from the Premier League at the end of the season. To add to their supporters' disappointment the club was also beaten in the finals of the League Cup and FA Cup in the same campaign – no other club has suffered three such disappointments in one season.

• **Goalkeeper Mark Schwarzer is Boro's highest capped international, playing 51 times for Australia while at the Riverside between 1997 and 2008.**

• In 1926/27 striker George Camsell hit an astonishing 59 league goals, including a record nine hat-tricks, as the club won the Second Division championship. His tally set a new Football League record and, although it was beaten by Everton's Dixie Dean the following season, Camsell still holds the divisional record. An ex-miner, Camsell went on to score a club record 325 league goals for Boro – a tally only surpassed by Dean's incredible 349 goals for Everton.

• Beaten in the Championship play-off semi-finals in 2018, Middlesbrough made their record signing in July 2017 when striker Britt Assombalonga signed from Nottingham Forest for £15 million. The following year Boro's bank balance was boosted by a club record £15 million following the departure of highly rated defender Ben Gibson to Burnley.

HONOURS
First Division champions 1995
Division 2 champions 1927, 1929, 1974
League Cup 2006
FA Amateur Cup 1895, 1898

MILLWALL

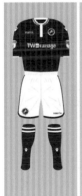

Year founded: 1885
Ground: The Den (20,146)
Previous name: Millwall Rovers
Nickname: The Lions
Biggest win: 9-1 v Torquay (1927) and v Coventry (1927)
Heaviest defeat: 1-9 v Aston Villa (1946)

The club was founded as Millwall Rovers in 1885 by workers at local jam and marmalade factory, Morton and Co. In 1920 they joined the Third Division, gaining a reputation as a club with some of the most fiercely passionate and partisan fans in the country.

• In 1988 Millwall won the Second Division title to gain promotion to the top flight for the first time in their history. The Lions enjoyed a few brief weeks at the top of the league pyramid in the autumn of 1988 but were relegated two years later.

• The club's greatest moment, though, came in 2004 when they reached their first FA Cup final. Despite losing 3-0 to Manchester United, the Lions made history by becoming the first club from outside the top flight to contest the final in the Premier League era, while substitute Curtis Weston set a new record for the youngest player to appear in the final (17 years and 119 days).

• Lions boss Neil Harris is the club's all-time leading scorer with 125 goals in two spells at the Den between 1998 and 2011. In 2017 he cemented his place in the hearts of Lions fans by leading Millwall out of League One and into the Championship after a 1-0 play-off final win against Bradford City.

• On their way to winning the Division Three (South) championship in 1928 Millwall scored 87 goals at home, an all-time Football League record. Altogether, the Lions managed 127 goals that season – a figure only ever bettered by three other clubs.

• Striker Moses Ashikodi became Millwall's youngest ever player when he came on as a sub in a 1-0 defeat to Brighton in February 2003 aged 15 and 240 days.

HONOURS
Division 2 champions 1988
Second Division champions 2001
Division 3 (South) champions 1928, 1938
Division 4 champions 1962

MILTON KEYNES DONS

Year founded: 2004
Ground: Stadium MK (30,500)
Nickname: The Dons
Biggest win: 7-0 v Oldham (2014)
Heaviest defeat: 0-6 v Southampton (2015)

The club was effectively formed in 2004 when Wimbledon FC were controversially allowed to re-locate to Milton Keynes on the ruling of a three-man FA commission despite the opposition of the club's supporters, the Football League and the FA.

• Despite pledging to Wimbledon fans that they would not change their name, badge or colours, within a few seasons all three of these things had happened, reinforcing the impression amongst many in the game that the MK Dons are English football's first 'franchise'. The MK Dons have since handed back to Merton Council all the honours and trophies won by Wimbledon FC and claimed by rivals AFC Wimbledon.

Millwall love a good chuckle down at the Den

MILTON KEYNES DONS

105

- Club captain Dean Lewington, the son of former England coach Ray, has made a record 573 league appearances for the Dons since making his debut in 2004. Striker Izale McLeod is the club's leading scorer, with 62 goals in two spells at the Stadium MK between 2004 and 2014.
- **Striker Simon Church won a club record nine caps for Wales during a season with MK Dons in 2015/16.**
- **Relegated to League Two in 2018, MK Dons sold dynamic midfielder Dele Alli to Tottenham for a club record £5 million in January 2015.**

HONOURS
League Two champions 2008
Football League Trophy 2008

LUKA MODRIC

Born: Zagreb, Croatia, 9th September 1985
Position: Midfielder
Club career:
2003-08 Dinamo Zagreb 112 (31)
2003 Zrinjski Mostar (loan) 22 (8)
2004 Inter Zapresic (loan) 18 (4)
2008-12 Tottenham Hotspur 127 (13)
2012- Real Madrid 166 (9)
International record:
2006- Croatia 113 (14)

After helping Real Madrid win the Champions League in 2014, 2016, 2017 and 2018, floppy-haired midfielder Luka Modric became the first Croatian player to win the trophy four times.
- **Modric started out with Croatian side Dinamo Zagreb, winning three league titles and the national Player of the Year award with his hometown club before joining Tottenham in 2008. He recovered from a broken leg to help Spurs qualify for the Champions League for the first time in 2010, but the following summer he agitated for a move to Chelsea until being forced to honour his contract by Tottenham chairman Daniel Levy. He finally left White Hart Lane in 2012, joining Real for around £33 million.**
- A gifted playmaker who is known as 'the Croatian Cruyff' in his home country, Modric made his international debut in 2006 and two years later starred at Euro 2008, where he was voted into the Team of the Tournament after some magnificent displays – only the second Croatian player ever to achieve this honour.

Luka Modric plays one of his 2.5 million passes at the 2018 World Cup

- **At the World Cup in Russia in 2018 Modric skippered Croatia in their first ever major final. Luck was against them on the day and they went down to a 4-2 defeat against France, but there was consolation for the talented midfielder when he was voted the tournament's best player and awarded the Golden Ball.**

MONACO

Year founded: 1924
Ground: Stade Louis II (26,768)
Nickname: Les rouge et blanc (The red and whites)
League titles: 8
Domestic cups: 5

AS Monaco were founded in 1924, following the merger of a number of small clubs in the principality and the surrounding region. In 2011 the club was bought by an investment group led by Russian billionaire Dmitry Rybolovlev and they have since splashed the cash on some big-name players, including

a then French record £51 million on Colombian striker Radamel Falcao from Atletico Madrid in 2013.
- **The club was managed by a young Arsène Wenger between 1987 and 1994, a team including former Tottenham midfielder Glenn Hoddle claiming the French title in thrilling style in 1988. Monaco's total of eight league titles is only bettered by Marseille and Saint Etienne.**
- Monaco have never won a European trophy, but they came close in 2004 when they reached the Champions League final, only to lose 3-0 to Jose Mourinho's Porto. The red and whites also reached the Cup Winners' Cup final in 1992, but went down 2-0 to German outfit Werder Bremen.
- **Monaco have never lost to an English club in the knock-out stages of the Champions League, beating Manchester United (1998), Chelsea (2004), Arsenal (2015) and Manchester City (2017).**
- Monaco won the French league for the first time in 17 years in 2017, along the way setting a new record for Ligue 1 with 12 consecutive victories.

HONOURS
French League champions 1961, 1963, 1978, 1982, 1988, 1997, 2000, 2017
French Cup 1960, 1963, 1980, 1985, 1991

MONEY

The Premier League is easily the richest league in world football. In the 2016/17 season the league's revenues hit a record £4.5 billion – a 25 per cent increase on the previous campaign – with domestic and worldwide TV rights accounting for more than half of that money.
- **Barcelona's Lionel Messi is the world's richest footballer, raking in £83.1 million per year in earnings and endorsements. He is followed on the rich list by Cristiano Ronaldo (£80.9 million) and Neymar, who has to get by on just £67.4 million.**
- According to Forbes, Manchester United are the most valuable club in the world, worth $4.12 billion in 2018. The Red Devils lead the way ahead of Spanish giants Real Madrid ($4.08

billion) and Barcelona ($4.06 billion), while fellow Premier League clubs Manchester City, Arsenal, Chelsea, Liverpool and Tottenham also feature in the top 10.

• The wealthiest manager in the world is Marcello Lippi, who earns £18 million every year as boss of the Chinese national team.

ALVARO MORATA

Born: Madrid, Spain, 23rd October 1992
Position: Striker
Club career:
2010-13 Real Madrid B 83 (45)
2010-14 Real Madrid 37 (10)
2014-16 Juventus 63 (15)
2016-17 Real Madrid 26 (15)
2017- Chelsea 31 (11)
International record:
2014- Spain 23 (13)

Spain international Alvaro Morata became Chelsea's record signing at the time when he moved from Real Madrid to west London for a cool £60 million in July 2017. In his first season at Stamford Bridge he was the most prolific player in the air in the Premier League, scoring seven headed goals, but he only added four more with his feet and a dip in form saw him dropped to the bench for the Blues' FA Cup final win against Manchester United. He also somewhat surprisingly missed out on Spain's squad for the World Cup in Russia.

• A hard-working striker who possesses excellent movement, Morata came through Real's youth system to score on his first start for the Spanish giants against Rayo Vallecano in February 2012. Two years later he came on as a sub for Real in their 4-1 defeat of city rivals Atletico Madrid in the 2014 Champions League final.

• That summer he moved on to Juventus for around £16 million, and in his first season in Turin scored in his team's Champions League final defeat against Barcelona. In October 2015 he equalled a club record held by Juve legend Alessandro Del Piero when he scored in a fifth consecutive Champions League match against Sevilla.

• After helping Juve win two league titles and scoring the winner in the 2016 Coppa Italia final against AC Milan, Morata returned to Real in a £27 million deal. He contributed 15 league goals as Real won La Liga in 2017 and also made a brief substitute appearance in their Champions League final victory against Juventus.

MORECAMBE

Year founded: 1920
Ground: Globe Arena (6,476)
Nickname: The Shrimps
Biggest win: 8-0 v Fleetwood Town (1993)
Heaviest defeat: 0-7 v Chesterfield (2016)

Founded in 1920 after a meeting at the local West View Hotel, Morecambe joined the Lancashire Combination League that same year and subsequently spent the next 87 years of their history in non-league football.

• The greatest moment in the club's history came in 2007 when the Shrimps beat Exeter 2-1 in the Conference play-off final at Wembley to win promotion to the Football League. The Shrimps have remained in League Two ever since, and are now the division's longest-serving club.

• Appointed in May 2011, Morecambe boss Jim Bentley is now the longest-serving manager in the Football League/ Premier League.

• Morecambe narrowly avoided relegation from League Two in the 2017/18 season and their poor form hardly had the fans flocking to the Globe Arena as the club's average attendance, 1,492, was the lowest in the Football League.

"Now, if I can just flick the ball up I should be able to head it in"

Jose Mourinho's audition for Strictly Come Dancing left his players a bit cold

MOTHERWELL

Year founded: 1886
Ground: Fir Park (13,677)
Nickname: The Well
Biggest win: 12-1 v Dundee United (1954)
Heaviest defeat: 0-8 v Aberdeen (1979)

Motherwell were founded in 1886 following the merger of two local factory-based sides, Alpha and Glencairn. The club turned pro in 1893 and, in the same year, joined the newly formed Scottish Second Division.

• **The club enjoyed its heyday in the 1930s, winning the league title for the first and only time in 1932 and finishing as runners-up in the Scottish Cup three times in the same decade.**

• Striker Willie McFadyen scored a remarkable 52 league goals for the Well when they won the title in 1931/32, a Scottish top-flight record that still stands today. His team-mate Bob Ferrier played in a Scottish record 626 league games between 1917 and 1937.

• **Motherwell had to wait until 1952 before they won the Scottish Cup for the first time, and they did it in some style by thrashing Dundee 4-0 in the final. Another success followed in 1991, the Well beating Dundee United 4-3 in an exciting final.**

• Defender Stephen Craigan made a club record 51 appearances for Northern Ireland between 2003 and 2011.

• **In May 2010 Motherwell were involved in the highest scoring game ever in the SPL, coming from 6-2 down to draw 6-6 with Hibs.**

> **HONOURS**
> *Division 1 champions* 1932
> *First Division champions* 1982, 1985
> *Division 2 champions* 1954, 1969
> *Scottish Cup* 1952, 1991
> *League Cup* 1951

JOSE MOURINHO

Born: Setúbal, Portugal, 26th January 1963
Managerial career:
2000 Benfica
2001-02 Uniao Leiria
2002-04 Porto
2004-07 Chelsea
2008-10 Inter Milan
2010-13 Real Madrid
2013-15 Chelsea
2016- Manchester United

In 2016/17 Jose Mourinho enjoyed the best ever debut season of a Manchester United manager as his team won both the League Cup, beating Southampton 3-2 in the final, and the Europa League, following a 2-0 win against Ajax in the final.

• **Mourinho started out as Bobby Robson's assistant at Sporting Lisbon, Porto and Barcelona before briefly** managing Benfica in 2000. Two years later he returned to Porto, where he won two Portuguese league titles and the UEFA Cup before becoming Europe's most sought-after young manager when his side claimed the Champions League trophy in 2004.

• Shortly after this triumph, Mourinho replaced Claudio Ranieri as Chelsea manager, styling himself as a 'Special One' in his first press conference. He certainly lived up to his billing, as his Blues team won back-to-back Premier League titles in 2005 and 2006, the FA Cup in 2007, and the League Cup in both 2005 and 2007.

• **After falling out with owner Roman Abramovich, Mourinho left Stamford Bridge in September 2007. He made a sensational return to west London in 2013 and in his second season back with the Blues guided them to both the Premier League and the League Cup, picking up a third Manager of the Year award in the process. However, after a calamitous start to the following campaign Mourinho was sacked in December 2015. Six months later he was appointed United manager, succeeding Louis van Gaal.**

• In between his stints at Chelsea, Mourinho took charge of Italian giants Inter Milan and Real Madrid. He led Inter to the first ever Treble, including the Champions League, by an Italian club in 2010, and guided Real to the Spanish title two years later with record tallies for points (100) and goals (121), making him the only manager to have won the championship in England, Italy and Spain.

NATIONAL LEAGUE

The pinnacle of the non-league system which feeds into the Football League, the fifth tier of English football was rebranded as the National League in 2015, having previously been called the Football Conference. The league was founded as the Alliance Premier League in 1979 and has been divided into three sections – National, North and South – since 2004.

• **Promotion and relegation between the Football League and the Conference became automatic in 1987, when Scarborough United replaced Lincoln City.**

• However, clubs have to satisfy the Football League's minimal ground requirements before their promotion can be confirmed and Kidderminster Harriers, Macclesfield Town and Stevenage Borough all failed on this count in the mid-1990s after topping the Conference table.

• **Barnet (1991, 2005 and 2015) and Macclesfield Town (1995, 1997 and 2018) have both won the division a record three times.**

• In 2011 Crawley Town won the league with a record 105 points. Three years later Hyde accumulated just 10 points – an all-time low for the division.

IS THAT A FACT?
A record National League crowd of 11,085 turned up for Bristol Rovers' home match against Alfreton on 25th April 2015. The vast majority of fans enjoyed the occasion hugely, as the Pirates romped to a 7-0 victory.

PHIL NEVILLE

Born: Bury, 21st January 1977
Managerial career:
2015 Salford City (caretaker)
2018- England Women

Appointed head coach of the England women's team in January 2018, Phil Neville got off to a great start in his new job when he led the Lionesses to a 4-1 win over France in the SheBelieves Cup in the USA in his first match in charge.

• **Neville is the first former male international to lead the women's team, but his appointment was criticised by some on the grounds that he had no previous experience in the women's game. However, he had previously worked as a coach for the England Under-21 team, Manchester United and Valencia and briefly managed Salford City, the National League club he co-owns with several of his former United team-mates.**

• In a long career spent mostly with Manchester United, Neville won six Premier League titles, three FA Cups and was an unused substitute when United beat Bayern Munich in the 1999 Champions League final in Barcelona to clinch a remarkable Treble.

• **A steady full-back who could also play in midfield, Neville won 59 caps for England between 1996 and 2007, including a record 31 alongside his brother Gary.**

THE NETHERLANDS

First international: Belgium 1 Netherlands 4, 1905
Most capped player: Wesley Sneijder, 133 caps (2003-17)
Leading goalscorer: Robin van Persie, 50 goals (2005-)
First World Cup appearance: Netherlands 2 Switzerland 1, 1934
Biggest win: Netherlands 11 San Marino 0, 2011
Heaviest defeat: England amateurs 9 Netherlands 1, 1909

Long associated with an entertaining style of attacking football, the Netherlands have only won one

Johan Cruyff, the Netherlands' greatest ever player

major tournament, the European Championships in 1988. In the final that year the Dutch beat Russia with goals from their two biggest stars of the time, Ruud Gullit and Marco van Basten.

• **The Netherlands are the only country to have lost all three World Cup finals they have played in. On the first two of these occasions they had the misfortune to meet the hosts in the final, losing to West Germany in 1974 and Argentina in 1978. Then, in the 2010 final, they went down 1-0 in extra-time to Spain in Johannesburg following a negative, at times brutal, Dutch performance which was totally at odds with the country's best footballing traditions. At the next World Cup, the Netherlands again did well, coming third.**

• A professional league wasn't formed in the Netherlands until 1956, and it took some years after that before the country was taken seriously as a football power. Their lowest ebb was reached in 1963 when the Dutch were humiliatingly eliminated from the European Championships by minnows Luxembourg.

• **However, the following decade saw a renaissance in Dutch football. With exciting players like Johan Cruyff, Johan Neeskens and Ruud Krol in their side, the Netherlands were considered the best team in Europe. Pivotal to their success was the revolutionary 'Total Football' system devised by manager Rinus Michels which allowed the outfield players constantly to switch positions during the game.**

• In 2011 the Netherlands strolled to their biggest ever win, 11-0 against San Marino in a Euro 2012 qualifier – just two goals shy of Germany's record European championship victory against the same hapless opposition five years earlier.

• To the disappointment of their orange-clad fans, the Netherlands failed to qualify for Euro 2016 and also missed out on the 2018 World Cup in Russia, after being narrowly pipped on goal difference to a play-off place by Sweden.

HONOURS
European Championships winners
1988
World Cup Record
1930 Did not enter
1934 Round 1
1938 Round 1
1950 Did not enter
1954 Did not enter
1958 Did not qualify
1962 Did not qualify
1966 Did not qualify
1970 Did not qualify
1974 Runners-up
1978 Runners-up
1982 Did not qualify
1986 Did not qualify
1990 Round 2
1994 Quarter-finals
1998 Fourth place
2002 Did not qualify
2006 Round 2
2010 Runners-up
2014 Third place
2018 Did not qualify

MANUEL NEUER

Born: Gelsenkirchen, Germany, 27th March 1986
Position: Goalkeeper
Club career:
2004-08 Schalke II 26
2006-11 Schalke 156
2011- Bayern Munich 190
International record:
2009- Germany 79

World Goalkeeper of the Year in 2013, 2014, 2015 and 2016, Bayern Munich's Manuel Neuer is only the second player to win the award four times on the trot (after Real Madrid's Iker Casillas, who won five consecutive awards). In the second of those years Neuer became the first goalkeeper to figure in the top three of the FIFA Ballon D'or when he

Manuel Neuer is a four-time World Goalkeeper of the Year

came third behind Cristiano Ronaldo and Lionel Messi.

• **A magnificent shot-stopper with excellent reflexes and a good distributor of the ball, Neuer signed for Bayern from Schalke for £19 million in 2011, at the time the second biggest transfer fee ever for a goalkeeper. Since then he has helped Bayern Munich win the Champions League in 2013, and a record six consecutive Bundesliga titles between 2013 and 2018.**

• In 2012 Neuer's penalty saves from Cristiano Ronaldo and Kaka in the semi-final shoot-out against Real Madrid enabled Bayern to reach the Champions League final, where they faced Chelsea at their home ground, the Allianz Arena. In the subsequent shoot-out that settled the match, Neuer became the first ever goalkeeper to score in a Champions League final, although he still finished on the losing side.

• **Neuer impressed at the 2010 World Cup, helping Germany come third in South Africa. Four years later he was instrumental in Germany's success in Brazil, keeping four clean sheets and collecting the Golden Glove award. He captained his country four years later in Russia but gifted a goal in spectacular fashion to South Korea in a 2-0 defeat which sealed the reigning champions' group-stage elimination.**

NEWCASTLE UNITED

Year founded: 1892
Ground: St James' Park (52,354)
Nickname: The Magpies
Biggest win: 13-0 v Newport County (1946)
Heaviest defeat: 0-9 v Burton Wanderers (1895)

The club was founded in 1892 following the merger of local sides Newcastle East End and Newcastle West End, gaining election to the Football League just a year later.

• **In 1895 Newcastle suffered their worst ever defeat, going down 9-0 to Burton Wanderers in a Second Division match. However, their most embarrassing loss was a 9-1 home hammering by Sunderland in December 1908. The Toon recovered, though, to win the title that season, making that defeat by their local rivals the heaviest ever suffered by the eventual league champions. The Magpies recorded their best ever win in 1946, thrashing Newport County 13-0 to equal Stockport County's record for the biggest ever victory in a Football League match. Star of** the show at St James' Park was Len Shackleton, who scored six of the goals on his Newcastle debut to set a club record.

• Newcastle have a proud tradition in the FA Cup, having won the competition on six occasions. In 1908 the Magpies reached the final after smashing Fulham 6-0, the biggest ever win in the semi-final. Then, in 1924, 41-year-old defender Billy Hampson became the oldest player ever to appear in the cup final, when he turned out for the Toon in their rain-swept 2-0 defeat of Aston Villa at Wembley.

• **The club's best cup era was in the 1950s when they won the trophy three times, boss Stan Seymour becoming the first man to lift the cup as a player and a manager. Legendary centre-forward Jackie Milburn was instrumental to Newcastle's success, scoring in every round in 1951 and then notching after just 45 seconds in the 1955 final against Manchester City – the fastest Wembley cup final goal ever at the time. In 1952 Chilean striker George Robledo notched the winner against Arsenal to become the first foreign player to score in the FA Cup final.**

• Milburn is the club's leading goalscorer in league matches with 178 strikes between 1946 and 1957. However, Alan Shearer holds the overall club goalscoring record, finding the net 206 times in all competitions after his then world record £15 million move from Blackburn Rovers in 1996. Shearer's predecessor Andy Cole scored 41 goals in all competitions in 1993/94 to set another club record.

• **Newcastle's only success in Europe came in 1969 when they won the Fairs Cup following a 6-2 aggregate win against Hungarian outfit Ujpest Dozsa. Skipper Bobby Moncur was the unlikely hero of that triumph, the central defender pitching in with three goals over the two legs.**

• The club's leading appearance maker is goalkeeper Jimmy Lawrence, who featured in 432 league games between 1904 and 1921. Another goalkeeper, Shay Given, is easily Newcastle's most honoured international with 83 caps for the Republic of Ireland between 1997 and 2009.

• **In January 2011 Newcastle sold striker Andy Carroll to Liverpool for £35 million, the highest fee at the time for a British player moving from**

one Premier League club to another. **Michael Owen is Newcastle's most expensive player, joining the Magpies from Real Madrid for £16 million in 2005 – the longest-standing record transfer among current Premier League clubs.**

• The club's youngest ever player is midfielder Steve Watson, who was aged 16 and 233 days when he made his debut against Wolves in November 1990.

> HONOURS
> **Division 1 champions** 1905, 1907, 1909, 1927
> **Championship champions** 2010, 2017
> **First Division champions** 1993
> **Division 2 champions** 1965
> **FA Cup** 1910, 1924, 1932, 1951, 1952, 1955
> **Fairs Cup** 1969

NEWPORT COUNTY

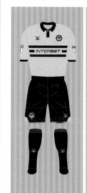

Year founded: 1912
Ground: Rodney Parade (7,850)
Nickname: The Ironsides
Biggest win: 10-0 v Merthyr Town (1930)
Heaviest defeat: 0-13 v Newcastle United (1946)

Founded in 1912, Newport County joined the Football League eight years later. After finishing bottom of the old Fourth Division in 1988 the club dropped into the Conference, only to be expelled in February 1989 for failing to fulfil their fixtures. The club reformed later that year in the Hellenic League, four divisions below the Football League.

• **The road back for Newport was a long one, but they eventually returned to the Football League after beating Wrexham 2-0 in the Conference play-off final in 2013, in the first ever final at Wembley between two Welsh clubs.**

• The club's greatest days came in the early 1980s when, after winning the Welsh Cup for the only time, County reached the quarter-finals of the European Cup Winners' Cup in 1981 before falling 3-2 on aggregate to eventual finalists Carl Zeiss Jena of East Germany.

• Goalkeeper Len Weare played in a club record 525 games for County between 1955 and 1970, while Reg Parker holds Newport's scoring record with 99 goals between 1948 and 1954.

> HONOURS
> **Division 3 (South) champions** 1939
> **Welsh Cup** 1980

NEYMAR

> **Born:** Mogi das Cruzes, Brazil, 5th February 1992
> **Position:** Striker/winger
> **Club career:**
> 2009-13 Santos 103 (54)
> 2013-17 Barcelona 123 (68)
> 2017- Paris Saint-Germain 20 (19)
> **International record:**
> 2010- Brazil 90 (57)

In August 2017 Brazilian superstar Neymar became the most expensive footballer ever when he moved from Barcelona to Paris Saint-Germain for an incredible £200 million – more than double the previous record. In his first season with PSG he scored an impressive 26 goals in all competitions despite missing the last three months of the campaign through injury.

• **A superbly talented player who is stronger than his slight frame suggests, Neymar shot to fame soon after making his Santos debut in 2009 when he scored five goals in a cup match against Guarani. Two years later he helped Santos win the Copa Libertadores for the first time since 1963, scoring against Penarol in the final and earning the Man of the Match award. He was named South American Footballer of the Year in 2011 and 2012 before joining**

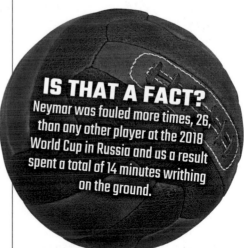

IS THAT A FACT?
Neymar was fouled more times, 26, than any other player at the 2018 World Cup in Russia and as a result spent a total of 14 minutes writhing on the ground.

Barcelona in 2013 for £48.6 million – making him the most expensive ever export from South America.

• After a mediocre first season with Barcelona, Neymar was on fire throughout 2014/15, impressing as part of a three-pronged strikeforce with Lionel Messi and Luis Suarez. He scored a total of 39 goals, including one against Juventus in the Champions League final and another in the final of the Copa del Rey against Athletic Bilbao as Barcelona stormed to a superb Treble. The following season he had to be satisfied with just a domestic Double, but again he scored in the Copa del Rey final, this time against Sevilla. In 2017 Neymar equalled a record set by the great Ferenc Puskas in 1962 when he scored in a third consecutive Copa Del Rey final, a 3-1 win over Alaves.

• **First capped by Brazil in 2010, Neymar has gone on to become the pin-up boy of Brazilian football and is now his country's third highest scorer of all time behind Pele and Ronaldo. At the 2014 World Cup he was Brazil's top scorer with four goals, despite missing his country's last**

Neymar's man-marker craftily hid inside the Brazil star's shirt

two matches through injury. Two years later he scored the winning goal in the shoot-out against Germany as Brazil won Olympic Gold on home soil.

NORTHAMPTON TOWN

Year founded: 1897
Ground: Sixfields Stadium (7,724)
Nickname: The Cobblers
Biggest win: 11-1 v Southend United (1909)
Heaviest defeat: 0-11 v Southampton (1901)

The club was founded at a meeting of local school teachers at the Princess Royal Inn in Northampton in 1897. After turning professional in 1901 Northampton were founder members of the Third Division in 1920.

• **The club's first full-time manager was Herbert Chapman (1907-12), who later became the first manager to win the league title with two different clubs, Huddersfield and Arsenal.**

• Despite being injured fighting in France during the Second World War, winger Tommy Fowler went on to make a record 552 appearances for the Cobblers between 1946 and 1961. His team-mate Jack English is the club's record scorer with a total of 143 goals.

• **Relegated from League One in 2018, the Cobblers enjoyed a rollercoaster decade in 1960s, rising from the old Fourth Division to the First in just six seasons. In the process they became the first club to rise through the three lower divisions to the top flight, before plummeting back down by 1969.**

• Cliff Holton scored a club record 36 league goals in 1961/62 – just two years after he had banged in a record 42 goals for Watford.

HONOURS
Division 3 champions 1963
League Two champions 2016
Division 4 champions 1987

Northern Ireland's talisman Norman Whiteside

NORTHERN IRELAND

First international: Northern Ireland 2 England 1, 1923
Most capped player: Pat Jennings, 119 caps (1964-86)
Leading goalscorer: David Healy, 36 goals (2000-13)
First World Cup appearance: Northern Ireland 1 Czechoslovakia 0 (1958)
Biggest win: Northern Ireland 7 Wales 0, 1930
Heaviest defeat: England 9 Northern Ireland 2, 1949

Until Trinidad and Tobago appeared at the 2006 tournament, Northern Ireland were the smallest country to qualify for a World Cup finals tournament. They have made it on three occasions, reaching the quarter-finals in 1958 and beating the hosts Spain in 1982 on their way to the second round.

• **Northern Ireland's Norman Whiteside is the youngest player ever to appear at the World Cup. He was aged just 17 years and 42 days when he played at the 1982 tournament in Spain, beating the previous record set by Pelé in 1958.**

• During the Euro 2008 qualifying campaign Northern Ireland's highest ever scorer David Healy scored a competition best 13 goals.

• **Under manager Michael O'Neill Northern Ireland qualified for the European Championships for the first** time in 2016. They did it in fine style too, becoming the first ever country from the fifth pot in the draw to top their qualifying group. At the finals they enjoyed their first ever win, beating Ukraine 2-0, before going out to Wales in the last 16.

• Northern Ireland were the last winners of the British Home Championship in 1984, topping the table on goal difference ahead of Wales, England and Scotland after all four countries finished level on points.

World Cup Record
1930 Did not enter
1934 Did not enter
1938 Did not enter
1950 Did not qualify
1954 Did not qualify
1958 Quarter-finalists
1962 Did not qualify
1966 Did not qualify
1970 Did not qualify
1974 Did not qualify
1978 Did not qualify
1982 Round 2
1986 Round 1
1990 Did not qualify
1994 Did not qualify
1998 Did not qualify
2002 Did not qualify
2006 Did not qualify
2010 Did not qualify
2014 Did not qualify
2018 Did not qualify

NORWICH CITY

Year founded: 1902
Ground: Carrow Road (27,244)
Nickname: The Canaries
Biggest win: 10-2 v Coventry City (1930)
Heaviest defeat: 2-10 v Swindon Town (1908)

Founded in 1902 by two school teachers, Norwich City soon found themselves in hot water with the FA and were expelled from the FA Amateur Cup in 1904 for being 'professional'. The club joined the Football League as founder members of the Third Division in 1920.

• Norwich were originally known as the Citizens, but adopted the nickname Canaries in 1907 as a nod

Guess which club culinary icon Delia Smith supports?

to the longstanding popularity of canary-keeping in the city – a result of 15th-century trade links with Flemish weavers who had brought the birds over to Europe from Dutch colonies in the Caribbean. Soon afterwards, the club changed their colours from blue and white to yellow and green.

• City fans enjoyed the greatest day in their history when Norwich beat Sunderland 1-0 at Wembley in 1985 to win the League Cup. However, joy soon turned to despair when the Canaries were relegated from the top flight at the end of the season, the first club to experience this particular mix of sweet and sour.

• Ron Ashman is the club's leading appearance maker, turning out in 592 league matches between 1947 and 1964. The Canaries' leading scorer is Ashman's team-mate John Gavin, who notched 122 league goals between 1948 and 1958.

• Now under the ownership of cook and recipe book author Delia Smith, Norwich came a best ever third in the inaugural Premiership season in 1992/93 – albeit with a goal difference of -4, the worst ever by a team finishing in the top three in the top flight. The following season the Canaries played in Europe for the first and only time, famously beating Bayern Munich away in the second round of the UEFA Cup – the only time a British club has won in the Olympic Stadium.

• **In January 2016 the Canaries splashed out a club record £9.1 million to bring Everton striker Steven Naismith to Carrow Road. In January 2017 Norwich received a club record £13 million when they sold midfielder Robbie Brady to Burnley.**

• Along with Crystal Palace, Middlesbrough, Sunderland and West Brom, Norwich have been relegated from the Premier League a record four times, most recently taking the plunge in 2016.

• **Defender Mark Bowen won a club record 35 caps for Wales while at Carrow Road between 1987 and 1996.**

HONOURS
First Division champions 2004
Division 2 champions 1972, 1986
League One champions 2010
Division 3 (South) champions 1934
League Cup 1985

NOTTINGHAM FOREST

Year founded: 1865
Ground: The City Ground (30,445)
Nickname: The Reds
Biggest win: 14-0 v Clapton (1891)
Heaviest defeat: 1-9 v Blackburn Rovers (1937)

One of the oldest clubs in the world, Nottingham Forest were founded in 1865 at a meeting at the Clinton Arms in Nottingham by a group of former players of 'shinty' (a form of hockey), who decided to switch sports to football.

• **Over the following years the club was at the forefront of important innovations in the game. For instance, shinguards were invented by Forest player Sam Widdowson in 1874, while four years later a referee's whistle** was first used in a match between Forest and Sheffield Norfolk. In 1890, a match between Forest and Bolton Wanderers was the first to feature goal nets.

• Forest enjoyed a golden era under legendary manager Brian Clough, who sat in the City Ground hotseat from 1975 until his retirement in 1993. After winning promotion to the top flight in 1977, the club won the league championship the following season – a feat that no promoted team has achieved since. Forest also won the League Cup to become the first side to win this particular double. Even more incredibly, the Reds went on to win the European Cup in 1979 with a 1-0 victory over Malmo in the final. The next year Forest retained the trophy, beating Hamburg 1-0 in the final in Madrid, to become the first and only team to win the European Cup more times than their domestic league.

• **Those glory days, however, felt very distant in 1999 when Forest became the first club to suffer the indignity of finishing rock bottom of the Premier League on three separate occasions.**

• In 1959, in the days before subs, Forest won the FA Cup despite being reduced to 10 men when Roy Dwight, an uncle of pop star Elton John, was carried off with a broken leg after 33 minutes of the final against Luton Town. It was the first time that a club had won the cup with fewer than 11 players.

• **Defender Bobby McKinlay, a member of that 1959 team, is Forest's longest serving player, turning out in 614 league games in 19 seasons at the club. The Reds' record scorer is Grenville Morris, who fell just one short of a double century of league goals for the club in the years before the First World War.**

• Hardman left-back Stuart 'Psycho' Pearce won a club record 76 caps for England while at the City Ground between 1987 and 1997.

• **The first club to spend a million pounds on a player (Birmingham City's Trevor Francis in 1979), Forest splashed out a club record £13.2 million on Benfica midfielder Joao Carvalho in June 2018. The previous summer Forest received a record £15 million when striker Britt Assombalonga moved to Middlesbrough.**

NOTTS COUNTY

Year founded: 1862
Ground: Meadow Lane (20,229)
Nickname: The Magpies
Biggest win: 15-0 v Rotherham (1885)
Heaviest defeat: 1-9 v Aston Villa (1888), v Blackburn (1889) and v Portsmouth (1927)

Notts County are the oldest professional football club in the world. Founded in 1862, the club were founder members of the Football League in 1888 and have since played a record 4,894 matches in the competition (losing a record 1,893 games).

• **In their long history County have swapped divisions more often than any other league club, winning 13 promotions and suffering the agony of relegation 16 times, most recently dropping into League Two in 2015.**

• The club's greatest ever day was way back in 1894 when, as a Second Division outfit, they won the FA Cup – the first time a team from outside the top flight had lifted the trophy. In the final at Goodison Park, County beat Bolton 4-1, with Jimmy Logan scoring the first ever hat-trick in the FA Cup final.

• **Striker Henry Cursham scored a competition record 48 goals for Notts County in the FA Cup between 1880 and 1887, playing alongside his two brothers in the same County team.**

• In their long and distinguished history Notts County have had 65 different managers, a record for an English club.

• **Notts County's Meadow Lane is just 330 yards from Nottingham Forest's City Ground, making the two clubs the nearest neighbours in the entire Football League.**

NUMBERS

Shirt numbers were first used in a First Division match by Arsenal against Sheffield Wednesday at Hillsborough on 25th August 1928. On the same day Chelsea also wore numbers for their Second Division fixture against Swansea at Stamford Bridge.

• **In 1933 teams wore numbers in the FA Cup final for the first time. Everton's players were numbered 1-11 while Manchester City's wore 12-22. Six years later, in 1939, the Football League made the use of shirt numbers obligatory for all teams.**

• England and Scotland first wore numbered shirts on 17th April 1937 for the countries' Home International fixture at

Richard Duffy of Notts County, the oldest football club in the world

After years in the doldrums, Rangers are taking off again

MARCUS RASHFORD

Born: Manchester, 31st October 1997
Position: Striker
Club career:
2016- Manchester United 78 (17)
International record:
2016- England 25 (3)

When, aged 18 and 208 days, Marcus Rashford opened the scoring for England in a 2-1 friendly win over Australia at the Stadium of Light in May 2016 he became the youngest ever scorer for his country on his debut, beating the record previously set by Tommy Lawton way back in 1938.

• On the books of Manchester United since the age of seven, Rashford enjoyed a sensational start to his Old Trafford career, scoring twice in a 5-1 thrashing of Danish side Midtjylland in the Europa League on 25th February 2016 to become the club's youngest ever scorer in European competition, eclipsing a record previously held by the legendary George Best.

• Three days later Rashford scored twice in a 3-2 home win over Arsenal, putting himself in third place in the list of United's youngest ever Premier League scorers behind Federico Macheda and Danny Welbeck. He then set another record by notching the winner away to Manchester City to become the youngest ever scorer in the Manchester derby.

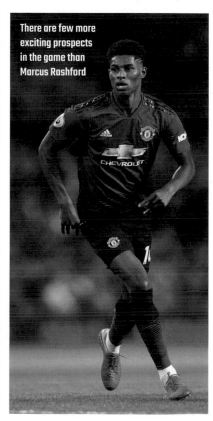

There are few more exciting prospects in the game than Marcus Rashford

• The club's record in the Scottish Cup is not quite as impressive, the Gers' 33 triumphs in the competition being bettered by Celtic's 38. However, it was in the Scottish Cup that Rangers recorded their biggest ever victory, thrashing Blairgowrie 14-2 in 1934. Striker Jimmy Fleming scored nine of the goals on the day to set a club record. Way back in 1887 Rangers reached the semi-final of the English FA Cup, but were beaten 3-1 by eventual winners Aston Villa.

• **Former Rangers boss Bill Struth is the most successful manager in the history of the British game, winning an incredible 18 league titles in a 34-year stint in the Ibrox hotseat between 1920 and 1954.**

• No player has turned out in the royal blue shirt of Rangers more often than former captain John Greig, who made 755 appearances in all competitions between 1961 and 1978. Famously, Greig led the Gers to their one success in continental competition, the European Cup Winners' Cup in 1972 when they beat Dynamo Moscow in the final.

• **Rangers are the only club to have won four different Scottish divisional titles, completing this feat in 2016 when the Gers topped the Championship table – the last stage of their return to the top flight after**

they were forced into liquidation in 2012 and made to start from scratch in the bottom tier.

HONOURS
SPL champions 1999, 2000, 2003, 2005, 2009, 2010, 2011
Premier League champions 1976, 1978, 1987, 1989, 1990, 1991, 1992, 1993, 1994, 1995, 1996, 1997
Division 1 champions 1891 (shared), 1899, 1900, 1901, 1902, 1911, 1912, 1913, 1918, 1920, 1921, 1923, 1924, 1925, 1927, 1928, 1929, 1930, 1931, 1933, 1934, 1935, 1937, 1939, 1947, 1949, 1950, 1953, 1956, 1957, 1959, 1961, 1963, 1964, 1975
Championship champions 2016
League One champions 2014
Third Division champions 2013
Scottish Cup 1894, 1897, 1898, 1903, 1928, 1930, 1932, 1934, 1935, 1936, 1948, 1949, 1950, 1953, 1960, 1962,1963, 1964, 1966, 1973, 1976, 1978, 1979, 1981, 1992, 1993, 1996, 1999, 2000, 2002, 2003, 2008, 2009
Scottish League Cup 1947, 1949, 1961, 1962, 1964, 1965, 1971, 1976, 1978, 1979, 1982, 1984, 1985, 1987, 1988, 1989, 1991, 1993, 1994, 1997, 1999, 2002, 2003, 2005, 2008, 2010, 2011
European Cup Winners' Cup 1972

• After enduring a disappointing 20-match run without a goal, Rashford ended the 2016/17 season on a high after helping United win the Europa League. At the end of the year he came third in the 'Golden Boy' poll for the best young player in Europe under the age of 21, behind winner Kylian Mbappe and Barcelona forward Ousmane Dembele.

• Fast, strong and a composed finisher in front of goal, Rashford was a surprise choice by then England manager Roy Hodgson for the 2016 European Championships, and when he came on in a 2-1 win against Wales became his country's youngest ever player at the finals, aged 18 and 229 days.

READING

Year founded: 1871
Ground: Madejski Stadium (24,161)
Nickname: The Royals
Biggest win: 10-2 v Crystal Palace (1946)
Heaviest defeat: 0-18 v Preston (1894)

Reading were founded in 1871, making them the oldest Football League club south of Nottingham. After amalgamating with local clubs Reading Hornets (in 1877) and Earley FC (in 1889), the club was eventually elected to the new Third Division in 1920.

• **The oldest club still competing in the FA Cup never to have won the trophy, Reading have got as far as the semi-finals just twice, losing to Cardiff City in 1927 and Arsenal in 2015.**

• In the 1985/86 season Reading set a Football League record by winning their opening 13 matches, an outstanding start which provided the launch pad for the Royals to go on to top the old Third Division at the end of the campaign.

• **Reading's greatest moment, though, came in 2006 when, under manager Steve Coppell, they won promotion to the top flight for the first time in their history. They went up in fine style, too, claiming the Championship title with a Football League record 106 points and going 33 matches unbeaten (a record for the second tier) between 9th August 2005 and 17th February 2006.**

Real Madrid usually have plenty to smile about

• Prolific marksman Ronnie Blackman holds two scoring records for the club, with a total of 158 goals between 1947 and 1954 and a seasonal best of 39 goals in the 1951/52 campaign. Defender Martin Hicks played in a record 500 league games for the Royals between 1978 and 1991.

• **During the 1978/79 season Reading goalkeeper Steve Death went 1,074 minutes without conceding a goal – a Football League record until 2009, when Manchester United's Edwin van der Sar beat it.**

• The Royals forked out a club record £7.5 million for Fulham striker Sone Aluko in August 2017. The club's bank balance was boosted by a record £6.6 million in August 2010 when stylish Icelandic midfielder Gylfi Sigurdsson joined German outfit Hoffenheim.

• **When Reading were beaten on penalties by Huddersfield Town in the 2017 Championship play-off final they matched Sheffield United's record of having lost four play-off finals.**

HONOURS
Championship champions 2006, 2012
Second Division champions 1994
Division 3 champions 1986
Division 3 (South) champions 1926
Division 4 champions 1979

REAL MADRID

Year founded: 1902
Ground: Estadio Bernabeu (81,044)
Previous name: Madrid
Nickname: Los Meringues
League titles: 33
Domestic cups: 18
European cups: 19
International cups: 6

Founded by students as Madrid FC in 1902, the title 'Real' (meaning 'Royal') was bestowed on the club by King Alfonso XIII in 1920.

• **One of the most famous names in world football, Real Madrid won the first ever European Cup in 1956 and went on to a claim a record five consecutive victories in the competition with a side featuring greats such as Alfredo di Stefano, Ferenc Puskas and Francisco Gento. Real's total of 13 victories in the European Cup/Champions League is also a record, and following their most recent success – a 3-1 defeat of Liverpool in the final in Kiev in 2018 – Real became the first club to win the trophy three times on the trot in the Champions League era.**

Sime Vrsaljko is a big fan of the old "What did I do ref?" defence

IS THAT A FACT?

Real Madrid scored in a European record 73 consecutive matches in all competitions between 30th April 2016 and 17th September 2017, the incredible run finally coming to an end with a shock 1-0 home defeat against Real Betis.

• The club have dominated Spanish football over the years, winning a record 33 league titles (eight more than nearest rivals Barcelona), including a record five on the trot on two occasions (1961-65 and 1986-90).

• **Real were unbeaten at home for a Spanish record 121 matches between February 1957 and March 1965.**

• Real have participated in the Champions League for a record 22 consecutive seasons since 1997/98.

HONOURS

Spanish League 1932, 1933, 1954, 1955, 1957, 1958, 1961, 1962, 1963, 1964, 1965, 1967, 1968, 1969, 1972, 1975, 1976, 1978, 1979, 1980, 1986, 1987, 1988, 1989, 1990, 1995, 1997, 2001, 2003, 2007, 2008, 2012, 2017
Spanish Cup 1905, 1906, 1907, 1908, 1917, 1934, 1936, 1946, 1947, 1962, 1970, 1974, 1975, 1980, 1982, 1989, 1993, 2011, 2014
European Cup/Champions League 1956, 1957, 1958, 1959, 1960, 1966, 1998, 2000, 2002, 2014, 2016, 2017, 2018
UEFA Cup 1985, 1986
European Super Cup 2002, 2014, 2016, 2017
Intercontinental Cup/Club World Cup 1960, 1998, 2002, 2014, 2016, 2017

REFEREES

In the 19th century Colonel Francis Marindin was the referee at a record nine FA Cup finals, including eight on the trot between 1883 and 1990. His record will never be beaten as the FA now appoints a different referee for the FA Cup final every year.

• **The first referee to send off a player in the FA Cup final was Peter Willis,** who dismissed Manchester United defender Kevin Moran in the 1985 final for a foul on Everton's Peter Reid. Video replays showed that it was a harsh decision.

• Uzbek referee Ravshan Irmatov has taken charge of a record 11 World Cup matches across the 2010, 2014 and 2018 tournaments.

• **On 9th February 2010 Amy Fearn became the first woman to referee a Football League match when she took charge of the last 20 minutes of Coventry's home game with Notts Forest after the original ref, Tony Bates, limped off with a calf injury.**

• In the 2003/04 season Rob Styles brandished a record 12 red cards in Premier League matches. Meanwhile, card-happy refs Martin Atkinson (in 2009/10 and 2014/15) and Bobby Madley (in 2016/17) share the record for yellows with 125 each.

• **In one of the most bizarre incidents ever in the history of football, a referee scored in a Division Three fixture between Plymouth and Barrow in 1968. A shot from a Barrow player was heading wide until it deflected off the boot of referee Ivan Robinson and into the Pilgrims' net for the only goal of the match.**

RELEGATION

Birmingham City boast the unwanted record of having been relegated from the top flight more often than any other club, having taken the drop 12 times – most recently in 2010/11. However, the Blues have not experienced that sinking feeling as often as Notts County, who have suffered 16 relegations in total. Meanwhile, Bristol City were the first club to suffer three consecutive relegations, dropping from Division One to Division Four between 1979/80 and 1981/82 – a fate matched by Wolves between 1983/84 and 1985/86.

• **In the Premier League era Crystal Palace, Middlesbrough, Norwich City, Sunderland and West Brom have dropped out of the top flight on a joint-record four occasions. In 1993 the Eagles were desperately unlucky to go down with a record 49 points, a tally matched by Norwich in 1985 in the old First Division. Southend in 1988/89 and Peterborough in 2012/13 were even more unfortunate, being relegated from the old Third Division and the Championship respectively despite amassing 54 points.**

• Manchester City are the only club to be relegated a year after winning the league title. Following their championship success in 1937 City went down in 1938 despite being top scorers in the First Division with 80 goals. The Mancunians also suffered another bizarre relegation in 1909 when they stayed out of the drop zone all season until Liverpool's 1-0 win at Newcastle two days after City's last fixture sent them down.

• **When Derby County went down from the Premier League in 2008, they did so with the lowest points total of any club in the history of English league football. The Rams accumulated only 11 points in a miserable campaign, during which they managed to win just one match out of 38.**

• SV Lohhof (2000-2003) and FC Kempton (2008-2011) have both suffered a record four consecutive relegations in German regional football.

REPLAYS

In the days before penalty shoot-outs, the FA Cup fourth qualifying round tie between Alvechurch and Oxford City went to a record five replays before Alvechurch reached the first round proper with a 1-0 win in the sixth match between the two clubs.

• **The first FA Cup final to go to a replay was the 1875 match between Royal Engineers and Old Etonians, Engineers winning 2-0 in the second match. The last FA Cup final to require** a replay was the 1993 match between Arsenal and Sheffield Wednesday, the Gunners triumphing 2-1 in the second game. In 1999 the FA elected to scrap final replays, ruling that any drawn match would be settled on the day by a penalty shoot-out.

• In 1912 Barnsley required a record six replays in total before getting their hands on the FA Cup. Fulham also played six replays in their run to the FA Cup final in 1975, but the extra games appeared to have taken their toll on the team as they lost limply 2-0 to West Ham at Wembley.

• **The only European Cup final to go to a replay was in 1974 when Bayern Munich drew 1-1 with Atletico Madrid in Brussels before the Germans won the second match 4-0 two days later.**

Andy Robertson has come a long way since his days with Queen's Park

REPUBLIC OF IRELAND

First international: Republic of Ireland 1 Bulgaria 0, 1924
Most capped player: Robbie Keane, 146 caps (1998-2016)
Leading goalscorer: Robbie Keane, 68 goals (1998-2016)
First World Cup appearance: Republic of Ireland 1 England 1, 1990
Biggest win: 8-0 v Malta (1983)
Heaviest defeat: 0-7 v Brazil (1982)

The Republic of Ireland enjoyed their most successful period under English manager Jack Charlton in the late 1980s and early 1990s. 'Big Jack' became a legend on the Emerald Isle after guiding the Republic to their first ever World Cup in 1990, taking the team to the quarter-finals of the tournament – despite not winning a single match – before they were eliminated by hosts Italy.

• **Ireland have since appeared at two more World Cups in 1994 and 2002, reaching the second round on both occasions before losing to the Netherlands and Spain respectively.**

• In 2009, in a World Cup play-off against France, the Republic were on the wrong end of one of the worst refereeing decisions of all time when Thierry Henry's blatant handball went unpunished before he crossed for William Gallas to score the goal that ended

Ireland's hopes of reaching the 2010 finals in South Africa. The Republic were also in a play-off for a place at Russia 2018 but could have no complaints about a 5-1 aggregate defeat to a Christian Eriksen-inspired Denmark.

• **The Republic have qualified for the European Championships on three occasions, reaching the knock-out stages for the first time at Euro 2016 thanks to a famous 1-0 win over Italy. However, a 2-1 defeat against hosts France ended their hopes of any further progress.**

• Republic of Ireland striker Robbie Keane has won more caps (146) and scored more international goals (68) than any other player from the British Isles.

World Cup Record
1930 Did not enter
1934 Did not qualify
1938 Did not qualify
1950 Did not enter
1954-86 Did not qualify
1990 Quarter-finals
1994 Round 2
1998 Did not qualify
2002 Round 2
2006 Did not qualify
2010 Did not qualify
2014 Did not qualify
2018 Did not qualify

ANDY ROBERTSON

Born: Glasgow, 11th March 1994
Position: Defender
Club career:
2012-13 Queen's Park 34 (2)
2013-14 Dundee United 36 (3)
2014-17 Hull City 99 (3)
2017- Liverpool 22 (1)
International record:
2014- Scotland 22 (2)

In his debut season at Liverpool pacy left-back Andy Robertson was one of the Reds' outstanding performers in a memorable campaign which saw them finish fourth in the Premier League and reach the final of the Champions League, which they lost 3-1 to Real Madrid.

• **Robertson started out as an amateur at Queen's Park before joining Dundee United in 2013. In his one season at Tannadice he helped the Terrors reach the Scottish Cup final, which they lost to St Johnstone, and was voted Scotland's Young Player of the Year.**

• His impressive displays earned Robertson a £2.85 million move to Hull City, with whom he won promotion to the Premier League via the play-offs in 2016. The Tigers fell back down to the Championship the following year, but Robertson's consistent performances persuaded Liverpool to part with £8 million for his services in the summer of 2017.

• After winning four caps at Under-21 level, Robertson was rewarded with his senior Scotland debut in a friendly against Poland in March 2014. Later that year he scored his first goal for his country with a low left-foot shot in a 3-1 friendly defeat to arch rivals England at Celtic Park.

ROCHDALE

Year founded: 1907
Ground: Spotland Stadium (10,249)
Nickname: The Dale
Biggest win: 8-1 v Chesterfield (1926)
Heaviest defeat: 1-9 v Tranmere Rovers (1931)

Founded at a meeting at the town's Central Council Office in 1907, Rochdale were elected to the Third Division (North) as founder members in 1921.

• The proudest day in the club's history came in 1962 when they reached the League Cup final. Rochdale lost 4-0 on aggregate to Norwich City, then in the Second Division, but took pride in becoming the first team from the bottom tier to reach a major cup final. The Dale's manager at the time was Tony Collins, the first ever black boss of a league club.

• Rochdale failed to win a single game in the FA Cup for 18 years from 1927 – the longest period of time any club has gone without victory in the competition. The appalling run finally came to an end in 1945 when the Dale beat Stockport 2-1 in a first-round replay.

• There was more misery for fans of the Dale in 1973/74 when their heroes won just two league games in the old Third Division – the worst ever return in a 46-match campaign.

• Midfielder Gary Jones made a record 467 league

appearances for the Dale in two spells at the club between 1998 and 2012. The club's top marksman is Reg Jenkins, who scored 119 league goals between 1964 and 1973.

BRENDAN RODGERS

Born: Carnlough, 26th January 1973
Managerial career:
2008-09 Watford
2009 Reading
2010-12 Swansea City
2012-15 Liverpool
2016- Celtic

When Celtic beat Motherwell 2-0 in the 2018 Scottish Cup final Brendan Rodgers became the first manager in British football history to lead his club to a 'Double-Treble', the Glasgow giants cleaning up all three domestic trophies for a second successive season.

• **Since being appointed Celtic boss in May 2016 Rodgers has enjoyed unparalleled success. In his first season in charge he led his new club through the Premiership campaign undefeated – the first time this had happened in the Scottish top flight since 1899 – as Celtic won the league with a record 106 points. Rodgers**

Brendan Rodgers is aiming for a 'Treble-Treble'

also saw his team set a new British record by going 69 domestic matches undefeated, a run which finally ended with a shock 4-0 defeat at Hearts on 17th December 2017.

• After injury forced him to retire aged just 20, Rodgers moved into youth coaching at Reading and Chelsea. He became Watford manager in 2008 and the following year took over as Reading, but was soon sacked after a bad run of results. He enjoyed greater success at Swansea, who he led into the Premier League via the play-offs in 2011.

• In June 2012 Rodgers became Liverpool manager and enjoyed a great season with the Reds in 2013/14, leading them to second place in the Premier League. His efforts saw him voted LMA Manager of the Year – the first Liverpool boss ever to win this award – but a steady decline in the club's fortunes led to him being dismissed from his post in October 2015.

AS ROMA

Year founded: 1927
Ground: Stadio Olimpico (70,634)
Nickname: I Lupi ('The Wolves')
League titles: 3
Domestic cups: 9
European cups: 1

Associazione Sportiva Roma were founded in 1927 following the merger of four clubs from the Italian capital and have since spent all but one season in the top flight of Italian football.

• **I Lupi ('The Wolves'), as they are known, have only occasionally managed to break the domination of their main rivals in northern Italy, winning just three Italian league titles. They've had more success in the Coppa Italia with nine wins, a record only bettered by Juventus' 13 triumphs.**

• Champions League semi-finalists in 2018, Roma have just one European title to their name, beating Birmingham City 4-2 on aggregate in the 1961 Fairs

Cup final. In 1984 they reached the European Cup final but lost on penalties on their own ground to Liverpool after a 1-1 draw.

• **Roma legend Francesco Totti is the second highest goalscorer in the history of Serie A, with an incredible 250 goals, including a record 71 from the penalty spot. His total of 619 appearances in Serie A (all for Roma) puts him third on the all-time list behind former AC Milan defender Paolo Maldini (647) and Juventus goalkeeper Gianluigi Buffon (638).**

> **HONOURS**
> *Italian champions* 1942, 1983, 2001
> *Italian Cup* 1964, 1969, 1980, 1981, 1984, 1986, 1991, 2007, 2008
> *Fairs Cup* 1961

CRISTIANO RONALDO

> **Born:** Madeira, Portugal, 5th February 1985
> **Position:** Winger/striker
> **Club career:**
> 2001-03 Sporting Lisbon 25 (3)
> 2003-09 Manchester United 196 (84)
> 2009-18 Real Madrid 292 (311)
> 2018- Juventus
> **International record:**
> 2003- Portugal 154 (85)

Now with Juventus following his £99.2 million transfer from Real Madrid in July 2018, Cristiano Ronaldo is the all-time leading scorer in the Champions League with a total of 120 goals for Manchester United and Real, including a record 58 in the knock-out stages and a record 17 in the 2013/14 season. He is also Real's all-time leading scorer with an incredible 450 goals in all competitions, a total which includes a record 34 hat-tricks in La Liga.

• **Born on the Portuguese island of Madeira, Ronaldo began his career with Sporting Lisbon before joining Manchester United in a £12.25 million deal in 2003. The following year he won his first trophy with the Red Devils, opening the scoring as United beat Millwall 3-0 in the FA Cup final. He later helped United win a host of major honours, including three Premiership titles and the Champions League in 2008 before signing for Real for a then world record £80 million in 2009.**

• In 2007 Ronaldo was voted PFA Player of the Year and Young Player of the Year, the first man to achieve this double since Andy Gray in 1977. The following season he scored a remarkable 42 goals for United in all competitions, and won the European Golden Boot. Three years later, in his second season with Real, he became the first player ever to win the award in two different countries. He has gone on to win two La Liga titles and the Champions League four times with Real, in 2014, 2016, 2017 and 2018, and is the only player in the modern era to score in three finals.

• **Arguably the most exciting talent in world football today, Ronaldo is the only player from the Premier League to have been voted World Footballer of the Year, having collected this most prestigious of awards in 2008. After playing second fiddle for some years to his great rival Lionel Messi, he is now equalled the** Barcelona magician's five awards after collecting the FIFA Best Men's Player gong in 2016 and 2017.

• Captain of Portugal since 2008, Ronaldo has played for his country a record 154 times and scored an incredible 85 goals – a tally unmatched by any European player in history. After coming close a number of times, he finally led his nation to glory at Euro 2016, although he had to limp off in the first half of Portugal's eventual 1-0 defeat of hosts France in the final in Paris. His tally of nine goals at the European Championships is a joint record, and he has also made a record 21 appearances at the finals.

The great Cristiano Ronaldo, the top scorer in the history of the Champions League

TOP 10

EUROPEAN INTERNATIONAL GOALSCORERS

1. Cristiano Ronaldo (Portugal, 2003-) — 85
2. Ferenc Puskas (Hungary, Spain, 1945-62) — 84
3. Sandor Kocsis (Hungary, 1948-56) — 75
4. Miroslav Klose (Germany, 2001-14) — 71
5. Gerd Muller (Germany, 1966-74) — 68
   Robbie Keane (Republic of Ireland, 1998-2016) — 68
7. Zlatan Ibrahimovic (Sweden, 2001-16) — 62
8. Imre Schlosser (Hungary, 1906-27) — 59
   David Villa (Spain, 2005-17) — 59
10. Jan Koller (Czech Republic, 1999-2009) — 55
    Robert Lewandowski (Poland, 2008-) — 55

England's all-time top scorer Wayne Rooney

WAYNE ROONEY

Born: Liverpool, 24th October 1985
Position: Striker/midfielder
Club career:
2002-04 Everton 67 (15)
2004-17 Manchester United 393 (183)
2017-18 Everton 31 (10)
2018- DC United 6 (1)
International record:
2003-16 England 119 (53)

With 53 goals for England and 253 in all competitions for Manchester United, Wayne Rooney is the leading all-time scorer for both the Red Devils and the Three Lions. In both cases, he passed longstanding benchmarks set in the early 1970s by another United and England legend, Sir Bobby Charlton. Rooney's total of 119 England caps, meanwhile, is a record for an outfield player and only surpassed by goalkeeper Peter Shilton.

• Rooney burst onto the scene with Everton in 2002, scoring his first league goal for the Toffees with a magnificent 20-yarder against reigning champions Arsenal at Goodison Park just five days before his 17th birthday. At the time he was the youngest ever Premiership scorer, but his record has since been surpassed by both James Milner and James Vaughan.

• After starring for England at Euro 2004 Rooney signed for Manchester United later that summer for £25.6 million, to become the world's most expensive teenage footballer. He started his Old Trafford career in sensational style with a hat-trick against Fenerbahce and until he returned on a free transfer to Everton in July 2017 played a pivotal role for the Red Devils, winning five Premier League titles, three League Cups, the FA Cup, the Champions League and, in his last match for United, the Europa League.

• When his career in England ended in June 2018 with a move to MLS outfit DC United, Rooney had amassed 208 Premier League goals – a total only bettered by Alan Shearer. During the 2016/17 season he also became United's record scorer in European football, when he banged in his 39th goal against Feyenoord. His total of 30 goals in the Champions League is a record for a British player.

• Rooney is the youngest ever England player to play 100 times for his country, reaching the landmark against Slovenia on 15th November 2014 aged 29 and 22 days. He fittingly marked the occasion with a goal from the penalty spot in a 3-1 Wembley win.

• When Wayne Rooney scored his first goal for England, against Macedonia in a Euro 2004 qualifier on 6th September 2003, he was aged just 17 years and 317 days – the youngest player ever to find the net for the Three Lions.

ROTHERHAM UNITED

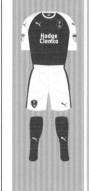

Year founded: 1925
Ground: New York Stadium (12,021)
Nickname: The Millers
Biggest win: 8-0 v Oldham Athletic (1947)
Heaviest defeat: 1-11 v Bradford City (1928)

The club had its origins in Thornhill FC (founded in 1878, later becoming Rotherham County) and Rotherham

Town, who merged with County to form Rotherham United in 1925.

• **The club's greatest moment came in 1961 when they reached the first ever League Cup final, losing 3-2 on aggregate to Aston Villa.** Six years earlier Rotherham had missed out on goal average on securing promotion to the First Division – the closest they've ever been to playing top-flight football.

• Gladstone Guest scored a record 130 goals for the Millers between 1946 and 1956, while his team-mate Danny Williams played a club best 459 games in midfield.

• **Centre back Kari Arnason played in a club record 36 matches for Iceland while with the Millers between 2012 and 2015.**

• Relegated from the Championship in 2017, Rotherham bounced back at the first attempt thanks to a 2-1 victory against Shrewsbury Town in the League One play-off final. With Blackburn and Wigan accompanying the Millers back up, it was the first time since 2007 that three relegated clubs from the same division had won promotion the following season.

HONOURS
Division 3 champions 1981
Division 3 (North) champions 1951
Division 4 champions 1989
Football League Trophy 1996

RUSSIA

First international: Soviet Union 3 Turkey 0, 1924
Most capped player: Sergei Ignashevich, 120 caps (2002-)
Leading goalscorer: Oleg Blokhin, 42 goals (1972-88)
First World Cup appearance: Soviet Union 2 England 2, 1958
Biggest win: Soviet Union 11 India 1, 1955
Heaviest defeat: Germany 16 Russian Empire 0, 1912

The successor to the old Soviet Union which broke up into its constituent parts in the early 1990s, Russia hosted the World Cup for the first time in 2018 and

Russia's Artem Dzyuba is either celebrating scoring against Saudi Arabia at the 2018 World Cup or showing people just how proud he is of his thighs!

reached the quarter-finals before losing on penalties to Croatia.

• **Russia gained its only major success as the Soviet Union way back in 1960 when they came from behind to beat Yugoslavia 2-1 in the final of the inaugural European Championships in Paris.** The Soviets also reached the final of the same competition in 1988 but lost 2-0 to a highly talented Netherlands team in Munich.

• The country's best showing at the World Cup was in 1966 when a Soviet team featuring legendary black-clad goalkeeper Lev Yashin reached the semi-finals of the tournament in England before losing 2-1 to West Germany

• **Four years later the Soviet Union became the first country ever to use a substitute at the World Cup finals when Anatoliy Puzach replaced Viktor Serebryanikov at half-time during the tournament's opening fixture, a drab 0-0 draw with hosts Mexico.**

• Since the demise of the Soviet Union, Russia have performed disappointingly for such a large country, although they did reach the semi-finals of Euro 2008.

• Russia hosted the Confederations Cup for the first time in 2017, but sadly for their passionate fans made an early exit after failing to qualify from the group stages.

HONOURS
European Championships winners 1960
World Cup Record
1930-54 Did not enter
1958 Quarter-finals
1962 Quarter-finals
1966 Fourth place
1970 Quarter-finals
1974 Disqualified
1978 Did not qualify
1982 Round 2
1986 Round 2
1990 Round 1
1994 Round 1
1998 Did not qualify
2002 Round 1
2006 Did not qualify
2010 Did not qualify
2014 Round 1
2018 Quarter-finals

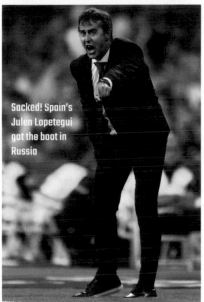

Sacked! Spain's Julen Lopetegui got the boot in Russia

SACKINGS

A joint-record 10 managers were sacked during the 2017/18 Premier League season, equalling the benchmark set in 2013/14. Among those to get the boot were Tony Pulis and Alan Pardew (both West Brom), Ronald Koeman (Everton) and fellow Dutchman Frank de Boer, whose reign at Crystal Palace lasted just five matches – the shortest ever tenure for a permanent Premier League boss.

• In 1959 Bill Lambton got the boot from Scunthorpe United after just three days in the managerial hotseat, an English league record. His reign at the Old Showground took in just one match – a 3-0 defeat at Liverpool in a Second Division fixture.

• In May 2007 Leroy Rosenior was sacked as manager of Conference side Torquay United after just 10 minutes in charge! No sooner had the former West Ham and QPR striker been unveiled as the Gulls' new boss when he was told that the club had been bought by a business consortium and his services were no longer required.

• **Notts County have sacked more managers than any other Football League club. When Harry Kewell took**

over at Meadow Lane in August 2018 he was the Magpies' 66th boss in their 149-year history.

• In 1998 Saudi Arabia boss Carlos Alberto Parreira was sacked during the World Cup after his side were eliminated having lost their first two matches. Mohammed Al-Kharashy took over for the final group game, a 2-2 draw with South Africa.

• **Even more shocking, though, was the dismissal of Spain boss Julen Lopetegui, just two days before the team's opening fixture at the 2018 World Cup against Portugal. Lopetegui was sacked after Real Madrid announced he would be their new coach for the 2018/19 season, with former Real star Fernando Hierro taking over his national team role for the tournament.**

ST JOHNSTONE

Year founded: 1884
Ground: McDiarmid Park (10,696)
Nickname: The Saints
Biggest win: 13-0 v Tulloch (1887)
Heaviest defeat: 0-12 v Cowdenbeath (1928)

St Johnstone were founded in 1884 by a group of local cricketers in Perth who wanted to keep fit in winter.

• **The Saints enjoyed their best ever day in 2014, when they beat Dundee United 2-0 in the Scottish Cup final at Celtic Park. Previously, the club had appeared in two League Cup finals, but lost in 1969 to Celtic and again in 1998 to Rangers.**

• Stalwart defender Steven Anderson has made a record 361 appearances for the Saints since making his debut in 2004. The club's leading scorer is John Brogan who rifled in 140 goals in all competitions between 1977 and 1984.

• **Along with Falkirk, St Johnstone have won the Scottish second tier a record seven times, most recently claiming the First Division title in 2009 while going on a club record unbeaten run of 21 games.**

• Midfielder Nick Dasovic won a club record 26 caps for Canada while at McDiarmid Park between 1996 and 2002.

ST MIRREN

Year founded: 1877
Ground: St Mirren Park (8,023)
Nickname: The Buddies
Biggest win: 15-0 v Glasgow University (1960)
Heaviest defeat: 0-9 v Rangers (1897)

Named after the patron saint of Paisley, St Mirren were founded in 1877 by a group of local cricketers and rugby players. The club were founder members of the Scottish League in 1890, but have never finished higher than third in the top flight.

• **Championship title winners in 2018, the Buddies have triumphed in the Scottish Cup three times, most recently in 1987 when they beat Dundee United 1-0 in the final after extra-time – the last time that the winners have fielded an all-Scottish line-up.**

• St Mirren have won the League Cup just once, beating Hearts 3-2 in an exciting final at Hampden Park in 2013.

• **Midfielder Hugh Murray played in a club record 424 games for the Buddies between 1996 and 2012. The club's top scorer is David McCrae who notched an impressive 221 goals between 1923 and 1934.**

• St Mirren defender Andy Millen holds the record for the oldest player ever to appear in the SPL, turning out for the Buddies for the last time in a 1-1 draw with Hearts aged 42 and 279 days on 15th March 2008.

"I wouldn't mind having that scarf, actually – it gets quite chilly at Anfield sometimes"

MOHAMED SALAH

Born: Basyoun, Egypt, 15th June 1992
Position: Winger/striker
Club career:
2010-12 El Mokawloon 38 (11)
2012-14 Basel 47 (9)
2014-16 Chelsea 13 (2)
2015 Fiorentina (loan) 16 (6)
2015-16 Roma (loan) 34 (14)
2016-17 Roma 31 (15)
2017- Liverpool 36 (32)
International record:
2011- Egypt 59 (35)

In a glorious debut season with Liverpool in 2017/18 following a £36.9 million move from Roma, Egypt international Mohamed Salah won the Golden Boot after scoring 32 Premier League goals – a record for a 38-match campaign. He also won both Player of the Year awards and became the first man ever to win three Premier League Player of the Month awards. However, Salah's season ended in deep disappointment when he had to be subbed off in Liverpool's Champions League final defeat by Real Madrid with a shoulder injury.

• A speedy and direct striker who began his career as a winger, Salah started out with Cairo club El Mokawloon before moving to Basel in 2012. After winning consecutive Swiss championships, Salah joined Chelsea in 2014, having impressed the Londoners' hierarchy by scoring in three European matches against the Blues.

• He failed to establish himself at Stamford Bridge, though, and in February 2015 he was loaned out to Fiorentina. Another loan at Roma followed, and after Salah topped the club's scoring charts with 14 Serie A goals in 2015/16 the move was made permanent in a £16 million deal.

• First capped by Egypt in 2011, Salah was joint-top scorer in the African section of the 2014 World Cup qualifiers with six goals. In 2017 he was part of the Egypt team which reached the final of the Africa Cup of Nations, losing 2-1 to Cameroon. Despite not being fully fit at the 2018 World Cup in Russia, he became the first Egyptian to score twice at the tournament since 1934 with strikes against Russia and Saudi Arabia.

ALEXIS SANCHEZ

Born: Tocopilla, Chile, 19th December 1988
Position: Winger/striker
Club career:
2005-06 Cobreloa 47 (12)
2006-07 Colo-Colo 32 (5)
2007-08 River Plate 23 (4)
2008-11 Udinese 95 (20)
2011-14 Barcelona 88 (39)
2014-18 Arsenal 122 (60)
2018- Manchester United 12 (2)
International record:
2006- Chile 121 (39)

Manchester United forward Alexis Sanchez is the only South American to score in two FA Cup finals. The Chilean achieved this feat before joining the Red Devils from Arsenal in January 2018 in an exchange deal with Henrikh Mkhitaryan, hitting the target in the Gunners' victories over Aston Villa in 2015 and Chelsea two years later.

• Sanchez made his name with Italian side Udinese, before joining Barcelona in 2011. He won the Copa del Rey with the Catalan giants in 2012 and La Liga the following year.

Alexis Sanchez is Chile's all-time top scorer

• When he scored three goals for Arsenal in a 5-2 win at Leicester in September 2015 Sanchez became the first ever player to score hat-tricks in the Premier League, La Liga and Serie A. His impressive tally of 15 league goals away from home in 2016/17 was the best return for an Arsenal player for 82 years.

• Sanchez made his debut for Chile against New Zealand in 2006 and is now his country's highest scorer of all time with 39 goals in a record 121 appearances. In 2015 he starred in Chile's first ever Copa America triumph, scoring the winning penalty as the hosts beat Argentina on spot-kicks in the final, and the following year he was named Player of the Tournament as Chile retained the trophy in the USA.

Leroy Sane, the 2018 PFA Young Player of the Year

LEROY SANE

Born: Essen, Germany, 11th January 1996
Position: Winger
Club career:
2014-16 Schalke 47 (11)
2016- Manchester City 58 (15)
International record:
2015- Germany 12 (0)

A talented winger who can race past defenders with a sudden blistering burst of acceleration, Leroy Sane was voted PFA Young Player of the Year in 2018 after an excellent campaign with Premier League champions Manchester City. The German's total of 15 assists was only bettered by team-mate Kevin de Bruyne, and he also chipped in with 14 goals in all competitions.

• Sane joined City from Schalke for £37 million in August 2016. After a relatively slow start at the Etihad, Sane's form improved to such an extent that he was nominated for the PFA Young Player of the Year award in 2017, although he was pipped in the final poll by Tottenham's Dele Alli.

• Sane can thank both his parents for providing him with excellent sporting genes. His father was an international footballer for Senegal, while his mother was a gymnast who competed for West Germany at the 1984 Olympics.

• After representing Germany at both Under-19 and Under-21 level, Sane made his full international debut in a 2-0 friendly defeat by France in Paris in November 2015 – a match which was overshadowed by a series of terrorist attacks in the French capital on the same night. To the surprise of many pundits, he was left out of Germany's squad for the 2018 World Cup in Russia.

MAURIZIO SARRI

Born: Naples, Italy, 10th January 1959
Managerial career:
2005-06 Pescara
2006-07 Arezzo
2007 Avellino
2008 Hellas Verona
2008-09 Perugia
2010-11 Alessandria
2011-12 Sorrento
2012-15 Empoli
2015-18 Napoli
2018- Chelsea

Appointed Chelsea manager in July 2018, Maurizio is the sixth Italian to occupy the Stamford Bridge hotseat,

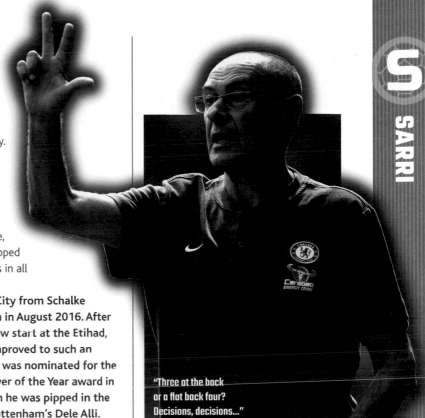

"Three at the back or a flat back four? Decisions, decisions..."

following Gianluca Vialli, Claudio Ranieri, Carlo Ancelotti, Roberto di Matteo and his predecessor Antonio Conte. No other English club has had so many managers from a single country outside of the British Isles.

• After playing amateur football and working for the world's oldest bank, the Banca Monte dei Paschi di Siena, Sarri devoted himself to coaching, taking a string of jobs with lowly Italian clubs. He got his first big break with Serie B outfit Pescara in 2005 but had to wait until 2014 for his first real success, guiding Empoli back into Serie A after a six-year absence.

• In 2015 Sarri replaced Rafa Benitez as boss of Napoli, and over the next three seasons he turned his hometown club into the main challengers to perennial champions Juventus. After leading Napoli to second place in 2016, the attack-minded Sarri was voted Serie A Coach of the Year the following year after the southern Italians scored an all-time league record 94 goals when finishing third. In 2018 Napoli again came third, this time with a club record 91 points.

• A fiery character who is often seen with a cigarette dangling between his lips, Sarri was fined 20,000 euros and banned for two Coppa Italia matches in January 2016 after directing homophobic abuse at Roberto Mancini, then the manager of Inter Milan. He subsequently apologised.

KASPER SCHMEICHEL

Born: Copenhagen, Denmark, 5th November 1986
Position: Goalkeeper
Club career:
2005-09 Manchester City 8
2006 Darlington (loan) 4
2006 Bury (loan) 29
2007 Falkirk (loan) 15
2007-08 Cardiff City (loan) 14
2008 Coventry City (loan) 9
2009-10 Notts County 43
2010-11 Leeds United 37
2011- Leicester City 263
International record:
2013- Denmark 39

Kasper Schmeichel became the first biological son of a Premier League-winning father to also lift the trophy when he helped surprise package Leicester City top the table in 2016, playing every minute of the campaign. His father, Peter, had previously won the title five times with Manchester United, a record for a goalkeeper. The following season he became the first goalkeeper in Champions League history to save a penalty in both legs of a knock-out tie when he twice denied Sevilla from the spot during the Foxes' 3-2 aggregate last-16 win.

• Schmeichel started out with **Manchester City but failed to hold down a first-team place and was loaned out to five other clubs before moving to Notts County in 2009, with whom he won the League Two title the following year.**

• After spending a season with Leeds United in 2010/11, Schmeichel joined Leicester and began to impress with some tremendous performances between the goalposts. He was voted into the Championship Team of the Year in 2013 and the next season was in fine form again as the Foxes won the Championship at a canter with a club record 102 points.

• **During the 2017/18 season Schmeichel went 571 minutes without conceding a goal for Denmark, breaking a record previously held by his father. At the World Cup in Russia he saved a penalty from Luka Modric in extra-time during Denmark's last 16 tie with Croatia but, despite making two more saves in the shoot-out that followed the two teams' 1-1 draw, couldn't prevent his country losing on spot-kicks.**

SCOTLAND

First international: Scotland 0 England 0, 1872
Most capped player: Kenny Dalglish, 102 caps (1971-86)
Leading goalscorer: Denis Law (1958-74) and Kenny Dalglish (1971-86), 30 goals
First World Cup appearance: Scotland 0 Austria 1, 1954
Biggest win: Scotland 11 Ireland 0, 1901
Heaviest defeat: Scotland 0 Uruguay 7, 1954

Along with England, Scotland are the oldest international team in the world. The two countries played the first official international way back in 1872, the match at Hamilton Crescent, Partick, finishing 0-0. Scotland were by far the dominant team in Britain in those early years, losing just two of their first 43 internationals.

• **It took the Scots a while to make an impression on the world scene, however. After withdrawing from the 1950 World Cup, Scotland competed in the finals for the first time in 1954 but were eliminated in the first round after suffering their worst ever defeat, 7-0 to reigning champions Uruguay.**

• Scotland have taken part in the World Cup finals on eight occasions but have never got beyond the group stage – a record for the tournament. They have been unlucky, though, going out in 1974, 1978 and 1982 only on goal difference. Since a poor showing at the 1998 finals the Scots have failed to qualify for five consecutive finals – the worst run in their history.

• **Scotland have a pretty poor record in the European Championships, only qualifying for the finals on two occasions, in 1992 and 1996. Again, they failed to reach the knockout stage both times, although they were unfortunate to lose out on the 'goals scored' rule to Holland at Euro '96.**

• Scotland had a good record in the Home Championships until the tournament was scrapped in 1984, winning the competition 24 times and sharing the title another 17 times. Only England (34 outright wins and 20 shared) have a better overall record.

• A European record crowd of 149,415 watched Scotland beat England 3-1 at Hampden Park in the Home Championships in 1937.

• Scotland's only foreign manager was German World Cup winner Berti Vogts, who lifted the trophy as a player in 1974. Vogts was in charge from 2002 to 2004 but the experiment was not successful, with Scotland slipping to their lowest ever ranking, 77, at the time of his departure.

World Cup Record
1930-38 Did not enter
1950 Withdrew
1954 Round 1
1958 Round 1
1962-70 Did not qualify
1974 Round 1
1978 Round 1
1982 Round 1
1986 Round 1
1990 Round 1
1994 Did not qualify
1998 Round 1
2002 Did not qualify
2006 Did not qualify
2010 Did not qualify
2014 Did not qualify
2018 Did not qualify

SCOTTISH CUP

The Scottish Cup was first played for in 1873/74, shortly after the formation of the Scottish FA. Queen's Park, who the previous year had competed in the English FA Cup, were the first winners, beating Clydesdale 2-0 in the final in front of a crowd of 3,000 at the original Hampden Park.

• **Queen's Park were the dominant force in the early years of the competition, winning 10 of the first 20 finals, including one in 1884 when their opponents, Vale of Leven, failed to turn up! Since then, Celtic have been the most successful side in the competition, winning the trophy for a 38th time in 2018 with a 2-0 victory over Motherwell at Hampden Park.**

• Celtic winger Bobby Lennox is the most successful player in the history of the competition, with eight wins in the final between 1965 and 1980.

• **Incredibly, the biggest ever victories in the history of British football took place in the Scottish Cup on the same day, 12th September 1885. Dundee Harp beat Aberdeen Rovers 35-0 and were confident that they had set a new record. Yet, no doubt to their utter**

Celtic won the Scottish Cup for a record 38th time in 2018

amazement, they soon discovered that Arbroath had thrashed Bon Accord, a cricket club who had been invited to take part by mistake, 36-0!

• Celtic legend Jimmy McGrory is the all-time leading scorer in the competition with 77 goals between 1922 and 1937, including three scored while on loan at Clydebank.

SCOTTISH LEAGUE CUP

The Scottish League Cup came into being in 1946, some 14 years before the English version. The following April, Rangers won the first final by thrashing Aberdeen 4-0 at Hampden Park.

• **Surprisingly, minnows East Fife were the first club to win the trophy three times (in 1947, 1949 and 1953) but since those early years the Glasgow giants have predictably dominated the competition, Rangers leading the way with 27 triumphs to Celtic's 17.**

• Ayr United (1952) and Partick Thistle (1993) jointly hold the record for the biggest win in the competition, with 11-1 hammerings of Dumbarton and Albion Rovers respectively. Celtic hold the record for the most emphatic win in the final, demolishing Rangers 7-1 at Hampden Park in 1957 in the biggest ever margin of victory in a major British final.

• Celtic also hold the record for the most consecutive appearances in the final, with an incredible 14 between 1965 and 1978. Surprisingly, though, the Glasgow giants somehow only managed to lift the trophy on six of those occasions.

• Prolific striker Joe Harper is the top scorer in the competition with 74 goals for Morton, Aberdeen and Hibs between 1963 and 1981.

TOP 10

BIGGEST SCOTTISH CUP WINS

1. **Arbroath 36 Bon Accord 0, 1885**
2. **Dundee Harp 35 Aberdeen Rovers 0, 1885**
3. **Victoria 1 Cowlairs Glasgow 21, 1889**
4. **Arbroath 20 Orion Aberdeen 0, 1886**
   Stirling Albion 20 Selkirk 0, 1984
6. **Arbroath 18 Orion 0, 1887**
7. **Yoker 17 Tayavalla 0, 1884**
   Redding Athletic 0 Camelon 17, 1887
9. **Cowlairs Glasgow 18 Temperance Athletic 2, 1888**
10. **Partick Thistle 16 Royal Albert 0, 1931**

SCUNTHORPE UNITED

Year founded: 1899
Ground: Glanford Park (9,088)
Previous name: Scunthorpe & Lindsey United
Nickname: The Iron
Biggest win: 9-0 v Boston United (1953)
Heaviest defeat: 0-8 v Carlisle United (1952)

The club was founded in 1899 when Brumby Hall linked up with some other local teams. Between 1910 and 1958 they were known as Scunthorpe and Lindsey United after amalgamating with the latter team.

• **Elected to the Third Division (North) when the league expanded in 1950, Scunthorpe won the division eight years later. In 1962 the Iron finished a best ever fourth in the old Second Division, missing out on promotion to the top flight by just five points.**

• In that same 1961/62 season striker Barrie Thomas set a club record by scoring 31 league goals. Incredibly, he had reached that tally by the end of January when, to the dismay of United's fans, he was sold to Newcastle.

- In the 2013/14 season Scunthorpe boss Russ Wilcox made the best ever start of a manager in Football League history, remaining unbeaten in his first 28 matches in charge as the Iron secured promotion to League One.
- Beaten in the League One play-off semi-finals in 2018, Scunthorpe made their record signing in 2009 when giant defender Rob Jones moved from Hibs for around £700,000. Striker Gary Hooper became the most expensive player to leave Glanford Park when he joined Celtic for £2.5 million in 2010.

> **HONOURS**
> *League One champions* 2007
> *Division 3 (North) champions* 1958

SHEFFIELD UNITED

> **Year founded:** 1889
> **Ground:** Bramall Lane (32,702)
> **Nickname:** The Blades
> **Biggest win:** 10-0 v Port Vale (1892) and v Burnley (1929)
> **Heaviest defeat:** 0-13 v Bolton (1890)

The club was founded at a meeting at the city's Adelphi Hotel in 1899 by the members of the Sheffield United Cricket Club, partly to make greater use of the facilities at Bramall Lane.

- **The Blades enjoyed their heyday in the late Victorian era, winning the title in 1898, and lifting the FA Cup in both 1899 and 1902. The club won the FA Cup again in 1915, beating Chelsea 3-0 at Old Trafford, in what was to be the last final to be played before the First World War brought a halt to the sporting calendar. They chalked up another victory in 1925.**
- The club's leading scorer is Harry Johnson, who bagged 201 league goals between 1919 and 1930. His successor at centre-forward, Jimmy Dunne, scored in a Football League record 12 consecutive games in the 1931/32 season.
- **The Blades' home, Bramall Lane, is one of the oldest sporting arenas in the world. It first hosted cricket in 1855, before football was introduced to the ground in 1862. Sixteen years later, in 1878, the world's first ever floodlit match was played at** the stadium between two sides picked from the Sheffield Football Association, the lights being provided by two generators.

- During an 18-year career with the club between 1948 and 1966, Joe Shaw made a record 631 appearances for the Blades. Goalkeeper Jack Smith made a record 203 consecutive appearances for the Blades between 1936 and 1947, and also saved 11 penalties to establish another club record.
- **One of just five clubs to top all four English divisions, Sheffield United hold the record for the most number of points, 90 in 2011/12, for a team failing to win promotion from the third tier.**
- To the dismay of their fans, United have appeared in four play-off finals and lost them all – a miserable record only matched by Reading. Most recently, the Blades lost the 2012 League One play-off final to Huddersfield on penalties after all 22 players on the pitch had been required to take a spot-kick – the first time this had happened in a Wembley final.
- **Striker Peter Ndlovu won a club record 26 of his 100 caps for Zimbabwe while at Bramall Lane between 2001 and 2004.**

> **HONOURS**
> *Division 1 champions* 1898
> *Division 2 champions* 1953
> *League One champions* 2017
> *Division 4 champions* 1982
> *FA Cup* 1899, 1902, 1915, 1925

SHEFFIELD WEDNESDAY

> **Year founded:** 1867
> **Ground:** Hillsborough (39,732)
> **Previous name:** The Wednesday
> **Nickname:** The Owls
> **Biggest win:** 12-0 v Halliwell (1891)
> **Heaviest defeat:** 0-10 v Aston Villa (1912)

The club was formed as The Wednesday in 1867 at the Adelphi Hotel in Sheffield by members of the Wednesday Cricket Club, who originally met on that particular day of the week. In 1929 the club added 'Sheffield' to their name, but are still often referred to by their fans as simply 'Wednesday'.

- **In 1904 the Owls became the first club in the 20th century to win consecutive league championships, despite scoring just 48 goals in 34 matches – the lowest total ever by a title-winning side. Wednesday won back-to-back titles again in 1929 and 1930 but have not lifted the league trophy since.**
- In 1935 Wednesday won the FA Cup for the third and last time beating Arsenal 1-0 in the final at Wembley, striker Ellis Rimmer scoring in every round of the competition.
- **Scottish international striker Andrew Wilson made a club record 560 appearances and scored a record 199 league goals while with Wednesday between 1900 and 1920.**

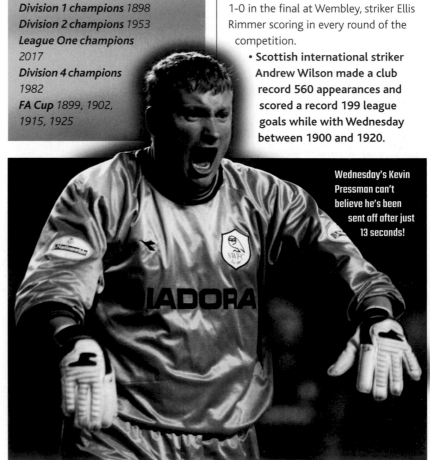

Wednesday's Kevin Pressman can't believe he's been sent off after just 13 seconds!

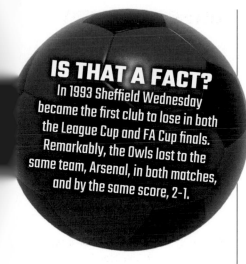

• In 1991, while residing in the old Second Division, the Owls won the League Cup for the first and only time in their history, beating Manchester United 1-0 at Wembley. It was the last time that a club from outside the top flight has lifted a major domestic cup.

• Defender Nigel Worthington made a club record 50 appearances for Northern Ireland during a decade at Hillsborough between 1984 and 1994.

• On the opening day of the 2000/01 season Wednesday goalkeeper Kevin Pressman was sent off after just 13 seconds at Molineux for handling a Wolves shot while outside the penalty area – the fastest dismissal ever in elite British football.

HONOURS
Division 1 champions 1903, 1904, 1929, 1930
Division 2 champions 1900, 1926, 1952, 1956, 1959
FA Cup 1896, 1907, 1935
League Cup 1991

JONJO SHELVEY

Born: Romford, 27th February 1992
Position: Midfielder
Club career:
2008-10 Charlton Athletic 42 (7)
2010-13 Liverpool 47 (2)
2011 Blackpool (loan) 10 (6)
2013-16 Swansea City 79 (10)
2016- Newcastle United 87 (6)
International record:
2012- England 6 (0)

A central midfielder who specialises in hitting accurate long balls from deep, Jonjo Shelvey was one of Newcastle's outstanding performers in 2017/18 as the newly-promoted Magpies defied expectations to finish in the upper half of the Premier League.

• Shelvey began his career with Charlton Athletic, becoming the Addicks' youngest ever player when he made his debut against Barnsley in April 2008 aged 16 and 59 days. The following year he became the club's youngest ever scorer when he netted in an FA Cup tie against Norwich while still 54 days short of his 17th birthday.

• In 2010 Shelvey joined Liverpool, but he made little impact at Anfield before signing for Swansea for £5 million three years later. His time with the Swans was marked by some spectacular goals, but also moments when the red mist descended.

• Shelvey's disciplinary problems followed him to Newcastle, where he was banned for five games and fined £100,000 after racially abusing Wolves' Romain Saiss in September 2016. However, in the same season the bald-headed midfielder helped the Geordies win promotion to the Premier League and was voted into the Championship Team of the Year.

• Shelvey has played for England from Under-16 level onwards, and was captain of the Under-21 team. When he made his first start for the senior team against San Marino in September 2015 he became the first ever Swansea player to represent the Three Lions.

SHREWSBURY TOWN

Year founded: 1886
Ground: Montgomery Waters Meadow (9,875)
Nickname: The Shrews
Biggest win: 11-2 v Marine (1995)
Heaviest defeat: 1-8 v Norwich City (1952) and v Coventry City (1963)

Founded at the Lion Hotel in Shrewsbury in 1886, the club played in regional football for many years until being elected to the Football League in 1950.

• Prolific striker Arthur Rowley is the club's record scorer, hitting 152 goals between 1958 and 1965 to complete his all-time league record of 434 goals (he also turned out for West Bromwich Albion, Fulham and Leicester City). His best season for the Shrews was in 1958/59 when he banged in a club best 38 goals.

• Defender Mickey Brown played in a club record 418 league games in three spells with the Shrews between 1986 and 2001, and famously scored the decisive goal in a 2-1 win at Exeter in 2000 that saved the club from relegation from the Football League.

• In 1971 Shrews striker Alf Wood became the first player in the post-

Jonjo has found his mojo on Tyneside

war era to score four headers in a Football League match. He ended the game with five goals in a 7-1 drubbing of Blackburn Rovers.

• Beaten by Rotherham in the 2018 League One play-off final, Shrewsbury have won the Welsh Cup six times – a record for an English club.

BERNARDO SILVA

Born: Lisbon, Portugal, 10th August 1994
Position: Midfielder
Club career:
2013-15 Benfica B 38 (7)
2013-15 Benfica 1 (0)
2014-15 Monaco (loan) 15 (2)
2015-17 Monaco 86 (22)
2017- Manchester City 35 (6)
International record:
2015- Portugal 30 (2)

In his first season with Manchester City in 2017/18 Portuguese midfielder Bernardo Silva played in more games (53) than any of the club's players as the Citizens won both the League Cup and the Premier League title.

Silva is like gold for Manchester City

• A skilful player who is adept at making quick, incisive passes around the opponents' box, Silva came through the Benfica youth system to be named the second tier Breakthrough Player of the Year in 2014 while representing the club's B team.

• In the same year he joined Monaco on loan, and six months later completed a £13 million move to the principality. In 2017 he helped Monaco win the French league title before joining City for £43.5 million.

• **Silva made his senior debut for Portugal in a 2-0 friendly defeat against Cape Verde in March 2015. The following year he missed his country's surprise triumph at Euro 2016 through injury but he started all four of Portugal's games at the 2018 World Cup.**

DAVID SILVA

Born: Las Palmas, Spain, 8th January 1986
Position: Midfielder
Club career:
2003-04 Valencia B 14 (1)
2004-10 Valencia 119 (21)
2004-05 Eibar (loan) 35 (5)
2005-06 Celta (loan) 34 (4)
2010- Manchester City 249 (48)
International record:
2006- Spain 125 (35)

A tricky midfielder who can wriggle out of the tightest of situations before delivering an astute pass, David Silva became the first Spanish player to win the Premier League three times after helping his club Manchester City top the table in 2012, 2014 and 2018.

• **Prior to moving to the Etihad stadium, Silva was a key player in the Valencia side that regularly managed to upset Real Madrid and Barcelona. His best moment with the Spanish side came in 2008, when Valencia won the Copa del Rey after beating Getafe 3-1 in the final.**

• Nicknamed 'El Mago' (The Magician) for his sublime skills on the ball, Silva

"And with a name like Silva you'll probably play for City too!"

joined City for £24 million in 2010 and in his first season in Manchester helped the Sky Blues win their first trophy for 35 years when they beat Stoke City 1-0 in the FA Cup final at Wembley. In the same campaign he topped the Premier League assists chart with 15 and he is now in the top 10 on the all-time list with 75.

• **First capped by his country in 2006, Silva was an integral figure in the Spain side that won Euro 2008, but was restricted to just two appearances as the Spanish became world champions in South Africa two years later. However, he returned to the starting line-up at Euro 2012, heading the first goal in Spain's 4-0 thrashing of Italy in the final. Silva has won 77 of his 125 caps with Manchester City, making him the club's most decorated international.**

SIZE

The heaviest player in the history of the professional game was Willie 'Fatty' Foulke, who played in goal for Sheffield United, Chelsea and Bradford City. By the end of his career, the tubby custodian weighed in at an incredible 24 stone.

- At just 5ft tall, Fred Le May is the shortest player ever to have appeared in the Football League. He played for Thames, Clapton Orient and Watford between 1930 and 1933. The shortest England international ever was Frederick 'Fanny' Walden, a 5ft 2in winger with Tottenham who won the first of his two caps in 1914.
- No prizes for guessing who the tallest ever England international is. It is, of course, towering striker Peter Crouch, who stands 6ft 7in in his socks. Crouch, though, is a full inch shorter than Watford goalkeeper Costel Pantilimon, who claims the record as the tallest ever Premier League player.
- The world's tallest player is Danish goalkeeper Simon Bloch Jorgensen, once a trialist with Everton, who towers over opposition strikers at 6ft 10 inches.

SON HEUNG-MIN

Born: Chuncheon, South Korea, 8th July 1992
Position: Winger/striker
Club career:
2010 Hamburg II 6 (1)
2010-13 Hamburg 73 (20)
2013-15 Bayer Leverkusen 62 (21)
2015- Tottenham Hotspur 99 (30)
International record:
2010- South Korea 70 (23)

A hard-working frontman who loves to run at defenders before unleashing a powerful shot, Tottenham's Son Heung-min is the highest-scoring Asian player in the history of the Premier League with 30 goals. No fewer than 12 of those came in the 2017/18 season, making the South Korean hitman the first Asian player to reach double figures in a Premier League campaign and he also matched a club record set by Jermain Defoe in 2004 by scoring in five consecutive home games.
- Son began his career in Germany, setting a record as the youngest player to score a league goal for Hamburg when he was on target against Cologne, aged 18, in 2010. Three years later he moved on to Bayer Leverkusen for a club record fee of around £8 million.
- In 2015 Son became the most expensive Asian player ever when he signed for Tottenham for £22 million, and in the same year he was named Asian

Son Heung-min, the highest-scoring Asian player in the history of the Premier League

International Footballer of the Year – the first South Korean to win this award.
- First capped in 2010, Son was on the scoresheet in the 2015 Asian Cup final but had to settle for a runners-up medal after Australia won 2-1 in extra-time. He scored twice at the 2018 World Cup in Russia, including a memorable goal in South Korea's shock 2-0 victory against reigning champions Germany.

SOUTHAMPTON

Year founded: 1885
Ground: St Mary's (32,505)
Previous name: Southampton St Mary's
Nickname: The Saints
Biggest win: 14-0 v Newbury Town (1894)
Heaviest defeat: 0-8 v Tottenham (1936) and v Everton (1971)

Founded as Southampton St Mary's by members of St Mary's Church Young Men's Association in 1885, the club joined the Southern League in 1894 and became simply 'Southampton' the following year.
- The Saints won the Southern League six times in the decade up to 1904

and also appeared in two FA Cup finals during that period, losing to Bury in 1900 and to Sheffield United two years later.
- The club finally won the cup in 1976. Manchester United were hot favourites to beat the Saints, then in the Second Division, but the south coast side claimed the trophy thanks to Bobby Stokes' late strike. As scorer of the first (and only) goal in the final, Stokes was rewarded with a free car... unfortunately, he still hadn't passed his driving test!
- **Mick Channon, a member of that cup-winning team and now a successful racehorse trainer, is the Saints' leading scorer with a total of 185 goals in two spells at The Dell, the club's old ground. Incredibly, Channon was top scorer in the old First Division in the 1973/74 season with 21 goals but Southampton were still relegated – the first club to go down after finishing third bottom under the then new 'three up, three down' system.**
- Winger Terry Paine, a member of England's 1966 World Cup-winning squad, is Southampton's longest serving player. Between 1956 and 1974 he wore the club's colours in no fewer than 713 league games before moving to Hereford United. Paine's amazing total of 824 league games puts him fourth in the all-time list, behind Peter Shilton, Tony Ford and Graham Alexander.
- **England goalkeeper Shilton is the club's most capped player, winning 49 of his record 125 caps during his time at The Dell.**
- In January 2018 the Saints forked out a record £19 million to buy Argentinian striker Guido Carillo from Monaco. In the same month Southampton received £75 million from Liverpool for Dutch centre-back Virgil van Dijk in a world record deal for a defender.
- **The Saints enjoyed their best European run in 1977, reaching the quarter-finals of the Cup Winners' Cup before bowing out to Belgian giants Anderlecht 3-2 on aggregate.**
- Southampton are the only English club to have had three Dutch managers: Jan Poortvliet (2008-09), Mark Woote (2009) and Ronald Koeman (2014-16).

HONOURS
Division 3 champions 1960
Division 3 (South) champions 1922
FA Cup 1976
Football League Trophy 2010

SOUTHEND UNITED

Year founded: 1906
Ground: Roots Hall (12,392)
Nickname: The Shrimpers
Biggest win: 10-1 v Golders Green (1934), v Brentwood (1968) and v Aldershot (1990)
Heaviest defeat: 1-9 v Brighton and Hove Albion (1965)

Southend United were founded in 1906 at the Blue Boar pub, just 50 yards away from the club's home, Roots Hall.

• After joining the Football League in 1920 the Shrimpers remained in the third tier for a record 46 years, before finally dropping into the Fourth Division in 1966.

• The club's top appearance maker is Sandy Anderson, who turned out in 452 league games between 1950 and 1962. His team-mate Roger Hollis is Southend's leading marksman, rifling in 120 league goals in just six years at the club between 1954 and 1960.

• Southend were relegated from the third tier in 1988/89 despite amassing a record points total for a demoted team (54). In all, the Shrimpers have dropped down to the fourth tier a record seven times.

• The club's most decorated international is defender Jason Demetriou, who has won 12 caps for Cyprus since arriving at Roots Hall from Walsall in 2016.

• In January 2017 Southend sold 13-year-old defender Finley Burns to Manchester City for £175,000 – a record fee for a player of that age.

HONOURS
League One champions 2006
Division 4 champions 1981

GARETH SOUTHGATE

Born: Watford, 3rd September 1970
Managerial career:
2006-09 Middlesbrough
2013-16 England Under-21
2016- England

In 2018 Gareth Southgate became the first England manager since Bobby Robson at Italia '90 to lead the Three Lions to the semi-finals of the World Cup. However, his dreams of glory were shattered by Croatia, who beat his young team 2-1 after extra-time in a pulsating tie in Moscow.

• Southgate became England manager, initially on a four-match temporary basis, following the sudden resignation of Sam Allardyce in September 2016. Two months later he was appointed full-time boss of the Three Lions on a four-year contract. He had previously been in charge of the England Under-21 team for three years.

• Southgate began his managerial career with Middlesbrough in 2006. Two years earlier he had become the first Boro captain to lift a major trophy when the Teesiders beat Bolton 2-1 in the League Cup final. However Southgate's long association with the club ended in the sack in October 2009, a few months after Boro' lost their Premier League place.

• A ball-playing centre-back, Southgate started out with Crystal Palace before moving to Aston Villa in 1995. The following year he helped Villa win the League Cup for a then joint-record fifth time and in 2000 he captained the Birmingham outfit in their 1-0 FA Cup final defeat to Chelsea. During a six-year spell at Villa

"Yesss! Surely nobody will ever mention my penalty miss again now!"

Park he won a club record 42 caps for England, but his international career is best remembered for a penalty shoot-out miss against Germany which cost the Three Lions a possible place in the final of Euro '96.

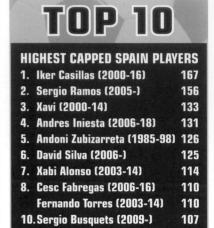

TOP 10

HIGHEST CAPPED SPAIN PLAYERS

1.	Iker Casillas (2000-16)	167
2.	Sergio Ramos (2005-)	156
3.	Xavi (2000-14)	133
4.	Andres Iniesta (2006-18)	131
5.	Andoni Zubizarreta (1985-98)	126
6.	David Silva (2006-)	125
7.	Xabi Alonso (2003-14)	114
8.	Cesc Fabregas (2006-16)	110
	Fernando Torres (2003-14)	110
10.	Sergio Busquets (2009-)	107

SPAIN

First international: Spain 1 Denmark 0, 1920
Most capped player: Iker Casillas, 167 caps (2000-)
Leading goalscorer: David Villa, 59 goals (2005-17)
First World Cup appearance: Spain 3 Brazil 1, 1934
Biggest win: Spain 13 Bulgaria 0, 1933
Heaviest defeat: Italy 7 Spain 1, 1928 and England 7 Spain 1, 1931

Spain are the first country in football history to win three major international titles on the trot following their successes at Euro 2008, the 2010 World Cup in South Africa and Euro 2012 in Poland and Ukraine.

• Spain secured their first ever World Cup triumph with a 1-0 victory over Holland at Soccer City Stadium in Johannesburg,

Andres Iniesta holds aloft the World Cup trophy in 2010

midfielder Andres Iniesta drilling home the all-important goal four minutes from the end of extra-time. Despite their entertaining close passing style of play, Spain only managed to score eight goals in the tournament – the lowest total ever by the winning nation at a World Cup.

• Along with Germany, Spain have won the European Championships a record three times. Their first success came in 1964 when they had the advantage of playing the semi-final and final, the latter against holders the Soviet Union, on home soil at Real Madrid's Bernabeu Stadium. Then, in 2008, a single Fernando Torres goal was enough to see off Germany in the final in Vienna. Finally, in 2012, Spain made it a hat-trick of victories after annihilating Italy 4-0 in the final in Kiev.

• Between 2007 and 2009 Spain went 35 matches without defeat (winning 32 and drawing just three) to equal the world record set by Brazil in the 1990s. The run came to an end when Spain lost 2-0 to USA at the 2009 Confederations Cup, but the Spanish were soon back on form, going into the 2010 World Cup on the back of 18 consecutive victories – including a record 10 in qualification – before they surprisingly lost their opening match at the finals against Switzerland. That setback, though, was soon forgotten as Vicente del Bosque's men went on to lift the trophy, sparking jubilant scenes across Spain from Santander to Seville.

• Along with Italy and England, Spain have been beaten in a record three penalty shoot-outs at the World Cup, their most recent failure coming at the 2018 tournament against hosts Russia in the last 16.

HONOURS

World Cup winners 2010
European Championships winners 1964, 2008, 2012

World Cup Record

1930 Did not enter
1934 Quarter-finals
1938 Did not enter
1950 Fourth place
1954 Did not qualify
1958 Did not qualify
1962 Round 1
1966 Round 1
1970 Did not qualify
1974 Did not qualify
1978 Round 1
1982 Round 2
1986 Quarter-finals
1990 Round 2
1994 Quarter-finals
1998 Round 1
2002 Quarter-finals
2006 Round 2
2010 Winners
2014 Round 1
2018 Round 2

SPONSORSHIP

Manchester United's £53 million-a-year shirt sponsorship deal with US car manufacturers Chevrolet, which started in 2014, is a record for the Premier League. In European football, Real Madrid's deal with Dubai-owned airline Emirates is the most lucrative, being worth around £64 million a year.

• On 24th January 1976 Kettering Town became the first senior football club in the UK to feature a sponsor's logo on their shirts, Kettering Tyres, for their Southern League Premier Division match against Bath City. The Football Association ordered the removal of the logo, but finally accepted shirt sponsorship in June 1977. Two years later Liverpool became the first top-flight club to sport a sponsor's logo after signing a deal with Hitachi.

• The first FA Cup final to feature sponsored shirts was in 1984 between Everton and Watford. The Toffees wore the logo of canned meat company Hania, while the Hornets advertised industrial vehicles manufacturer Iveco.

• **The League Cup was the first major English competition to be sponsored,** being renamed the Milk Cup after receiving backing from the Milk Marketing Board in 1982. It has since been rebranded as the Littlewoods Cup, the Rumbelows Cup, the Coca-Cola Cup, the Worthington Cup, the Carling Cup, the Capital One Cup, the EFL Cup and, from 2017, the Carabao Cup. Since 1994 the FA Cup has been sponsored by Littlewoods, AXA, E.ON, Budweiser, and from the 2015/16 season, Emirates. Meanwhile, the Premier League has been sponsored by Carling, Barclaycard and Barclays, but has had no sponsor since 2016.

• The first competition in England to be sponsored was the Watney Cup in 1971, a pre-season tournament between the highest scoring teams in the different divisions of the Football League.

• **Arsenal's shirt sponsorship deal with Emirates airline, which first began in 2006, is the longest running in the Premier League.**

STADIUMS

With a capacity of 114,000 the Rungrado 1st of May Stadium in Pyongyang, North Korea is the largest football stadium anywhere in the world. As well as football matches, the stadium also hosts athletic meetings and mass displays of choreographed gymnastics. In the late 1990s a number of North Korean army generals were burned to death in the stadium after being implicated in a plot to assassinate the country's then dictator, Kim Jong-il.

• **Barcelona's Nou Camp is the largest football stadium in Europe and the second largest in the world with a capacity of 99,354.** Old Trafford (75,643) has the largest capacity of any dedicated Premier League ground.

• Built at a cost of $2.3 billion, the Yankee stadium in New York is the world's most expensive sporting venue.

Opened in 2009, the stadium has been the home of MLS outfit New York City since 2015.

• With a capacity of just 11,464 Bournemouth's Vitality Stadium is the smallest ever to host Premier League football. However, that's a relative giant compared to Eibar's Ipurua Municipal Stadium in northern Spain which has a capacity of just 7,083 and is the smallest venue in Europe's top four leagues.

RAHEEM STERLING

Born: Kingston, Jamaica, 8th December 1994
Position: Winger/striker
Club career:
20012-15 Liverpool 91 (18)
2015- Manchester City 97 (31)
International record:
2012- England 44 (2)

Speedy winger Raheem Sterling became the most expensive English player ever when he moved from Liverpool to Manchester City for £49 million in July 2015. He enjoyed his most prolific season at the Etihad in 2017/18, pitching in with 23 goals in all competitions as City won the Premier League title and the League Cup.

• **Jamaican-born Sterling started his career with QPR, before switching to Liverpool for a bargain £600,000 in** 2010. He became the third youngest player ever to make his debut for the Reds when he came on as a sub in a 2-1 home defeat against Wigan Athletic on 24th March 2012. Seven months later he became the club's second youngest goalscorer at the time (behind England striker Michael Owen) when he notched his first goal for the Merseysiders in a 1-0 win against Reading.

• Sterling was a star of Liverpool's magnificent 2013/14 Premier League campaign, during which he chipped in with nine league goals. At the end of the year he became only the second English player (after Wayne Rooney in 2004) to win the Golden Boy award for the most promising player aged under-21 in European football. However, Sterling's performances the following season were affected by a contract dispute with Liverpool, which ended with him demanding to leave Anfield.

• **Sterling rose through the England youth ranks to make his senior debut in a 4-2 friendly defeat away to Sweden in November 2012. In only his fourth game for the Three Lions he was sent off in a pre-2014 World Cup friendly against Ecuador to become the youngest ever England player to see red. He was a regular starter for England at the 2018 World Cup in Russia but missed a number of good chances and failed to add to his international tally.**

STEVENAGE

Year founded: 1976
Ground: Broadhall Way (6,722)
Previous name: Stevenage Borough
Nickname: The Boro
Biggest win: 7-0 v Merthyr (2006)
Heaviest defeat: 1-7 v Luton Town (2017)

The club was founded in 1976 as Stevenage Borough, following the bankruptcy of the town's former club, Stevenage Athletic. In 2010 the club decided to become simply 'Stevenage'.

• **Stevenage rose through the football pyramid to gain promotion to the Conference in 1994. Two years later they won the title but were denied promotion to the Football League as their tiny Broadhall Way Stadium did not meet the league's standards.**

• Stevenage finally made it into the league in 2010 after topping the Conference table with an impressive 99 points. If the club's two victories against Chester City, who were expelled from the league during the season, had not been expunged then Stevenage would have set a new Conference record of 105 points. The following season Stevenage were promoted again, after beating Torquay United 1-0 in the League Two play-off

Raheem Sterling, the most expensive English player ever

final at Old Trafford, but their three-year stay in League One ended in 2014 when they finished bottom of the pile.

• In 2007 Stevenage became the first club to lift a trophy at the new Wembley, beating Kidderminster Harriers 3-2 in the final of the FA Trophy watched by a competition record crowd of 53,262.

• Veteran goalkeeper Chris Day made a record 223 appearances in the Football League for the Boro between 2010 and 2018.

STOKE CITY

Year founded: 1863
Ground: Bet365 Stadium (30,089)
Previous name: Stoke Ramblers, Stoke
Nickname: The Potters
Biggest win: 11-0 v Stourbridge (1914)
Heaviest defeat: 0-10 v Preston (1889)

Founded in 1863 by employees of the North Staffordshire Railway Company, Stoke are the second oldest league club in the country. Between 1868 and 1870 the club was known as Stoke Ramblers, before simply becoming Stoke and then adding the suffix 'City' in 1925.

• Stoke were founder members of the Football League in 1888 but finished bottom of the table at the end of the season. After another wooden spoon in 1890 the club dropped out of the league, but returned to the big time after just one season.

• The club's greatest moment came in 1972 when they won the League Cup, beating favourites Chelsea 2-1 in the final at Wembley, thanks to a late winner by George Eastham – aged 35 and 161 days at the time, the oldest player ever to score in the League Cup final. The Potters had a great chance to add to their meagre haul of silverware in 2011 when they reached the FA Cup final for the first time, but they lost 1-0 to Manchester City.

• Freddie Steele is Stoke's leading scorer with 140 league goals between 1934 and 1949, including a club record 33 in the 1936/37 season. Stalwart defender Eric Skeels played in a record 507 league games for the Potters between 1960 and 1976.

• Midfielder Greg Whelan is Stoke's most capped player, with 81 appearances for the Republic of Ireland between 2008 and 2017.

• Relegated from the Premier League in 2018, Stoke splashed out a club record £18.3 million in January 2016 to bring French midfielder Giannelli Imbula to the Potteries from Porto. The club received a record £20 million in July 2017 when Austrian forward Marko Arnautovic joined West Ham.

• On 27th January 1974 Stoke became the first top-flight club to host Sunday football when they played Chelsea at their former home, the Victoria Ground. Ignoring the complaints of religious groups, a crowd of nearly 32,000 turned up to see Stoke win 1-0.

• Stoke defender Ryan Shawcross has conceded a record 11 penalties in the Premier League.

JOHN STONES

Born: Barnsley, 28th May 1994
Position: Defender
Club career:
2012-13 Barnsley 24 (0)
2013- Everton 77 (1)
2016- Manchester City 45 (0)
International record:
2014- England 33 (2)

An elegant ball-playing defender who loves to launch attacks from deep inside his own half,

John Stones became the second most expensive defender in the world at the time (after David Luiz) when he signed for Manchester City from Everton for £47.5 million in July 2016. Although he missed much of the season through injury in 2018 he helped City win the Premier League title.

• Stones started out with his hometown club, Barnsley, coming through the Tykes' academy before making his first-team debut against Reading in March 2012. At the start of the following year he moved to Everton for £3 million, but had to wait until August 2013 before he made his first appearance for the Toffees.

• The young defender scored his first goal for Everton in a 3-0 home defeat of Manchester United in April 2015 and that summer was the subject of three large bids from reigning Premier League champions Chelsea, all of which were rejected by the Goodison club hierarchy despite Stones reportedly handing in a transfer request.

• Stones made his debut for England in a 3-0 friendly win against Peru at Wembley in May 2014. At Russia 2018 he became the first ever England defender to score twice in a World Cup match when he grabbed a brace in a 6-1 demolition of Panama.

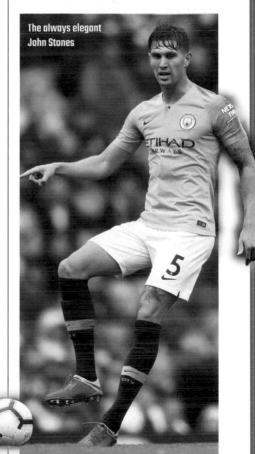

The always elegant John Stones

"I'll just pop this in the net, then it'll be time for a mid-match snack!"

LUIS SUAREZ

Born: Salto, Uruguay, 24th January 1987
Position: Striker
Club career:
2005-06 Nacional 27 (10)
2006-07 Groningen 29 (10)
2007-11 Ajax 110 (81)
2011-14 Liverpool 110 (69)
2014- Barcelona 130 (110)
International record:
2007- Uruguay 103 (53)

A quick-witted striker who is famed for his ability to score from the tightest of angles, Luis Suarez became the third most expensive player in football history at the time when he joined Barcelona from Liverpool in July 2014 for £75 million. Since then he has helped the Catalan giants win the domestic Double in 2015, 2016 and 2018 and the Champions League in 2015, scoring in the final against Juventus. In 2016 he won the European Golden Shoe after scoring a career-best 40 goals in La Liga.

• Suarez enjoyed a rollercoaster three years with Liverpool after signing for the Merseysiders from Ajax for £22.8 million in January 2011. In his first full season with the Reds he helped them win the Carling Cup but, significantly less impressively,

was given an eight-match ban by the FA and fined £40,000 for racially abusing Manchester United and France defender Patrice Evra.

• The following season Suarez was in hot water again after he bit Chelsea defender Branislav Ivanovic on the arm in an unprovoked attack. The striker, who had been banned for seven games after a similar incident while playing for his previous club Ajax, was hit with a 10-game ban – the fifth longest in Premier League history.

• However, the Uruguayan appeared to turn over a new leaf in 2013/14 when he topped the Premier League scoring charts with 31 goals, won both Player of the Year awards and became the first player ever to score 10 Premier League goals in a single month in December 2013.

• The temperamental Suarez was involved in another shocking incident at the 2014 World Cup when he bit Italy defender Giorgio Chiellini, earning a four-month ban from all football activities in the stiffest ever sanction handed out by FIFA at the World Cup for on-field misconduct. In happier days with Uruguay, Suarez was named Player of the Tournament when his country won the 2011 Copa America, and two years later he became the South Americans' all-time leading scorer.

TOP 10

PREMIER LEAGUE GOALS BY SUBSTITUTES

1.	Jermain Defoe (2001-)	24
2.	Olivier Giroud (2012-)	19
3.	Ole Gunnar Solskjaer (1996-2007)	17
	Nwankwo Kanu (1999-2010)	17
5.	Javier Hernandez (2010-)	16
	Daniel Sturridge (2007-)	16
	Peter Crouch (2002-)	16
8.	Victor Anichebe (2006-17)	14
9.	Edin Dzeko (2011-16)	13
	Darren Bent (2001-15)	13

SUBSTITUTES

Substitutes were first allowed in the Football League in the 1965/66 season. The first player to come off the bench was Charlton's Keith Peacock, who replaced injured goalkeeper Mike Rose after 11 minutes of the Addicks' match away to Bolton on 21st August 1965. On the same afternoon Barrow's Bobby Knox became the first substitute to score a goal when he notched against Wrexham.

• The fastest ever goal scored by a substitute was by Arsenal's Nicklas Bendtner, who headed in a corner against Tottenham at the Emirates on 22nd December 2007, just 1.8 seconds after replacing Emmanuel Eboue.

• The most goals ever scored in a Premier League game by a substitute is four by Ole Gunnar Solskjaer in Manchester United's 8-1 win at Nottingham Forest in 1999. Incredibly, the Norwegian striker was only on the pitch for 19 minutes. However, Jermain Defoe has scored the most Premier League goals as a sub with 24 for his various clubs. Stoke striker Peter Crouch has made a record 152 Premier League appearances as a sub since 2002.

• Substitutes were first allowed at the World Cup in 1970, with Holland's Dick Nanninga becoming the first sub to score in the final eight years later. The most goals scored by a sub at the tournament in a single match is three by Hungary's Lazlo Kiss against El Salvador in 1982. Brazilian winger Denilson made a record 11 appearances as a substitute at the finals in 1998 and 2002.

• At the 2018 World Cup Russia's Aleksandr Yerokhin became the first fourth substitute to be used at the tournament when he came on in extra-time during the host nation's last 16 tie with Spain.

• Jermain Defoe made a record 35 substitute appearances for England between 2004 and 2017, scoring a record seven goals for the Three Lions off the bench.

• In the 2014/15 season Manchester City became the first club to use all three of their permitted substitutions in every one of their 38 Premier League matches.

SUNDERLAND

Year founded: 1879
Ground: Stadium of Light (49,000)
Previous name: Sunderland and District Teachers' AFC
Nickname: The Black Cats
Biggest win: 11-1 v Fairfield (1895)
Heaviest defeat: 0-8 v Sheffield Wednesday (1911), v West Ham (1968), v Watford (1982) and v Southampton (2014)

The club was founded as the Sunderland and District Teachers' AFC in 1879 but soon opened its ranks to other professions and became simply 'Sunderland' the following year.

• Sunderland were the first 'new' club to join the Football League, replacing Stoke in 1890. Just two years later they won their first league championship and they retained the title the following year, in the process becoming the first club to score 100 goals in a league season. In 1895 Sunderland became the first club ever to win three championships, and their status was further enhanced when they beat Scottish champions Hearts 5-3 in a one-off 'world championship' match.

• In 1958 Sunderland were relegated after a then record 57 consecutive seasons in the top flight – a benchmark which lasted until Arsenal went one better in 1983/84.

• Sunderland were the first Second Division team in the post Second World War era to win the FA Cup, beating Leeds 1-0 at Wembley in 1973 in one of the biggest upsets of all time thanks to a goal by Ian Porterfield. Incredibly, their line-up featured not one international player. The following season the Wearsiders

had their one and only experience of European football, reaching the second round of the Cup Winners' Cup before losing 3-2 on aggregate to Sporting Lisbon.

• Goalkeeper Jim Montgomery, a hero of that cup-winning side, is the Black Cats' record appearance maker, turning out in 537 league games between 1960 and 1977. Inside forward Charlie Buchan is Sunderland's record scorer with 209 league goals between 1911 and 1925. Dave Halliday holds the record for a single season, hitting the target 43 times in 1928/29.

• Sunderland's record victory was an 11-1 thrashing of Fairfield in the FA Cup in 1895. However, the club's best ever league win, a 9-1 demolition of eventual champions and arch rivals Newcastle at St James' Park in 1908, probably gave their fans more pleasure. To this day, it remains the biggest ever victory by an away side in the top flight.

• Sunderland last won the league championship in 1935/36, the last time, incidentally, that a team wearing stripes has managed to top the pile. The Wearsiders' success, however, certainly wasn't based on a solid defence – the 74 goals they conceded that season is more than any other top-flight champions before or since.

• Relegated from the Championship in 2018, Sunderland have finished rock bottom of the Premier League on three occasions – in 2003, 2006 and 2017 – to match a record first set by Nottingham Forest in the 1990s. The Black Cats are also one of just five clubs to have been relegated from the league on four separate occasions.

HONOURS
Division 1 champions 1892, 1983, 1895, 1902, 1913, 1936
Championship champions 2005, 2007
Division 2 champions 1976
Division 3 champions 1988
FA Cup 1937, 1973

SUPERSTITIONS

Many footballers, including some of the great names of the game, are highly superstitious and believe that performing the same personal routines before every game will bring them good luck. England midfielder Dele Alli, for instance, has been wearing the same 'lucky' shinpads since he was aged

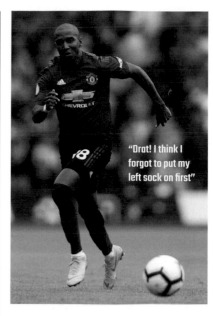

"Drat! I think I forgot to put my left sock on first"

11 while Three Lions skipper Harry Kane never shaves once he starts one of his scoring streaks.

• Kolo Toure's superstition almost cost his then club Arsenal dear in their 2009 Champions League clash with Roma. Believing that it would be bad luck to walk out of the dressing room before team-mate William Gallas, who was receiving treatment, Toure failed to appear for the start of the second half, leaving the Gunners to restart the match with just nine players!

• Juventus star Cristiano Ronaldo has a number of pre-match superstitions, including always sitting in the same spot on the team bus, insisting on being the last player out on the pitch (unless he is playing for Portugal, when he is always first) and taking a slug of water after the official team photo.

• England and Manchester United left-back Ashley Young always puts his left sock on first, and then makes sure that his left leg goes into his shorts before his right leg.

IS THAT A FACT?
Superstitious Argentina boss Carlos Bilardo refused to let his players eat chicken during the 1986 World Cup as he believed it would bring bad luck. The poultry ban paid off big time as the South Americans went on to win the tournament, beating West Germany 3-2 in the final in Mexico City.

• At the 2002 Africa Cup of Nations Cameroon coach Winfried Schafer and his assistant Thomas Nkono were arrested by police after placing a lucky charm on the pitch ahead of their team's semi-final against hosts Mali. However, the 'magic' still worked as Cameroon won the match 3-0 and went on to win the final against Senegal on penalties.

• **Some superstitions are not entirely irrational. For example, Arsenal always make sure that a new goalkeeper's jersey is washed before it is used for the first time. The policy stems from the 1927 FA Cup final, which the Gunners lost when goalkeeper Dan Lewis let in a soft goal against Cardiff. He later blamed his mistake on the ball slipping from his grasp and over the line as it brushed against the shiny surface of his new jumper.**

SWANSEA CITY

Year founded: 1912
Ground: Liberty Stadium (21,088)
Previous name: Swansea Town
Nickname: The Swans
Biggest win: 12-0 v Sliema Wanderers (1982)
Heaviest defeat: 0-8 v Liverpool (1990) and v Monaco (1991)

The club was founded as Swansea Town in 1912 and entered the Football League eight years later. The present name was adopted in 1970.

• **Under former Liverpool striker John Toshack the Swans climbed from the old Fourth Division to the top flight in just four seasons between 1978 and 1981, the fastest ever ascent through the Football League. The glory days soon faded, though, and by 1986 Swansea were back in the basement division once again.**

• In 2011, though, Swansea beat Reading 4-2 in the Championship play-off final at Wembley to become the first Welsh club to reach the Premier League. Again, their rise was a rapid one as they had been in the basement tier just six years earlier.

• **The club's greatest day came in 2013 when they won their first major trophy, the League Cup. The Swans triumphed in fine style, too, demolishing League Two outfit**

Swansea waved goodbye to the Premier League in 2018

Bradford City 5-0 at Wembley in the biggest ever victory in the final.

• Ivor Allchurch is the Swans' leading scorer, banging in 166 goals in two spells at the club between 1949 and 1968. One-club man Wilfred Milne is the Swans' leading appearance maker, turning out in 586 league games between 1920 and 1937.

• **In 1961 the club became the first from Wales to compete in Europe, but were knocked out of the Cup Winners' Cup in the first round by East German side Carl Zeiss Jena. In the same competition the Swans recorded their biggest ever win over Maltese minnows Sliema Wanderers 12-0 in 1982.**

• Iceland midfielder Gylfi Sigurdsson is the most expensive player to leave the Swans, signing for Everton for £45 million in August 2017. In January 2018 striker Andre Ayew re-signed for the club from West Ham for a record £18 million but he couldn't prevent the Swans from dropping out of the Premier League at the end of the season.

HONOURS
League One champions 2008
Division 3 (South) champions 1925, 1949
Third Division champions 2000
League Cup 2013
Football League Trophy 1994, 2006
Welsh Cup 1913, 1932, 1950, 1961, 1966, 1981, 1982, 1983, 1989, 1991

SWINDON TOWN

Year founded: 1879
Ground: The County Ground (15,728)
Previous name: Swindon Spartans
Nickname: The Robins
Biggest win: 10-1 v Farnham United Breweries (1925)
Heaviest defeat: 1-10 v Manchester City (1930)

The club was founded by the Reverend William Pitt in 1879, becoming Swindon Spartans two years later before adopting the name Swindon Town in 1883. In 1920 Swindon were founder members of the Third Division, kicking off their league career with a 9-1 thrashing of Luton.

• **The Robins' finest moment came in 1969 when, as a Third Division club, they beat mighty Arsenal 3-1 in the League Cup final on a mud-clogged Wembley pitch. Legendary winger Don Rogers was the star of the show, scoring two of Swindon's goals.**

• In 1993, three years after being denied promotion to the top flight for the first time because of a financial scandal, Swindon earned promotion to the Premiership via the play-offs. The following campaign, though, proved to be a miserable one as the Robins finished bottom of the pile and conceded 100 goals – a record for the Premier League that has yet to be beaten.

• **Swindon won the Fourth Division title in 1985/86 with a then Football League best 102 points, a total which remains a record for the bottom tier.**

• John Trollope is Swindon's longest serving player, appearing in 770 league games for the club between 1960 and 1980 – a record for a single club. Harry Morris scored a record 229 goals for the club between 1926 and 1933, including a seasonal best of 47 in the league in his first year with the Robins.

• **The Robins' coffers were boosted by a record £4 million in May 2015 when midfielders Massimo Luongo and Ben Gladwin both joined QPR.**

HONOURS
Second Division champions 1996
League Two champions 2012
Division 4 champions 1986
League Cup 1969

"Let's celebrate! Serge Aurier finally managed to do a proper throw-in!"

THROW-INS

Thomas Gronnemark from Denmark holds the world record for the longest ever throw. Employing a forward hand-spring technique he hurled the ball an incredible 51.33 metres on 18th June 2010.

• During the 2008/09 season Stoke City scored a record eight goals in the Premier League from throw-ins, thanks to the remarkable ability of Rory Delap, a one-time schoolboy javelin champion, to send the ball deep into the opposition box from as far away as the halfway line.

• The most bizarre goal from a throw-in came in a derby between Birmingham City and Aston Villa in 2002. Villa defender Olof Mellberg threw the ball back to goalkeeper Peter Enckelman and it dribbled under his foot and into the net. Despite Villa's protests, referee David Elleray ruled that the goal should stand because Enckelman had made contact with the ball.

• Perhaps, though, the most famous goal from a throw-in came at the European championships in 2016 in the last 16 tie between Iceland and England. Iceland skipper Aron Gunnarsson threw the ball into the box for Kari Arnason to flick on, and Ragnar Sigurdsson volleyed past Joe Hart for the underdogs' equaliser in their eventual 2-1 win.

IS THAT A FACT?
Tottenham defender Serge Aurier became the first player ever to make three foul throws in the same Premier League match during Spurs' visit to Crystal Palace on 25th February 2018.

TOTTENHAM HOTSPUR

Year founded: 1882
Ground: Tottenham Hotspur Stadium (62,062)
Previous name: Hotspur FC
Nickname: Spurs
Biggest win: 13-2 v Crewe (1960)
Heaviest defeat: 0-8 v Cologne (1995)

The club was founded as Hotspur FC in 1882 by a group of local cricketers, most of whom were former pupils of Tottenham Grammar School. Three years later the club decided to add the prefix 'Tottenham'.

• Tottenham were members of the Southern League when they won the FA Cup for the first time in 1901, defeating Sheffield United 3-1 in a replay at Bolton's Burnden Park. Spurs' victory meant they were the first (and, so far, only) non-league club to win the cup since the formation of the Football League in 1888.

• In 1961 Tottenham created history when they became the first club in the 20th century to win the fabled league and cup Double. Their title success was based on a storming start to the season, Bill Nicholson's side winning their first 11 games to set a top-flight record which has not been matched since.

• As Arsenal fans like to point out, Tottenham have failed to win the league since those 'Glory, Glory' days

of skipper Danny Blanchflower, Dave Mackay and Cliff Jones. Spurs, though, have continued to enjoy cup success, and their total of eight victories in the FA Cup is only surpassed by the Gunners and Manchester United. Remarkably, five of those triumphs came in years ending in a '1', giving rise to the legend that these seasons were particularly lucky for Spurs.

• Tottenham have also enjoyed much success in the League Cup, winning the competition four times. The last of these triumphs, in 2008 following a 2-1 defeat of holders Chelsea in the final, saw Tottenham become the first club to win the League Cup at the new Wembley.

• Spurs have a decent record in Europe, too. In 1963 they thrashed Atletico Madrid 5-1 in the final of the European Cup Winners' Cup, striker Jimmy Greaves grabbing a brace, to become the first British club to win a European trophy. Then, in 1972, Tottenham defeated Wolves 3-2 on aggregate in the first ever UEFA Cup final and the first European final to feature two English clubs. A third European triumph followed in 1984 when Tottenham beat Anderlecht in the first UEFA Cup final to be settled by penalties.

• Ace marksman Jimmy Greaves holds two goalscoring records for Tottenham. His total of 220 league goals between 1961 and 1970 is a club best, as is his impressive tally of 37 league goals in 1962/63. Clive Allen, though, struck an incredible total of 49 goals in all competitions in 1986/87, including a record 12 in the League Cup.

- Stalwart defender Steve Perryman is the club's longest serving player, pulling on the famous white shirt in 655 league games between 1969 and 1986, including 613 in the old First Division – a top-flight record for a player at a single club. His team-mate Pat Jennings is the club's most decorated international, winning 74 of his record 119 caps for Northern Ireland while at the Lane.

- In August 2013 Spurs received a then world record transfer fee of £86 million from Real Madrid for Welsh winger Gareth Bale. The club's record buy is Colombian defender Davinson Sanchez, who cost £42 million from Ajax in August 2017. However, the following year Spurs became the first Premier League club ever not to buy a single player in the summer transfer window.

- **Tottenham's first title success was in 1950/51 when Arthur Rowe's stylish 'Push and Run' team topped the table just one year after winning the Second Division championship. In the years since, only Ipswich Town (in 1961 and 1962) have managed to claim the top two titles in consecutive seasons.**

- Spurs finished a best ever second in the Premier League in 2016/17 with a goal difference of +60 – a record for a club not winning the title.

- **Spurs' incredible 9-1 trouncing of Wigan on 22nd November 2009 was only the second time a club had scored nine goals in a Premier League game. Jermain Defoe struck five times after half-time to set a Premier League record for the most goals scored in a single half.**

- In 2017 Tottenham moved to Wembley for a season while work continued on their new 62,062-capacity stadium at White Hart Lane, and attracted a record Premier League crowd of 83,222 for the visit of local rivals Arsenal on 10th February 2018. The majority of them headed home happy, too, after a 1-0 Spurs victory.

TRANMERE ROVERS

Year founded: 1884
Ground: Prenton Park (16,567)
Previous name: Belmont FC
Biggest win: 13-0 v Oswestry United (1914)
Heaviest defeat: 1-9 v Tottenham Hotspur (1953)

Founded as Belmont FC in 1884 by members of two local cricket clubs, the club changed its name to Tranmere Rovers the following year and joined the Football League for the first time in 1921 as members of the newly-created Third Division (North).

- **Promoted back to League Two via the play-offs in 2018 after a three-year absence, Tranmere enjoyed their greatest day in 2000 when they played Leicester City in the League Cup final at Wembley, eventually going down 2-1.**

- Rovers' best league victory, 13-4 against Oldham on Boxing Day 1935, set a record for the highest scoring Football League match ever. Striker Robert 'Bunny' Bell scored nine goals in the match, a league record at the time until it was beaten by Luton's Joe Payne later that same season.

- **Between 1946 and 1955 Tranmere's Harold Bell appeared in 375 consecutive league games, a run unmatched by any other Football League player. He went on to make a club record 595 appearances before retiring in 1964.**

TRANSFERS

The world's most expensive player is Brazilian striker Neymar, who moved from Barcelona to Paris Saint-Germain in August 2017 for an incredible £200 million, more than double the previous record set a year earlier when Paul Pogba joined Manchester United from Juventus for £89.3 million.

- **Premier League clubs spent £1.4 billion on new players during the summer of 2017, a record for a**

James Maddison's £20m move to Leicester contributed to the Premiership's total spend of £1.26bn on transfers in summer 2018

single transfer window. The following summer the total dropped to £1.26 billion, possibly as a result of the transfer window closing three weeks earlier than previously.

- The world's most expensive teenager is Kylian Mbappe, who joined Paris Saint-Germain from Monaco for £166 million in the summer of 2017.

- **In August 2018 Spain international Kepa Arrizabalaga became the most**

TOP 10

TRANSFERS IN WORLD FOOTBALL

1. Neymar (Barcelona to PSG, 2017) £200 million
2. Kylian Mbappe (Monaco to PSG, 2017) £166 million
3. Philippe Coutinho (Liverpool to Barcelona, 2018) £142 million
4. Cristiano Ronaldo (Real Madrid to Juventus, 2018) £99.2 million
5. Ousmane Dembele (Borussia Dortmund to Barcelona, 2017) £97 million
6. Paul Pogba (Juventus to Manchester United, 2016) £89.3 million
7. Gareth Bale (Tottenham to Real Madrid, 2013) £86 million
8. Cristiano Ronaldo (Manchester United to Real Madrid, 2009) £80 million
9. Luis Suarez (Liverpool to Barcelona, 2014) £75 million
   Gonzalo Higuain (Napoli to Juventus, 2016) £75 million
   Romelu Lukaku (Everton to Manchester United, 2017) £75 million
   Virgil van Dijk (Southampton to Liverpool, 2018) £75 million

expensive goalkeeper in football history when he moved from Athletic Bilbao to Chelsea for £71.6 million.**

• Milene Domingues, the then wife of Brazil star Ronaldo, became the most expensive female footballer in the world when she moved from Italian side Fiamma Monza to Atletico Madrid Feminas for £200,000 in September 2002. Chelsea Ladies set a new British transfer record in July 2015 when they bought striker Fran Kirby from Reading for around £60,000.

TREBLES

Rangers first won the league title, Scottish Cup and Scottish League Cup all in the same season in 1949, and have gone on to win a world record seven 'Trebles'.

• In 1922 Northern Ireland outfit Linfield became the first club in the world to land a 'Treble', actually landing all seven trophies they competed for that season including the Irish league, Irish Cup and County Antrim Shield.

• In 2018 Celtic became the first English or Scottish side to win the 'Double-Treble' when they made a clean sweep of the Premiership, Scottish Cup and League Cup for a second successive season.

• No English side has ever won the domestic 'Treble', although Manchester United came mighty close in 1994 when they won the Premier League, FA Cup and reached the League Cup final, only to lose to Aston Villa. Five years, later, however, United claimed an even better 'Treble' when they won the traditional 'Double' and then lifted the Champions League as well.

KIERAN TRIPPIER

Born: Bury, 19th September 1990
Position: Defender
Club career:
2007-12 Manchester City 0 (0)
2010 Barnsley (loan) 3 (0)
2010-11 Barnsley (loan) 39 (2)
2011-12 Burnley (loan) 25 (1)
2012-15 Burnley 145 (4)
2015- Tottenham Hotspur 42 (1)
International record:
2015- England 13 (1)

Along with Bobby Charlton (1996) and Gary Lineker (1990), Tottenham defender Kieran Trippier is one of just three England players to have scored in a World Cup semi-final. The Bury-born right wing-back joined this elite club when he curled a delightful free kick over the wall to give England an early lead against Croatia at Russia 2018, but it wasn't enough to prevent the Three Lions going down to an eventual 2-1 defeat.

• Tripper started out at Manchester City but failed to break through into the first team, instead making his debut on loan at Barnsley, where he was voted the club's Young Player of the Year in 2011. A further loan at Burnley was made into a permanent move in 2012, and two years later he was voted into the Championship Team of the Year for a second time after helping the Clarets win promotion to the Premier League.

• In June 2015 Trippier joined Tottenham for £3.5 million, but found it hard to dislodge Kyle Walker from the right-back position, only really cementing a place in the Spurs first team after Walker moved on to Manchester City in the summer of 2017.

• An attack-minded wing-back who loves to put in dangerous crosses and is an expert at delivering set pieces, Tripper was part of the England Under-19 side that lost 2-0 to Ukraine in the European Championship final in 2009. He made his senior debut in a 3-2 friendly defeat to France in June 2017 and went on to enjoy an outstanding World Cup, with many pundits rating him as one of England's best players at the tournament.

In a desperate bid to thwart Croatia, Kieran Trippier superglued the ball to his head

TV AND RADIO

The first ever live radio broadcast of a football match was on 22nd January 1927 when the BBC covered the First Division encounter between Arsenal and Sheffield United at Highbury. The *Radio Times* printed a pitch marked into numbered squares, which the commentators used to describe where the ball was at any given moment (which some suggest gave rise to the phrase 'back to square one').

• The 1937 FA Cup final between Sunderland and Preston was the first to be televised, although only parts of the match were shown by the BBC. The following year's final between Preston and Huddersfield was the first to be screened live and in full, although the audience was only around 10,000 as so few people had TV sets at the time.

• The biggest British TV audience ever for a football match (and, indeed, the biggest ever for any TV broadcast in this country) was 32.3 million for the 1966 World Cup final between England and West Germany. The viewing figures for the match, which was shown live by both BBC and ITV, were all the more remarkable as only 15 million

"Oi, stop filming me – this isn't Big Brother, you know!"

households in the UK had TV sets. The biggest worldwide TV audience for any football match is 3.2 billion for the tense 2014 World Cup final between Germany and Argentina.

• **The BBC's *Match of the Day* is the longest-running football programme in the world. It was first transmitted on 22nd August 1964 when highlights of Arsenal's trip to Liverpool were broadcast to an audience estimated to be around 20,000.**

• The TV deal between Sky, BT and the Premier League which started in the 2016/17 season is the biggest in the history of the game. Under the terms of the deal the two companies will pay £5.136 billion over three years to show 168 live games per season – a 71 per cent increase on the previous three-year agreement. The Premier League's biggest deal outside of the UK is with Chinese digital broadcaster PPTV, who will pay £564 million over three years from the start of the 2019/20 season.

TWITTER

Cristiano Ronaldo has more followers on Twitter than any other footballer in the world, with over 75 million at the last count – putting him ahead of the likes of Justin Timberlake, Kim Kardashian and even US President Donald Trump. Ronaldo, though, can't compete with the world's most popular Twitter celebrity, the singer Katy Perry, who has around 110 million followers.

• **The 2018 World Cup in Russia attracted a record 115 billion 'Impressions' (views on Twitter), with the most tweeted match being the final between France and Croatia. Kylian Mbappe's goal for Les Bleus in that game was the most tweeted moment of the whole tournament.**

• Arsenal midfielder Mesut Ozil is comfortably the most popular Premier League footballer on Twitter, with around 23 million followers.

• **Chelsea defender Ashley Cole was fined a record £90,000 for a tweet in October 2012, when he posted abusive comments about the FA after the governing body had questioned the truth of his statements in the John Terry race abuse inquiry.**

• The most popular football club on Twitter are Real Madrid, with 31 million followers, followed by Barcelona (29 million). In England Manchester United lead the way (18 million), followed by two London clubs: Arsenal (14 million) and Chelsea (12 million).

UEFA

UEFA, the Union of European Football Associations, was founded in 1954 at a meeting in Basel during the World Cup. Holding power over all the national FAs in Europe, with 55 members it is the largest and most influential of the six continental confederations of FIFA.

• **UEFA competitions include the Champions League (first won as the European Cup by Real Madrid), the Europa League (formerly the UEFA Cup) and the UEFA Super Cup.**

• The longest serving UEFA President is Sweden's Lennart Johansson, who did the job for 17 years between 1990 and 2007. In 2015 the then President, former French international Michel

Platini, was forced to step down after an investigation by FIFA's Ethics Committee and was replaced the following year by Slovenian lawyer Aleksander Ceferin.

• **Countries to join UEFA in recent years include Montenegro (2007), Gibraltar (2013) and Kosovo (2016).**

UEFA NATIONS LEAGUE

A new UEFA competition largely designed to replace international friendlies, the first edition of the Nations League is scheduled to run from September 2018 to June 2019.

• **The competition will consist of four divisions or 'Leagues', A, B, C and D, each made up of 12-16 countries, based on their current world rankings. At the end of the round of matches four teams from each league will be promoted to the league above with four being relegated.**

• The winners of the four groups in League A will play in the Nations League finals, with two semi-final matches deciding which teams shall meet in the final.

• **The Nations League will provide a pathway into the 2020 European Championships for the four highest-finishing countries which did not reach the finals through the normal qualification process.**

"Thanks for the lovely trophy, UEFA!"

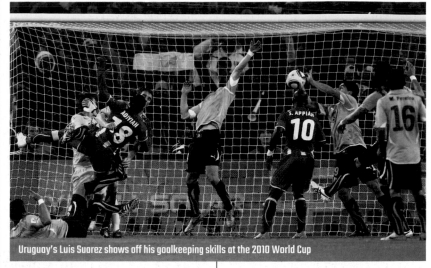

Uruguay's Luis Suarez shows off his goalkeeping skills at the 2010 World Cup

URUGUAY

First international: Uruguay 2 Argentina 3, 1901
Most capped player: Maxi Pereira, 125 caps (2005-)
Leading goalscorer: Luis Suarez, 53 goals (2007-)
First World Cup appearance: Uruguay 1 Peru 0, 1930
Biggest win: Uruguay 9 Bolivia 0, 1927
Heaviest defeat: Uruguay 0 Argentina 6, 1902

In 1930 Uruguay became the first winners of the World Cup, beating arch rivals Argentina 4-2 in the final on home soil in Montevideo. The match was a repeat of the Olympic final of 1928, which Uruguay had also won. In terms of population, Uruguay is easily the smallest nation ever to win the World Cup.

• **In 1950 Uruguay won the World Cup for a second time, defeating hosts Brazil 2-1 in 'the final' (it was actually the last and decisive match in a four-team final group). The match was watched by a massive crowd of 199,854 in the Maracana Stadium in Rio de Janeiro, the largest ever to attend a football match anywhere in the world.**

• Uruguay set a record at the 1970 World Cup when they started their group game with Italy with no fewer than eight players from the same club, Montevideo outfit Nacional. Although they only managed to draw 0-0 the South Americans went on to reach the semi-finals before losing 3-1 to Brazil.

• At the 2010 World Cup in South Africa Uruguay again finished fourth. However, their campaign is mostly remembered for a blatant handball on the line by striker Luis Suarez, which denied their opponents Ghana a certain winning goal in the teams' quarter-final clash.

• Uruguay are the most successful team in the history of the Copa America. Winners of the inaugural tournament in 1916, Uruguay have won the competition a total of 15 times, most recently lifting the trophy in 2011 after beating Paraguay 3-0 in the final.

HONOURS
World Cup winners 1930, 1950
Copa America winners 1916, 1917, 1920, 1923, 1924, 1926, 1935, 1942, 1956, 1959, 1967, 1983, 1987, 1995, 2011
World Cup Record
1930 Winners
1934 Did not enter
1938 Did not enter
1950 Winners
1954 Fourth place
1958 Did not qualify
1962 Round 1
1966 Quarter-finals
1970 Fourth place
1974 Round 1
1978 Did not qualify
1982 Did not qualify
1986 Round 2
1990 Round 2
1994 Did not qualify
1998 Did not qualify
2002 Round 1
2006 Did not qualify
2010 Fourth place
2014 Round 2
2018 Quarter-finals

VIRGIL VAN DIJK

Born: Breda, Netherlands, 8th July 1991
Position: Defender
Club career:
2011-13 Groningen 62 (7)
2013-15 Celtic 76 (9)
2015-18 Southampton 67 (4)
2018- Liverpool 14 (0)
International record:
2015- Netherlands 19 (1)

A strong, powerful and commanding centre-back, Virgil van Dijk became the world's most expensive defender when he moved from Southampton to Liverpool in January 2018 for £75 million. He helped the Reds reach the final of the Champions League in his first half-season at Anfield, but finished on the losing side after a 3-1 defeat to Real Madrid in Kiev.

• **Van Dijk began his career with Groningen before moving to Celtic for £2.6 million in 2013. In two successful seasons in Glasgow he won two league titles and was twice voted into the PFA Scotland Team of the Year.**

• He moved on to Southampton for £13 million in September 2015, and was named Saints captain a little over a year later. However, after missing the final of the 2017 League Cup through injury he became increasingly unhappy at St Mary's as speculation mounted about Liverpool's interest in him.

• **Van Dijk's Liverpool career got off to a great start when he headed the winner in a 2-1 defeat of Everton in the FA Cup third round – the first player to score on his debut in a Merseyside derby since 1901.**

• In October 2015 Van Dijk made his debut for the Netherlands in a Euro 2016 qualifier against Kazakhstan. He was made captain of his country by new boss Ronald Koeman in March 2018.

JAMIE VARDY

Born: Sheffield, 11th January 1987
Position: Striker
Club career:
2007-10 Stocksbridge Park Steels 107 (66)
2010-11 Halifax Town 37 (27)
2011-12 Fleetwood Town 36 (31)
2012- Leicester City 205 (82)
International record:
2015- England 26 (7)

In 2016 Jamie Vardy became the first ever Leicester City player to be voted Footballer of the Year by the football writers after his 24 goals helped fire the Foxes to the Premier League title. He also scored in 11 consecutive Premier League games to set a new record for the league.

• **After a subdued campaign the following year Vardy was back to his best in 2017/18, scoring 20 goals to finish the season as the fourth best marksman in the Premier League behind Mohamed Salah, Harry Kane and Sergio Aguero.**

• Vardy started out on £30 per week with non-league Stocksbridge Park Steels after being rejected by Sheffield Wednesday for being too short. Following spells with Halifax Town and Fleetwood Town, with whom he was top scorer in the Conference in 2011/12 with 31 goals, the Sheffield-born striker moved to Leicester City in the summer of 2012 for £1 million – a record fee for a non-league player. After initially struggling to adjust to higher level football, Vardy enjoyed a superb season in 2013/14, scoring 16 league goals as the Foxes claimed the Championship title at a canter.

• **A hard-working, pacy and clinical striker who is prepared to chase after long balls, Vardy made his England debut as a sub in a 0-0 friendly draw with the Republic of Ireland in June 2015. The following year he scored his first goal for his country with a clever backheel flick in a 3-2 win against Germany in Berlin, and he was also on the scoresheet in England's 2-1 victory over Wales at Euro 2016. He announced his retirement from international football in August 2018, although said he would still make himself available in the event of an injury crisis.**

JAN VERTONGHEN

Born: Saint-Niklaas, Belgium, 24th April 1987
Position: Defender
Club career:
2006-12 Ajax 155 (23)
2012 RKC Waalwijk (loan) 12 (3)
2011- Tottenham Hotspur 187 (4)
International record:
2007- Belgium 108 (9)

A composed and consistent central defender, Jan Vertonghen has been a mainstay of the Tottenham team which has finished in the top three in each of the past three Premier League seasons, conceding a club record low of just 26 goals in the 2016/17 campaign.

• **Vertonghen started out at Ajax, with whom he won two league titles and two Dutch Cups before moving to Tottenham in the summer of 2012. In the same year he was named the Dutch game's Footballer of the Year.**

Jamie Vardy holds the record for scoring in the most consecutive Premier League matches

• Although he has yet to win silverware with Spurs, Vertonghen did help the north Londoners reach the League Cup final in 2015 and he has twice been voted into the PFA Team of the Season.

• Vertonghen made his debut for Belgium against Portugal in 2007 and is now his country's most decorated player with over 100 caps to his name.

VIDEO ASSISTANT REFEREE

In March 2016 the International Football Association Board approved trials of the Video Assistant Referee (VAR) system allowing referees to review decisions with the help of video replays in four categories: potential penalties, red-card offences, goals scored and cases of possible mistaken identity.

• The first trial of the VAR system was in August 2016 in a match between New York Red Bulls II and Orlando City B in the third division of the United Soccer League. In the 35th minute referee Ismail Elfath decided to review a foul just outside the penalty area and sent off Orlando defender Conor Donovan for unfairly denying his opponent a goalscoring opportunity.

• The VAR system was first used in an international match in September 2016 when France beat Italy 3-1 in Bari. The experiment was judged to be a success, and the VAR system was later approved by FIFA for use at the 2018 World Cup. In the most controversial decision involving VAR at the tournament France were awarded a penalty for handball in the final against Croatia, Antoine Griezmann scoring from the spot in Les Bleus' 4-2 win.

• For the first time VAR was used in England for FA Cup matches shown live on TV in 2018. The first goal to be awarded after a video review was scored by Leicester striker Kelechi Iheanacho against Fleetwood Town. Referee Jon Moss originally disallowed the goal for offside but after consulting with his video assistant, Mike Jones, decided that the goal should stand.

"This is great! Now I just need a comfy sofa, a jumbo pizza and a can of fizzy pop from the fridge!"

WALES

First international: Scotland 4 Wales 0, 1876
Most capped player: Neville Southall, 92 caps (1982-98)
Leading goalscorer: Gareth Bale, 29 goals (2006-)
First World Cup appearance: Wales 1 Hungary 1, 1958
Biggest win: Wales 11 Ireland 0, 1888
Heaviest defeat: Scotland 9 Wales 0, 1878

Wales have only qualified for two major international tournaments, but on both occasions did their loyal fans more than proud. The country's finest moment came at Euro 2016 in France when a Welsh side including the likes of Gareth Bale, Aaron Ramsey and skipper Ashley Williams defied the odds to reach the last four.

• Despite losing to England in their second match, Wales topped their group after impressive victories against Slovakia and Russia. Following a narrow 1-0 win over Northern Ireland in the last 16, Wales produced a superb performance against Belgium in the quarter-finals, coming from a goal down to triumph 3-1. However, they were unable to repeat those heroics in the semi-final, losing 2-0 to eventual winners Portugal.

• Wales' only other tournament experience came in 1958 when a side including such great names as John Charles, Ivor Allchurch, Cliff Jones and Jack Kelsey qualified for the World Cup finals in Sweden after beating Israel in a two-legged play-off. After drawing all three of their group matches, Wales then beat Hungary in a play-off to reach the quarter-finals where they lost 1-0 to eventual winners Brazil.

• Wales winger Billy Meredith is the oldest international in the history of British football. He was aged 45 years and 229 days when he won the last of his 48 caps against England in 1920, a quarter of a century after making his international debut. Six months earlier he scored in a 2-1 win against England, to set a record for the oldest scorer in an international match (45 years and 73 days) which still stands today.

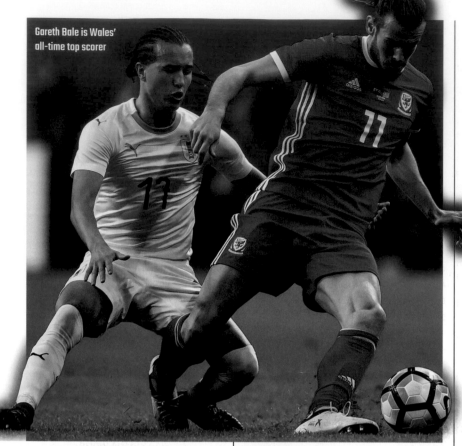

Gareth Bale is Wales' all-time top scorer

• Wales' youngest player is Liverpool's Harry Wilson, who was aged just 16 and 207 days when he made his debut as a sub against Belgium in October 2013. Having spotted his keen interest in football when he was just 18 months old, Wilson's grandfather had put a £50 bet on him playing international football at odds of 2,500/1 – and collected a cool £125,000 when the youngster made his three-minute cameo appearance for the Dragons!

World Cup Record
1930-38 Did not enter
1950-54 Did not qualify
1958 Quarter-finals
1962-2018 Did not qualify

IS THAT A FACT?
In March 2018 Gareth Bale became Wales' all-time top scorer, passing Ian Rush's old benchmark of 28 goals, when he scored a hat-trick in a 6-0 thrashing of hosts China in the China Cup.

KYLE WALKER

Born: Sheffield, 28th May 1990
Position: Defender
Club career:
2008-09 Sheffield United 2 (0)
2008 Northampton Town (loan) 9 (0)
2009-17 Tottenham Hotspur 183 (4)
2009-10 Sheffield United (loan) 26 (0)
2010-11 QPR (loan) 20 (0)
2011 Aston Villa (loan) 15 (1)
2017- Manchester City 32 (0)
International record:
2011- England 40 (0)

An athletic right-back who enjoys surging forward from deep, Kyle Walker became the second most expensive British defender ever (after John Stones) when he moved from Tottenham to Manchester City for an initial £45 million in July 2017. After being sent off on his home debut against Everton he went on to enjoy a great first season at the Etihad, helping City win the Premier League and the League Cup.
• Walker joined Sheffield United, his local club, when he was aged just seven, eventually going on to make his first-team debut in an FA Cup tie against Leyton Orient in January 2009. Later that year he became the youngest ever Blades player to appear at Wembley, when he turned out for United in their Championship play-off final defeat against Burnley three days short of his 19th birthday.
• That summer he joined Tottenham along with team-mate Kyle Naughton for a combined fee of £9 million, but was immediately loaned back to the Yorkshire outfit. Further loans at QPR and Aston Villa followed before Walker cemented his place in the Tottenham line-up at the start of the 2011/12 season. At the end of the campaign he was voted PFA Young Player of the Year.
• While representing England at Under-21 level Walker was named in the Team of the Tournament at the 2011 European Under-21 Championships. Later that year he made his senior debut as a sub in a 1-0 friendly win over Spain at Wembley. After establishing himself at right-back, he was switched by England manager Gareth Southgate to a central defensive position at the 2018 World Cup in Russia.

WALSALL

Year founded: 1888
Ground: Banks's Stadium (11,300)
Previous name: Walsall Town Swifts
Nickname: The Saddlers
Biggest win: 10-0 v Darwen (1899)
Heaviest defeat: 0-12 v Small Heath (1892) and v Darwen (1896)

The club was founded in 1888 as Walsall Town Swifts, following an amalgamation of Walsall Swifts and Walsall Town. Founder members of the Second Division in 1892, the club changed to its present name three years later.
• Now the longest-serving members of League One, Walsall have never played in the top flight, but they have a history of producing momentous cup shocks, the most famous coming back in 1933 when they sensationally beat eventual league champions Arsenal 2-0 in the FA Cup. The Saddlers' opening goal on that historic afternoon was scored by prolific striker Gilbert Alsop, who went on to score a record 22 hat-tricks for the club.
• Two players share the distinction of being Walsall's all-time leading scorer:

Tony Richards, who notched 184 league goals for the club between 1954 and 1963, and his strike partner Colin Taylor, who banged in exactly the same number in three spells with the Saddlers between 1958 and 1973.

• **After 127 years Walsall finally made it to Wembley in 2015 when they reached the final of the Football League Trophy. Sadly for their fans, the day did not end happily as the Saddlers lost 2-0 to Bristol City.**

• Loyal defender Colin Harrison played in a club record 473 league games for Walsall between 1964 and 1982.

> **HONOURS**
> *League Two champions* 1007
> *Division 4 champions* 1960

WATFORD

Year founded: 1881
Ground: Vicarage Road (21,500)
Previous name: Watford Rovers, West Herts
Nickname: The Hornets
Biggest win: 10-1 v Lowestoft Town (1926)
Heaviest defeat: 0-10 v Wolves (1912)

Founded as Watford Rovers in 1881, the club changed its name to West Herts in 1893. Five years later, following a merger with Watford St Mary's, the club became Watford FC.

• **The club's history was fairly nondescript until pop star Elton John became chairman in 1976 and invested a large part of his personal wealth in the team. With future England manager Graham Taylor at the helm, the Hornets rose from the Fourth to the First Division in just five years, and reached the FA Cup final in 1984. More recently, the club has become established in the Premier League after winning promotion from the Championship in 2015 with a club record 89 points.**

• After finishing second in the old First Division in 1983, Watford made their one foray into Europe, reaching the third round of the UEFA Cup before losing 7-2 on aggregate to Sparta Prague.

• **Luther Blissett, one of the star players of that period, is the club's**
record appearance maker. In three spells at Vicarage Road the energetic striker notched up 415 league appearances and scored 148 league goals (also a club record).

• In the 1959/60 season striker Cliff Holton scored a club record 42 league goals for the Hornets, helping them gain promotion from the third tier.

• **England winger John Barnes and Wales defender Kenny Jackett made a club record 31 appearances each for their respective countries while with Watford in the 1980s.**

• In August 2017 the Hornets splashed out £18.5 million on Burnley striker Andre Gray, their most expensive signing ever. In July 2018 the Hertfordshire side received a record £35 million when speedy Brazilian winger Richarlison joined Everton.

• **In May 2007 Watford goalkeeper Alec Chamberlain became the second oldest player in Premier League history when he came off the bench against Newcastle aged 42 years and 327 days.**

• Striker Keith Mercer became Watford's youngest ever player when he came on as a sub in a 1-0 defeat at Tranmere aged 16 and 125 days in February 1973.

> **HONOURS**
> *Second Division champions* 1998
> *Division 3 champions* 1969
> *Division 4 champions* 1978

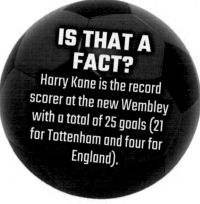

IS THAT A FACT?
Harry Kane is the record scorer at the new Wembley with a total of 25 goals (21 for Tottenham and four for England).

WEMBLEY STADIUM

Built at a cost of £798 million, the new Wembley Stadium is the most expensive sporting venue in Britain. With a capacity of 90,000, it is also the second largest in Europe and the largest in the world to have every seat under cover.

• **The stadium's most spectacular feature is a 315m-wide arch, the world's longest unsupported roof structure. Wembley also boasts a staggering 2,618 toilets, more than any other venue in the world.**

• Originally scheduled to open in 2003, the stadium was not completed until 2007 due to a variety of financial and legal difficulties. The first professional match was played at the new venue on 17th March 2007 when England Under-21s met their Italian counterparts, with the first goal arriving after just 28 seconds when Giampaolo Pazzini struck for the visitors. Half an hour later, David

Every club wants to play at Wembley – except Tottenham!

Bentley became the first Englishman to score at the new stadium.

• The first Wembley Stadium was opened in 1923, having been constructed in just 300 days at a cost of £750,000. The first match played at the venue was the 1923 FA Cup final between Bolton and West Ham, although the kick-off was delayed for nearly an hour when thousands of fans spilled onto the pitch because of overcrowding in the stands.

• Tottenham moved into Wembley for the 2017/18 season on a full-time basis while construction work continued on their new stadium at White Hart Lane. Spurs had previously played four European games at Wembley during the 2016/17 campaign, and have now played a record 38 games at the new national stadium.

• Arsenal and England defender Tony Adams played a record 60 games at the old Wembley between 1987 and 2000, a total boosted by the fact that the Gunners used the stadium for their home games in the Champions League in the late 1990s.

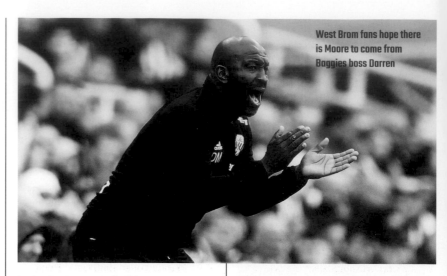

West Brom fans hope there is Moore to come from Baggies boss Darren

WEST BROMWICH ALBION

Year founded: 1878
Ground: The Hawthorns (26,688)
Previous name: West Bromwich Strollers
Nickname: The Baggies
Biggest win: 12-0 v Darwen (1892)
Heaviest defeat: 3-10 v Stoke City (1937)

Founded as West Bromwich Strollers in 1878 by workers at the local Salter's Spring Works, the club adopted the suffix 'Albion' two years later and were founder members of the Football League in 1888.

• **The Baggies were the first club to lose two consecutive FA Cup finals, going down to Blackburn Rovers in 1886 and Aston Villa the following year. In 1888, though, West Brom recorded the first of their five triumphs in the cup, beating favourites Preston 2-1 in the final.**

• In 1931 West Brom became the first and only club to win promotion and the FA Cup in the same season. The Baggies came close to repeating this particular double in 2008 when they topped the Championship, but they were beaten in the FA Cup semi-final by eventual winners Portsmouth.

• **West Brom claimed their only league title in 1920, in the first post-First World War season. The 60 points they amassed that season and the 104 goals they scored were both records at the time. The club's manager at the time, Fred Everiss, was in charge at the Hawthorns from 1902-48, his 46-year stint being the longest in European football history.**

• In 1966 West Brom won the last League Cup final to be played over two legs, overcoming West Ham 5-3 on aggregate. The next year they appeared in the first one-off final at Wembley, but surprisingly lost 3-2 to Third Division QPR after leading 2-0 at half-time.

• **The Baggies, though, returned to Wembley the following season and beat Everton 1-0 in the FA Cup final. West Brom's winning goal was scored in extra-time by club legend Jeff Astle, who in the process became one of just 12 players to have scored in every round of the competition. Astle also found the target in his side's 2-1 defeat by Manchester City in the 1970 League Cup final to become the first player to score in both domestic cup finals at Wembley.**

• In 1892 West Brom thrashed Darwen 12-0 to record their biggest ever win. The score set a record for the top flight which has never been beaten, although Nottingham Forest equalled it in 1909.

• **Cult hero Tony 'Bomber' Brown is West Brom's record scorer with 218 league goals to his name. The attacking midfielder is also the club's longest serving player, turning out in 574 league games between 1963 and 1980.**

• West Brom's record purchase is winger Oliver Burke who joined the club from Leipzig in August 2017 for £15 million, making him the most expensive Scottish player ever. The club's bank balance was boosted by a record £15 million when striker Saido Berahino joined Stoke City in January 2017.

• **West Brom were relegated from the Premier League for a joint-record fourth time in 2018, along the way enduring a club record run of 20 league games without a win. However, the Baggies had some good results at the end of the campaign, leading boss Darren Moore to become the first ever Manager of the Month winner in charge of a relegated club.**

HONOURS
Division 1 champions 1920
Championship champions 2008
Division 2 champions 1902, 1911
FA Cup 1888, 1892, 1931, 1954, 1968
League Cup 1966

WEST HAM UNITED

Year founded: 1895
Ground: London Stadium (57,000)
Previous name: Thames Ironworks
Nickname: The Hammers
Biggest win: 10-0 v Bury (1983)
Heaviest defeat: 2-8 v Blackburn (1963)

The club was founded in 1895 as Thames Ironworks by shipyard workers employed by a company of the same name. In 1900 the club was disbanded but immediately reformed under its present name.

• **The biggest and best supported club in east London, West Ham have** a proud tradition in the FA Cup. In 1923 they reached the first final to be played at the original Wembley Stadium, losing 2-0 to favourites Bolton Wanderers.

• The Hammers experienced a more enjoyable Wembley 'first' in 1965 when they became the first English side to win a European trophy on home soil, defeating Munich 1860 2-0 in the final of the Cup Winners' Cup.

• **The following year West Ham were the only club to provide three members – Bobby Moore, Geoff Hurst and Martin Peters – of England's World Cup-winning team. Between them Hurst and Peters scored all four of England's goals in the final against West Germany while Moore, as captain, collected the trophy.**

• West Ham's leading scorer is Vic Watson, with an impressive 298 league goals between 1920 and 1935, including a record 42 goals in the 1929/30 season.

• **No West Ham player has turned out more often for the club than former manager Billy Bonds. Between 1967 and 1988 'Bonzo', as he was dubbed by fans and team-mates alike, appeared in 663 league games.**

• FA Cup winners in 1964, West Ham lifted the trophy again in 1975 after a 2-0 victory against Fulham – the last time the winners have fielded an entirely English line-up. When the east Londoners triumphed for a third time in 1980 they became the last club from outside the top flight to win the FA Cup. The Hammers, then residing in the old Second Division, beat favourites Arsenal 1-0 thanks to a rare headed goal by Trevor Brooking.

• **The legendary Bobby Moore is the club's most capped international. He played 108 times for England to set a record that has since only been passed by Peter Shilton, David Beckham, Wayne Rooney and Steven Gerrard.**

• On 19th October 1968 Geoff Hurst scored a club record six goals in a 8-0 drubbing of Sunderland – a feat unmatched in the top flight since. Hurst later admitted that his first goal should have been disallowed as he had punched the ball into the net.

• **On Boxing Day 2006 Teddy Sheringham became the oldest player ever to score in the Premier League when he netted for West Ham against Portsmouth aged 40 years and 266 days. Four days later he made his last appearance for the Hammers at Manchester City, stretching his own record as the oldest outfield player in the league's history.**

• The Hammers smashed their transfer record in July 2018, buying Brazilian midfielder Felipe Anderson from Lazio for £36 million. In January 2017 they sold former fans' favourite Dimitri Payet to Marseille for a record £25 million.

> HONOURS
> *Division 2 champions 1958, 1981*
> *FA Cup 1964, 1975, 1980*
> *European Cup Winners' Cup 1965*

WIGAN ATHLETIC

Year founded: 1932
Ground: DW Stadium (25,138)
Nickname: The Latics
Biggest win: 7-0 v Oxford United (2017)
Heaviest defeat: 1-9 v Tottenham Hotspur (2009)

The club was founded at a public meeting at the Queen's Hotel in 1932 as successors to Wigan Borough, who the previous year had become the first ever club to resign from the Football League. After 34 failed attempts, including a bizarre application to join the Scottish Second Division in 1972, Wigan were finally elected to the old Fourth Division in 1978 in place of Southport.

• **The greatest day in the club's history came in 2013 when Wigan won their first major trophy, the FA Cup, after beating hot favourites Manchester City 1-0 in the final at Wembley thanks to a last-minute header by Ben Watson. Sadly for their fans, Wigan's eight-year stay in the Premier League ended just three days after that triumph, meaning that they became the first club ever to win the FA Cup and be relegated in the same season.**

• In November 2009 Wigan were hammered 9-1 at Tottenham, only the second time in Premier League history that a side had conceded nine goals. The eight goals the Latics let in after the break was a record for a Premier League half.

• **The club's record goalscorer is Andy Liddell, who hit 70 league goals between 1998 and 2003. No player has pulled on Wigan's blue-and-white stripes more often than Kevin Langley, who made 317 league appearances in two spells at the club between 1981 and 1994.**

Felipe Anderson is the most expensive Hammer ever

• Midfielder Jimmy Bullard made a club record 123 consecutive league appearances for Wigan between January 2003 and December 2005.

• **Wigan's most decorated international is flamboyant goalkeeper Ali Al Habsi who played 42 times for Oman between 2010 and 2015.**

• Promoted to the Championship as League One champions in 2018, Wigan became the first club to top the third tier twice in three seasons, having previously lifted the title in 2016.

HONOURS
League One champions 2016, 2018
Second Division champions 2003
Third Division champions 1997
FA Cup 2013
Football League Trophy 1985, 1999

WOLVERHAMPTON WANDERERS

Year founded: 1877
Ground: Molineux (31,700)
Previous name: St Luke's
Nickname: Wolves
Biggest win: 14-0 v Cresswell's Brewery
Heaviest defeat: 1-10 v Newton Heath

Founded as St Luke's by pupils at a local school of that name in 1877, the club adopted its present name after merging with Blakenhall Wanderers two years later. Wolves were founder members of the Football League in 1888, finishing the first season in third place behind champions Preston and Aston Villa.

• **The Black Country club enjoyed their heyday in the 1950s under manager Stan Cullis, a pioneer of long ball 'kick and rush' tactics. After a number of near misses, Wolves were crowned league champions for the first time in their history in 1954 and won two more titles later in the decade to cement their reputation as the top English club of the era. Incredibly, the Black Country outfit scored a century of league goals in four consecutive seasons between 1958 and 1961.**

• When Wolves won a number of high-profile friendlies against foreign opposition in the 1950s in some of the first ever televised matches they were hailed as 'champions of the world' by the national press, a claim which helped inspire the creation of the European Cup. In 1958 Wolves became only the second English team to compete in the competition, following in the footsteps of trailblazers Manchester United.

• **The skipper of that great Wolves team, centre-half Billy Wright, is the club's most capped international.**

Between 1946 and 1959 he won a then record 105 caps for England, captaining his country in 90 of those games (another record).

• Steve Bull is Wolves' record scorer with an incredible haul of 250 league goals between 1986 and 1999. His impressive total of 306 goals in all competitions included a record 18 hat-tricks for the club.

• **Stalwart defender Derek Parkin pulled on the famous gold shirt more often than any other player, making 501 appearances in the league between 1967 and 1982.**

• Wolves won the first of their four FA Cups in 1893 when they beat Everton 1-0 at the Fallowfield Stadium in Manchester. The Merseysiders complained that spectators in the 60,000 crowd had frequently encroached from the sidelines onto the pitch, but their demands for a replay were rejected.

• **Championship champions in 2018, Wolves were the first team in the country to win all four divisions of the Football League, completing the 'full house' in 1989 when they won the old Third Division title a year after claiming the Fourth Division championship.**

• On their way back to the big time, Wolves won the League One title in 2014 after amassing a third-tier record 103 points.

• **Wolves made their record signing in August 2018 when they splashed out £18 million on Middlesbrough winger Adama Traore. The club received a record £14 million in August 2012 when Scottish international striker Steven Fletcher joined Sunderland.**

The great Billy Wright is a legend at Wolves

HONOURS
Division 1 champions 1954, 1958, 1959
Championship champions 2009, 2018
Division 2 champions 1932, 1977
League One champions 2014
Division 3 champions 1989
Division 3 (North) champions 1924
Division 4 champions 1988
FA Cup 1893, 1908, 1949, 1960
League Cup 1974, 1980
Football League Trophy 1988

Chelsea were all smiles after beating Arsenal in the 2018 Women's FA Cup final in front of a record crowd

WOMEN'S FA CUP

The first Women's FA Cup final took place in 1971, two years after the Women's FA was founded. A total of 71 teams, including some from Scotland and Wales, entered the competition which was won by Southampton who beat Scottish outfit Stewarton and Thistle 4-1 in the final.

• **The most successful side in the competition are Arsenal with 14 victories, including a record four on the trot between 2006 and 2009.**
• In the biggest victory in the final, Southampton hammered QPR 8-2 in 1978, with striker Pat Chapman helping herself to a record six goals.
• **Since 2015 the final has been played at Wembley, with a record crowd of 45,423 watching Chelsea beat Arsenal 3-1 in the 2018 showpiece.**

WOMEN'S SUPER LEAGUE

In a bid to attract more fans to games, the top flight of women's football in England was reorganised in 2011 as a semi-professional summer league consisting of eight clubs (now expanded to 10 clubs), the FA Women's Super League. However, the FA decided to return to a winter league in 2017 with Chelsea finishing top of that year's one-off bridging competition, the Spring Series.

• **Arsenal, Liverpool and 2018 champions Chelsea have all won the WSL twice, while the only other club to win the title are Manchester City in 2016.**

• A number of important records were set in the WSL in the 2017/18 season: Chelsea won the league with a record 44 points, Manchester City scored a record 51 goals, Yeovil finished bottom with an all-time low of two points and Birmingham City's Ellen White was the league's top scorer with a record 15 goals.

WOMEN'S WORLD CUP

Since it was first competed for in China in 1991 there have been seven Women's World Cup tournaments. The USA won the first World Cup and have gone on to lift the trophy a record three times, most recently beating Japan 5-2 in the 2015 final in Vancouver at the first tournament to be played entirely on artificial turf.

Germany have won the tournament twice, while Norway (1995) and Japan (2011) are the only two other nations to take the trophy home.
• **The top scorer in the World Cup is Marta (Brazil) with 15 goals between 2003 and 2015. Michelle Akers of the USA scored a record 10 goals at the 1991 tournament, including a record five in one game against minnows Chinese Taipei.**
• The USA's Kristine Lilly played in a record 30 games at the World Cup between 1991 and 2007.
• **Germany hold the record for the biggest win at the Women's World Cup, thrashing Argentina 11-0 in 2007.**
• Midfielders Formiga (Brazil) and Homare Sawa (Japan) played in a record six World Cup tournaments between 1995 and 2015.

WORLD CUP

The most successful country in the history of the World Cup is Brazil, who have won the competition a record five times. Germany and Italy are Europe's leading nation with four wins each, the Germans becoming the first European nation to triumph in South America when they beat Argentina 1-0 in the 2014 final in Brazil. Neighbours Argentina and Uruguay have both won the competition twice, the Uruguayans emerging victorious when the pair met in the first ever World Cup final in Montevideo in 1930. France can also boast two triumphs, on home soil in 1998 and in 2018 in Russia, when they beat Croatia 4-2 in the final in Moscow.

Current holders the USA have won the Women's World Cup a record three times

The only other countries to have claimed the trophy are England (1966) and Spain (2010).

• Including both Japan and South Korea, who were joint hosts for the 2002 edition, the World Cup has been held in 16 different countries. The first nation to stage the tournament twice was Mexico (in 1970 and 1986), while Italy (1934 and 1990), France (1938 and 1998), Germany (1974 and 2006) and Brazil (1950 and 2014) have also welcomed the world to the planet's biggest football festival on two occasions each.

• Brazil are the only country to have played at all 21 tournaments and have recorded the most wins (73) and scored the most goals (229).

• However, Hungary hold the record for the most goals scored in a single tournament, banging in 27 in just five games at the 1954 finals in Switzerland. Even this

incredible tally, though, was not quite sufficient for the 'Magical Magyars' to lift the trophy as they went down to a 3-2 defeat in the final against West Germany, a team they had beaten 8-3 earlier in the tournament.

• Hungary also hold the record for the biggest ever victory at the finals, demolishing El Salvador 10-1 in 1982. That, though, was a desperately close encounter compared to the biggest win in qualifying, Australia's 31-0 annihilation of American Samoa in 2001, a game in which Aussie striker Archie Thompson helped himself to a record 13 goals.

• The legendary Pele is the only player in World Cup history to have been presented with three winner's medals. The Brazilian superstar enjoyed his first success in 1958 when he scored twice in a 5-2 rout of hosts Sweden in the final, and was a winner again four years later in Chile despite hobbling out of the tournament

with a torn leg muscle in the second match. He then made it a hat-trick in 1970, setting a sparkling Brazil side on the road to an emphatic 4-1 victory against Italy in the final with a trademark bullet header.

• The leading overall scorer in the World Cup is Germany's Miroslav Klose with 16 goals between 2002 and 2014. He is followed by Brazil legend Ronaldo with 15, including two in the 2002 final against Germany.

• England's Geoff Hurst had previously gone one better in 1966, scoring a hat-trick as the hosts beat West Germany 4-2 in the final at Wembley. His second goal, which gave England a decisive 3-2 lead in extra-time, was the most controversial in World Cup history and German fans still argue to this day that his shot bounced on the line after striking the crossbar, rather than over it. Naturally, England fans generally agree with the eagle-eyed Russian linesman, Tofik Bahramov, who awarded the goal.

• Germany midfielder Lothar Matthaus made a record 25 World Cup appearances for his country between 1982 and 1998. Mexico's Rafael Marquez captained his country in a record 17 matches between 2002 and 2018.

• England's Peter Shilton kept a record 10 clean sheets between 1982 and 1990, his tally later being matched by France's Fabien Barthez.

• Turkey striker Hakan Sukur scored the fastest goal at the finals after just 11 seconds of the play-off for third place against South Korea in 2002. The fastest goal in the final itself was scored by Netherlands midfielder Johan Neeskens from the penalty spot after 90 seconds against hosts West Germany in 1974.

• The oldest player to appear at the finals is Egypt goalkeeper Essam El-Hadary who played in a 2-1 defeat by Saudi Arabia in 2018 aged 45 and 161 days. The youngest player is Northern Ireland's Norman Whiteside, who was aged 17 and 41 days when he lined up against Yugoslavia in 1982.

• Mexico have suffered a record seven consecutive eliminations at the last 16 stage, most recently losing 2-0 to Brazil in 2018.

• Oleg Salenko scored a record five goals for Russia in their 6-1 hammering of Cameroon in 1994.

• A record 29 penalties were awarded at the 2018 finals in Russia, with a record 22 being converted.

Miroslav Klose celebrates the news that he is the all-time top scorer at the World Cup

WORLD CUP FINALS

1930 Uruguay 4 Argentina 2 (Uruguay)
1934 Italy 2 Czechoslovakia 1 (Italy)
1938 Italy 4 Hungary 2 (France)
1950 Uruguay 2 Brazil 1 (Brazil)
1954 West Germany 3 Hungary 2 (Switzerland)
1958 Brazil 5 Sweden 2 (Sweden)
1962 Brazil 3 Czechoslovakia 1 (Chile)
1966 England 4 West Germany 2 (England)
1970 Brazil 4 Italy 1 (Mexico)
1974 West Germany 2 Netherlands 1 (West Germany)
1978 Argentina 3 Netherlands 1 (Argentina)
1982 Italy 3 West Germany 1 (Spain)
1986 Argentina 3 West Germany 2 (Mexico)
1990 West Germany 1 Argentina 0 (Italy)
1994 Brazil 0* Italy 0 (USA)
1998 France 3 Brazil 0 (France)
2002 Brazil 2 Germany 0 (Japan/South Korea)
2006 Italy 1* France 1 (Germany)
2010 Spain 1 Netherlands 0 (South Africa)
2014 Germany 1 Argentina 0 (Brazil)
2018 France 4 Croatia 2 (Russia)

* Won on penalties

TOP 10

TOTAL WORLD CUP GOALS

1.	Brazil	229
2.	Germany	226
3.	Argentina	137
4.	Italy	128
5.	France	120
6.	Spain	99
7.	England	91
8.	Hungary	87
	Uruguay	87
10.	Netherlands	86

WORLD CUP GOLDEN BALL

The Golden Ball is awarded to the best player at the World Cup following a poll of members of the global media. The first winner was Italian striker Paolo Rossi, whose six goals at the 1982 World Cup helped the Azzurri win that year's tournament in Spain.

• Rossi was followed in 1986 by another World Cup winner, Argentina captain Diego Maradona, but since then only one player has claimed the Golden Ball and a winner's medal at the same tournament, Brazilian striker Romario in 1994.

• The only goalkeeper to win the award to date is Germany's Oliver Kahn, who finished on the losing side in the final against Brazil in 2002. The most controversial winner, meanwhile, was France's mercurial midfielder Zinedine Zidane, who was named as the outstanding performer at the 2006 World Cup before the final – a game which ended in disgrace for Zidane after he was sent off for headbutting Italian defender Marco Materazzi.

• Croatia's Luka Modric won the Golden Ball at Russia 2018, the fourth time in five tournaments that a losing finalist collected the award.

WORLD CUP GOLDEN BALL WINNERS

1982 Paolo Rossi (Italy)
1986 Diego Maradona (Argentina)
1990 Salvatore Schillaci (Italy)
1994 Romario (Brazil)
1998 Ronaldo (Brazil)
2002 Oliver Kahn (Germany)
2006 Zinedine Zidane (France)
2010 Diego Forlan (Uruguay)
2014 Lionel Messi (Argentina)
2018 Luka Modric (Croatia)

WORLD CUP GOLDEN BOOT

Now officially known as the 'adidas Golden Shoe', the Golden Boot is awarded to the player who scores most goals in a World Cup finals tournament. The first winner was Guillermo Stabile,

Golden Ball winner Harry Kane scores against Tunisia, one of his six goals at the 2018 World Cup

whose eight goals helped Argentina reach the final in 1930.

• French striker Just Fontaine scored a record 13 goals at the 1958 tournament in Sweden. At the other end of the scale, nobody managed more than four goals at the 1962 World Cup in Chile, so the award was shared between six players.

• Surprisingly, it wasn't until 1978 that the Golden Boot was won outright by a player, Argentina's Mario Kempes, whose country also won the tournament. Since then only Italy's Paolo Rossi in 1982 and Brazil's Ronaldo in 2002 have won both the Golden Boot and a World Cup winner's medal in the same year.

• **At the 2010 World Cup in South Africa Germany's Thomas Muller was one of four players to top the scoring charts with five goals, but FIFA's new rules gave him the Golden Boot because he had more assists than his three rivals for the award, David Villa, Wesley Sneijder and Diego Forlan.**

• At the 2018 World Cup in Russia England captain Harry Kane's six goals, including a hat-trick against Panama, won him the Golden Boot outright. Previously, the only other England player to win the award was Gary Lineker back in 1986.

WYCOMBE WANDERERS

Year founded: 1887
Ground: Adams Park (9,617)
Nickname: The Chairboys
Biggest win: 15-1 v Witney Town (1955)
Heaviest defeat: 0-8 v Reading (1899)

Wycombe Wanderers were founded in 1887 by a group of young furniture-makers (hence the club's nickname, The Chairboys) but had to wait until 1993 before earning promotion to the Football League.

• **In 2001 the Chairboys caused a sensation by reaching the semi-finals of the FA Cup where they lost 2-1 to eventual winners Liverpool at Villa Park. Wycombe also reached the semi-finals of the League Cup in 2007, but were beaten 5-1 on aggregate by eventual winners Chelsea.**

• On 23rd September 2000 Wycombe's Jamie Bates and Jermaine McSporran set a new Football League record for the shortest time between two goals when they both scored against Peterborough within nine seconds of each other either side of half-time.

• **Midfielder Steve Brown played in a record 371 league games for Wycombe between 1994 and 2004. Defender Mark Rogers won a record seven international caps for Canada while at Adams Park between 2000 and 2003.**

• Wycombe were promoted to League One in 2018 after winning a club record 24 league games. The Chairboys' top scorer with 17 goals was burly striker Adebayo Akinfenwa, at 103 kgs the heaviest player in the whole of the Football League.

> HONOURS
> *Conference champions 1993*
> *FA Amateur Cup 1931*

YEOVIL TOWN

Year founded: 1890
Ground: Huish Park (9,565)
Previous names: Yeovil, Yeovil Casuals
Nickname: The Glovers
Biggest win: 12-1 v Westbury United (1923)
Heaviest defeat: 0-8 v Manchester United (1949)

Founded in 1890, initially as Yeovil and then as Yeovil Casuals (1895-1907), the club had to wait until 2003 before finally entering the Football League when they were promoted as runaway Conference champions by a then record 17-point margin.

• **The Glovers adapted well to league football, beating Rochdale 3-1 away in their opening fixture – the last time a newcomer to the Football League has won on their debut. After two more promotions Yeovil reached the heady heights of the Championship in 2013, but the glory years were short-lived and following two consecutive relegations the Somerset club were back in the basement of league football two years later.**

• Before they made it into the Football League, Yeovil were famed FA Cup giant-killers, knocking out no fewer than 20 league clubs – a record for a non-league outfit. Their most notable scalp came in 1949 when they beat Sunderland 2-1 in the fourth round on their famously sloping Huish Park pitch.

• **Stalwart defender Terry Skiverton played in a record 328 league games for the Glovers between 1999 and 2010.**

• Only two players have won an international cap while with Yeovil: Latvia's Andrejs Stolcers in 2004, and Arron Davies, who came on as a sub for Wales in a 2-1 win against Trinidad and Tobago in 2006.

> HONOURS
> *League Two champions 2005*
> *Conference champions 2003*

ASHLEY YOUNG

Born: Stevenage, 9th July 1985
Position: Defender/winger
Club career:
2003-07 Watford 98 (19)
2007-11 Aston Villa 157 (30)
2011- Manchester United 150 (13)
International record:
2007- England 39 (7)

Recalled to the England squad by Gareth Southgate after a four-year absence, Ashley Young was a surprise choice at left wing-back in the Three Lions team which surpassed the public's expectations by reaching the semi-finals of the 2018 World Cup in Russia.

• **Now a 33-year-old veteran, Young began his career his career as a nippy winger at Watford, scoring on his debut for the Hornets against Millwall in 2003. He was voted Watford's Young Player of the Year in 2005 and the** following season he contributed 15 goals as the Hornets won promotion to the Premier League after beating Leeds 3-0 in the play-off final.

• In January 2007 Young joined Aston Villa for a then club record £9.75 million and later that month he scored on his debut for the Midlanders in a 3-1 defeat at Newcastle. His outstanding displays for Villa earned him three Player of the Month awards in 2008, making him the first player ever to win a trio of these awards in the same calendar year.

• **Young moved on to Manchester United in June 2011 for a £17 million fee. He helped the Red Devils win the Premier League title two years later and, after being converted to a wing-back by then manager Louis van Gaal, the FA Cup in 2016.**

• First capped by England in 2007, Young enjoyed a golden patch in the 2011/12 season when he scored in four consecutive internationals. Less happily, at the end of that campaign he missed his penalty in the shoot-out against Italy which saw England eliminated at the quarter-finals of the 2012 European Championships.

WILFRIED ZAHA

Born: Abidjan, Ivory Coast, 10th November 1992
Position: Winger
Club career:
2010-13 Crystal Palace 110 (12)
2013-15 Manchester United 2 (0)
2013 Crystal Palace (loan) 16 (1)
2014 Cardiff City (loan) 12 (0)
2014-15 Crystal Palace (loan) 12 (0)
2015- Crystal Palace 113 (27)
International record:
2012-13 England 2 (0)
2017- Ivory Coast 8 (2)

No player was more important to his club in the 2017/18 Premier League

Wilfried Zaha celebrates being the last entry in this book!

season than Wilfried Zaha. The pacy Crystal Palace winger scored an impressive nine goals in 29 appearances, while the Eagles certainly noted his absence in the nine matches he missed through injury, losing all of them.

• **Zaha moved from Africa to London with his family aged four. He came through the ranks of the Crystal Palace academy to make his debut, aged 17, in April 2010, and the following year gained national prominence when he starred in the Eagles' shock 2-1 victory away to Manchester United in the League Cup quarter-final. At the end of the 2011/12 campaign he was voted the Football League's Young Player of the Year.**

• A £15 million move to Manchester United followed in January 2013, making Zaha the most expensive player to leave Selhurst Park at the time. However, he was immediately loaned back to the Eagles, helping them gain promotion to the Premier League via the play-offs. When he eventually pitched up at Old Trafford Zaha soon fell out of favour with then United boss David Moyes and was loaned out to Cardiff City. A further loan to Palace resulted in a permanent move back to Selhurst Park, and he was a key figure in Palace's run to the 2016 FA Cup final – which, ironically, they lost to United.

• **After making two non-competitive appearances for England back in the 2012/13 season, Zaha disappointed Three Lions boss Gareth Southgate by switching his allegiance to his birth nation, Ivory Coast, ahead of the 2017 Africa Cup of Nations. Zaha went on to figure in all three of the reigning champions' group matches at the tournament but couldn't prevent Ivory Coast from being dumped out at the first stage.**

"Right lads, we've won a World Cup penalty shoot-out. Next time we're got to go all the way!"